Android™
Game
Programming
FOR
DUMMIES®

Android™ Game Programming

FOR

DUMMIES®

by Derek James

WILEY

John Wiley & Sons, Inc.

Android™ Game Programming For Dummies®

Published by
John Wiley & Sons, Inc.
111 River Street
Hoboken, NJ 07030-5774

www.wiley.com

For general information on our other products and services, please contact our Customer Care Department within the U.S. at 877-762-2974, outside the U.S. at 317-572-3993, or fax 317-572-4002.

For technical support, please visit www.wiley.com/techsupport.

Wiley publishes in a variety of print and electronic formats and by print-on-demand. Some material included with standard print versions of this book may not be included in e-books or in print-on-demand. If this book refers to media such as a CD or DVD that is not included in the version you purchased, you may download this material at http://booksupport.wiley.com. For more information about Wiley products, visit www.wiley.com.

Library of Congress Control Number: 2012950501

ISBN 978-1-118-02774-5 (pbk); 978-1-118-23599-7 (ebk); ISBN 978-1-118-26083-8 (ebk); ISBN 978-1-118-22218-8 (ebk)

Manufactured in the United States of America

10 9 8 7 6 5 4 3 2 1

WILEY

About the Author

Derek James is the founder and owner of Polyclef Software, one of the most successful Android indie game developers on Google Play. His apps and games have garnered over 1 million combined downloads, with multiple games receiving four-star or better ratings and holding top-ranking positions in their categories for many months. He was an early adopter of the Android platform and has been developing Android apps and games since the first device was released. He lives in Lafayette, Louisiana. You can follow Derek on Polyclef's Twitter feed (@polyclefapps), his blog (http://polyclefsoftware.blogspot.com), and his website (polyclefsoftware.com).

Dedication

To Jenna, who was there by my side throughout the writing of this book.

Author's Acknowledgments

Thanks to Acquisitions Editor Kyle Looper for contacting me to work on this book. I'm grateful for the opportunity.

Thanks for Project Editor Pat O'Brien for all the valuable and timely feedback in helping get this book put together.

Jeremy Breaux provided invaluable feedback as technical editor, helping to make sure that the code and examples worked well and were clear.

Finally, thanks to Laurie, as well as my friends and family for being supportive throughout the writing process.

Publisher's Acknowledgments

We're proud of this book; please send us your comments at http://dummies.custhelp.com. For other comments, please contact our Customer Care Department within the U.S. at 877-762-2974, outside the U.S. at 317-572-3993, or fax 317-572-4002.

Some of the people who helped bring this book to market include the following:

Acquisitions, Editorial, and Vertical Websites

Project Editor: Pat O'Brien

Acquisitions Editor: Kyle Looper

Copy Editor: Barry Childs-Helton

Technical Editor: Jeremy Breaux

Editorial Manager: Kevin Kirschner

Editorial Assistant: Leslie Saxman

Sr. Editorial Assistant: Cherie Case

Cover Photo: © iStockphoto.com / Cary Westfall

Cartoons: Rich Tennant (www.the5thwave.com)

Composition Services

Project Coordinator: Katherine Crocker

Layout and Graphics: Carrie A. Cesavice, Joyce Haughey, Christin Swinford

Proofreaders: Melissa Cossell, Shannon Ramsey

Indexer: BIM Indexing & Proofreading Services

Publishing and Editorial for Technology Dummies

    Richard Swadley, Vice President and Executive Group Publisher

    Andy Cummings, Vice President and Publisher

    Mary Bednarek, Executive Acquisitions Director

    Mary C. Corder, Editorial Director

Publishing for Consumer Dummies

    Kathleen Nebenhaus, Vice President and Executive Publisher

Composition Services

    Debbie Stailey, Director of Composition Services

Contents at a Glance

Table of Contents

Introduction

• •

*T*here's something special about games. The best games, the ones we remember, don't just relieve our boredom from time to time. They teach us new things, stretch our brains, or make us feel happy, excited, and sometimes angry! Social games can even bring us closer to our friends and family. We all have games that we think of fondly, that added something to our lives. Now, with the advent of smartphones, we can carry that experience around in our pockets and purses.

I still remember when my parents hooked up our first video game, Pong, to the family television. At the time that luminescent "ball" traversing the blurry screen was the coolest thing I'd ever seen. I've played a lot of games on a lot of platforms in the intervening years, but when my friend Philip gifted me with the first Android phone, the G1, I was skeptical that it would make a very good gaming platform. Who wants to play games by staring at a tiny screen on a device whose primary function is to make phone calls? Then again, the iPhone had by that time already proven that people were not only willing to play games on their smartphones, they were absolutely *ravenous* for games on their smartphones.

When the Android market launched, it took a little while to get some traction. I developed and published some of the first games on the market, when not many other developers were flocking to the platform. The G1 was a clunky, first-generation device, they said. It'll never compete with the iPhone, they said. Open platforms are never good for gaming, they said. Well, I was able to make enough games that generated enough income to let me develop for Android full-time. And the platform has come a long way in the meantime; now Google doesn't have a problem attracting game developers.

When I was approached to write this book, I jumped at the chance to write about a subject that blends my two passions of gaming and programming. I'm guessing you share those passions as well, and want to make cool, compelling games. I'm going to help you make that happen.

Why You Need This Book

Obviously you want to make games for Android, but you may not know where to get started. You may not even have any programming experience — if you do, great! — but I don't make too many assumptions about your level of experience. By default, Android apps are written in Java. All the examples in this book are also in Java, so it's helpful, but not necessary, to have some working knowledge of Java. However, even someone with little or no experience should be able to work through this book.

By the end, you'll have a good understanding of Android, two complete, working and playable games, and a solid foundation for developing and publishing your own games. Along the way, I also talk a bit about how you might get more downloads and actually make money from your games. If any or all of that interests you, this book is a great place to start.

Conventions Used in This Book

Code examples are all in the Java programming language. Android also uses XML files to define layouts and preferences in projects. I use a monospaced font to show examples of the content that lurks in these types of files. The idea is to set the examples apart from other text; they look like this:

```
System.out.println("Hello");
```

Java and XML are *case-sensitive* (it matters whether letters are capitalized), so be sure to capitalize letters in any code example from the book exactly as you see them. If you don't, you'll see compile errors in Eclipse.

URLs for websites will also appear in monospaced font

```
http://www.google.com
```

If you are ever confused about the contents of a given file in any of the projects discussed in this book, you can always refer to the actual source files here:

```
www.dummies.com/go/androidgameprogramming
```

Technical Considerations

To develop games for Android, you need a PC running a version of either Linus, Windows, or Mac OS that meets the requirements for both the Android SDK and the Java Development Kit (JDK). Both the SDK and JDK are freely available from their respective websites, where you can find more detail about specific system requirements:

```
http://developer.android.com/sdk
```

```
http://www.oracle.com/technetwork/java/javase/downloads/
          index.html
```

Android also uses the Eclipse IDE (integrated development environment), which we will be using throughout this book. Installation of all this software is covered in Chapter 3.

As I stated earlier, a working knowledge of Java and XML are helpful, but not necessary. If you're familiar with any high-level language and development environment, you should be fine. If not, you should still be able to work through the examples and put together workable games, but you'll likely have a bit more of a tussle.

If you're interested in developing for Android, you probably have an Android device, but you don't necessarily need one. The Android SDK provides an *emulator* which lets you configure virtual devices to test your games without the actual hardware.

But testing playability without actual devices is not advised. Especially if you're designing for multiple *form factors,* such as both phones and tablets, you'll probably want to invest in at least a couple of test devices.

How This Book Is Organized

Android Game Programming For Dummies is divided into six parts. The following section describes the contents of each part.

Part 1: Adopting the Android Gaming Mindset

Part I provides you with a history of Android and mobile gaming to this point in time. I contrast Android game development with other platforms and discuss its pros and cons. This part also helps you think through all the necessary decisions before you begin to program, including the basics of designing a mobile game for Android.

Part II: Starting to Program

Part II walks you through setting up your development environment and installing all the necessary frameworks and tools for building Android games. I show you how to create a simple Android project and run the resulting app on both virtual and real devices. I then walk you through the guts of an Android project to get a closer look at what all the pieces are and how they all fit together to make a game.

Part III: Making Your First Game: Crazy Eights

Part III involves making your first game, the two-player card game Crazy Eights. You create a title screen, load and display graphics, and implement UI elements such as buttons. You implement all the elements for a card game, including such tasks as loading, shuffling, and dealing a virtual deck of cards. You implement all the logic for playing cards and taking turns, and also conjure up a computer opponent to play against. By the end of this part, you'll have a complete, playable card game for Android.

Part IV: Moving On to Your Second Game: Whack-a-Mole

Part IV shows you how to make a second complete game, Whack-a-Mole. I use a different approach than our first game that's slightly more complex, but provides the additional rendering speed we need for real-time arcade games. I cover how to generate simple animations and how to load and play sounds in response to events in the game. I also show you how to store and retrieve data, allowing you to manage game states between sessions. By the end of this part, you'll have a second complete playable game.

Part V: Managing Your Game in the Market

Part V discusses how to make money from your game, if that interests you. I also discuss the nuts and bolts of exporting and digitally signing your game for upload to Google Play. I walk you through the process of creating an uploadable application file, but also all the promotional resources you'll need for the market listing. I then show you how to upload your game to the market and update it when it's there.

Part VI: The Part of Tens

Part VI provides you with some handy resources to help you develop your own games while working through this book and moving beyond it. I discuss some intriguing open-source game projects that cover genres and approaches that the two sample games here don't cover — such as side-scrolling platformers and word games. Then I point you to game engines you can leverage to save you lots of time, and point out some features like physics engines that handle chores like gravity and movement and would take months to implement otherwise. I also talk about free tools to help you create your own graphics and sound resources, as well as frameworks to help you promote and monetize your game.

Icons Used in This Book

This icon indicates useful information you should pay attention to.

This icon represents important overriding concepts that frame all the content in a particular section.

This icon indicates information that dives a bit deeper into the technical aspects of a particular subject. Usually it's not essential to your understanding of the associated material, but is provided to give you a better handle on the topic.

This icon points out potential problems you might encounter when you're dealing with a particular aspect of development. Pay particular attention to these and try to avoid these pitfalls when possible.

These links connect you to valuable internet resources.

Where to Go from Here

Are you ready to start developing games for Android? I hope you enjoy the process as much as I enjoyed putting this book together for you. I tried my best to make the subject informative and entertaining, but if you have any additional questions, you can contact me via e-mail at `polyclefsoftware@gmail.com`. If there are updates, they'll be posted at

`www.dummies.com/go/androidgameprogrammingfordummies`

Part I

Adopting the Android Gaming Mindset

In this part . . .

Part I gets you ready to build amazing games by giving you the background you need to understand Android as a gaming platform — and then by walking you through all the necessary steps for designing your game. I discuss the history of Android and mobile gaming, then I talk about all the things you need to consider before firing up your computer to start coding.

Chapter 1

Getting to Know Android Gaming

In This Chapter

▶ Learning the background of Android

▶ Approaching Android as a gaming platform

▶ Planning your first game

You love games and now want to make some of your own, specifically for smartphones and tablets. You're in luck! These are exciting times for the mobile game industry. Mobile device adoption is exploding, and mobile games are the hottest segment of mobile applications.

Android in particular is experiencing enormous growth. That means your games will be available to millions of users around the world. Android is also a great platform for developers, with flexibility and freedom unparalleled on other mobile platforms.

Seeing the Potential of the Android Platform

Whether you want to make games for Android as a personal project or as part of a plan to launch your own game studio, the platform has a lot of things going for it. For starters:

✔ Android is an open platform.

  That means fewer restrictions on what you have access to and what you can do.

✔ Android is the fastest-growing mobile platform.

  That means more people to download and play your games.

Where Android came from

Android started out as a secretive startup in 2003, and luckily got bought by Google in 2005 as a way to enter the mobile software market. The first version of Android was released on the G1 (also known as the HTC Dream) in late 2008.

Hard to believe there was a time when there was only one version of Android running on one phone. Now there are hundreds of different models running Android!

Android was built using Linux at its core, and the philosophy was simple: Make a powerful mobile operating system that is free and open-source.

- ✔ Manufacturers can focus more on hardware when they don't have to develop their own OS.
- ✔ Anyone can take Android and customize it any way they want!

Google bet big on this strategy to lead to widespread adoption, and it has worked like a dream.

And where it's going

As of this writing, Android is big and growing:

- ✔ Over 300 million people worldwide own Android devices.
- ✔ Over 850,000 new devices are activated every day. That's about another 300 million added per year.

Android is in version 4.0 (codename Ice Cream Sandwich), soon to release a new major version.

In just a few short years, the advances in screen size and resolution and processing power are staggering. Even though it started out on a single smartphone, Android is now used in phones, tablets, and even television!

The future is bright, and Android shows no signs of slowing:

- ✔ Market share is expected to continue to grow
- ✔ More powerful multi-core devices will continue to allow for richer, more sophisticated gaming.

What You Must Know about the Mobile Gaming Industry

Smartphones and app stores have revolutionized the way people play games, as well as how developers make them. The game industry has continued to boom, with the budgets of games for the PC and consoles sometimes exceeding those of Hollywood blockbusters. Teams of dozens or hundreds of professionals, working for months or years, are required to make such big-budget productions.

But mobile gaming has gone a long way in returning game development to its early roots, when lone developers working in their basements could churn out fun, cool games in their spare time and possibly hit it big.

Handhelds and smartphones

With the release of the Game Boy in the late '80s, Nintendo changed the way people play video games, allowing them to play on the go. The Game Boy ushered in a new era of handheld gaming devices, electronic gadgets that fit in the palm of your hand, dedicated to playing video games. The introduction of smartphones lets people game wherever they are, but without buying a specialized device.

Developing for smartphones is also a lot easier than for the handheld market, which usually requires an expensive software development kit (SDK) and authorization from the manufacturer. Smartphones have democratized mobile game development, lowering the bar of entry for those interested in making mobile games:

✔ Anyone can develop for Android

✔ Other than the expense of a computer and fees associated with selling through a market, it's free!

iOS or Android

These days smartphone users and developers usually fall into one of two camps when it comes to smartphones:

✔ iOS

✔ Android

They are both great platforms, with their own advantages and drawbacks for development.

iOS development has several advantages:

- ✔ Tight integration of software and hardware
- ✔ Fewer hardware/software configurations to develop for
- ✔ Apple actively checks applications for quality

But there are drawbacks to developing for iOS:

- ✔ Mac-only development environment
- ✔ More restrictive ecosystem
- ✔ Apple may reject applications for confusing or arbitrary reasons

Android development has a different balance of advantages and drawbacks.

Android is much easier and (in most cases) more flexible to develop for:

- ✔ Java development environment runs on Linux, Mac, or PC
- ✔ Less restrictive ecosystem
- ✔ No screening process to block releases

Okay, Android development also has a few drawbacks:

- ✔ May make less money than on iOS, because Android users generally buy fewer apps.
- ✔ Many more hardware/software configurations to worry about
- ✔ Absence of screening process, which can lead to
    - More spam
    - Lower-quality apps and games on the market
- ✔ If starting a business is your focus, you may have varying results between the platforms
    - Some studies have suggested that Android users are less willing than iOS users to purchase apps.
    - In-app purchases and advertising are other ways to monetize apps and may find more success on Android.

> I've had great success on Android with both
>
> - Selling apps
> - Generating ad revenue.

✔ Android has lots of other markets besides Google Play.

> The most notable at this time is the Amazon App Store. Like iTunes, it requires quality screening. I've had good success there, as have other developers, so it looks like a solid complement to Google's official market.

If you have a great game idea, consider developing your game for both of the dominant smartphone platforms. See Chapter 14 for tools that make cross-platform development easier.

How Android Is Suited to Mobile Gaming

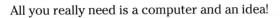

The biggest advantage to developing games for Android is the low level of investment needed to get started:

✔ The SDK and all associated development tools are free.

✔ A number of game engines are free.

All you really need is a computer and an idea!

But there are some aspects of Android that make it particularly appealing as a platform.

Growth

For the past few years Android has been the fastest-growing mobile gaming platform. The number of activations per day has risen steadily each quarter and continues to rise.

✔ A recent report showed that nearly 50 percent of cellphones in the US are smartphones. That means smartphone adoption will continue in the US.

✔ For the global market, Android is poised for even more growth.

Freedom

You want to develop

- ✔ The next great physics-based game?
- ✔ A local multiplayer game?
- ✔ An asynchronous multiplayer game?

With the standard SDK and the ability to use any number of third-party libraries to develop your games, the sky is the limit.

And (as mentioned earlier) with no review process for the official Android market, the moment you choose Submit your app is live.

Developing and publishing on Android is probably the easiest end-to-end process of any platform in gaming today.

Potential

Because Android is an open platform, it's going to be adapted to more and more uses:

- ✔ Although Google TV (which also runs on Android) has not panned out so far as a viable market for developers, potential exists for gaming with undreamed-of new systems running Android.
- ✔ With the rapid cycle of hardware and software development, gadgets sprout new
  - • Interfaces
  - • Mechanisms
  - • Form factors

That means all sorts of interesting possibilities for game design, such as augmented reality games (those that blend the digital and real worlds), which currently make up only a small percentage of games on the mobile market.

Thinking Through Your Game Project

Before you download the SDK or even boot up your development machine, the first thing you should do is flesh out your game plan. You have a lot of decisions to make before coding your game, and they are all important.

Chapter 2 delves into these questions more deeply and guides you through more specific design issues:

- What kind of game do you want to make?
- Who is your target audience?
- What range of devices are you going to target?
- Do you want to focus on tablets?
- Do you want to Target as wide a variety of devices as possible?
- How will a player navigate through your game?
- How will a player control what happens?
- Do you want to try to make money with your game?
- How can you monitize your game?

Initially, one of the best ways to think through a lot of design issues related to your game is to sketch out what the game might look like with either

- Pen and paper
- Your favorite graphics program

Designing first

Let's consider the broad design questions first:

- Simple turn-based games have been popular throughout history.

  The simpler they are, the wider their audience and appeal.

  So let's start with a simple card game that even kids can learn and play.
- We also want to learn how to make faster-paced games.

  Let's stick with the simple-is-better mantra and design a single-player game that can also be for all ages.

The games chosen for this book can be

- Played by one player
- Learned in only a few minutes
- Controlled with a purely touchscreen interface to promote universal compatibility.

Rules for Crazy Eights

Crazy Eights is a turn-based card game played with a standard 52-card deck. The goal of each hand is to get rid of all of your cards.

✔ Each player is dealt seven cards.

✔ The remaining cards become the draw pile.

✔ The top card is turned over to start the discard pile.

In turn, each player must discard exactly one card face up on the discard pile.

Except when an 8 is on top of the pile, the discarded card can be either

✔ The same *rank* as the topmost card on the discard pile.

   If the top card were the 6 of clubs, you could discard any 6.

✔ The same *suit* as the topmost card on the discard pile.

   If the top card were the 6 of clubs, you could discard any club.

✔ Any 8.

   You may discard an 8 at any time, and name a suit for the next player to play.

   When an 8 is on top of the pile, the next player must discard a card of the named suit.

If a player doesn't have an appropriate card to discard, the player must continue drawing cards from the draw pile until an appropriate card is drawn and played.

This book walks you through the development of two complete, fully functional games:

✔ Crazy Eights, the children's card game.

   This card game is played against a computer opponent.

✔ Whack-a-Mole, a fast-paced action game.

For our initial design considerations, let's mock up the two main screens in the game:

✔ A title screen

✔ A play screen.

A title screen should have

✔ The name of the game

✔ The main menu

Figure 1-1 shows my title screen mockup for Crazy Eights:

Figure 1-1:
Mockup title
screen.

My mockup only has two buttons for

- ✔ Starting a new game
- ✔ Displaying credits

For now, keep it simple. However, you may also want buttons for something like

- ✔ High scores
- ✔ A feature for sharing information about the game via e-mail or a social networking site

The other mockup is for the play screen (Figure 1-2), and we have a lot more decisions to make when designing this screen.

We'll definitely want to display the core game components,such as

- ✔ Each player's score
- ✔ Each player's hand
- ✔ The draw pile
- ✔ The discard pile

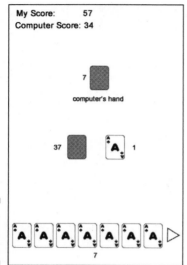

Figure 1-2:
Mockup
play screen.

In this mockup, text by each set of cards indicates how many cards are in that set.

In terms of playing the game, some of this information isn't all that useful (such as how many cards are in the discard pile), but when you're initially laying things out, it's often a good idea to include too much — with an eye toward paring down to essentials later.

Probably the biggest design decision is how to display the user's hand:

✔ In Crazy Eights, players must draw until they can play, so their hand size may grow very large.

A player could hold more than 20 cards! How do we want to display very large hands? There is simply not enough space on the screen to display more than 20 cards, unless we stack them or shrink them — both of which make them more difficult to interact with via a touch interface.

✔ My initial proposal is to only display seven cards at a time. If the hand gets larger than seven cards, the user may use an arrow button to cycle through his or her hand in "carousel" fashion. This may not be the best way to do this task, but we can always change it later.

Just get your initial ideas down somewhere, and you'll save yourself a lot of headache down the road when you start to code.

Following a structured development process

If you're working on a team, even a small one, most likely you'll want to use some form of software *version control*, such as

✔ Subversion (SVN)

✔ Concurrent Versions System (CVS)

These tools help organize any revisions made to your source code; it's a great help in keeping things straight if you need to roll back to a previous working build of your code.

Even if you work alone, you may want to consider using such a system:

✔ Games can often be very complex

✔ You may find yourself in a situation where something breaks and you may want to backtrack instead of banging your head against a particularly nasty bug.

Try to follow standard conventions for naming your packages, files, and variables. For variables, use mixed-case names that are descriptive, such as `highScore` instead of `x1`. Even if you don't extensively comment your code, naming elements in your code in an intuitive way will help others who may need to work with your code. If you revisit your code after a long period of time, good naming conventions will help you understand your own code as well!

Oracle maintains a resource on naming conventions at `http://www.oracle.com/technetwork/java/codeconv-138413.html`.

Whether or not you use formal source control, you will definitely need some way to back up and restore versions of your code. In terms of workflow, whether or not you follow a formal software development process, you will definitely want to follow some version of the following steps:

1. Think about what you want the user to experience.

2. Design with that experience in mind.

3. Build your game based on this design.

4. Test the build incrementally.

5. Revise based on testing.

You will end up iterating through a lot of changes late in the process, and with games especially you will want to do a lot of testing. Get the game into the hands of your friends and family (or random strangers if you can!) and let them play it.

The most important question is: Is it fun? But you might not even get there if the interface is confusing and the users can't figure out how to play your game.

Of course, playing games should be fun, and most of the time making games is fun, too. But the more disciplined you are about the development process, the better your game will be when you launch it into the world.

Deciding on distribution

How you distribute your game will depend on your goals. Do you want to make money?

- ✔ If you make your game available for free, life becomes a lot simpler:
    - You just upload it for free to every market you can find.
    - you may want to distribute it directly from your website.
- ✔ If you want to make money, things become a bit more complicated in terms of distribution.

    Some markets have restrictions on how much you can sell your game for (such as stating that the app can't sell for less on their store and more on another).

Chapter 11 is all about monetizing your games, but it is an issue you'll need to think seriously about up front, as it can drastically affect the design of your game:

- ✔ If you want to monetize using ads, you will have less room on the screen for game content.
- ✔ You want to think about where the best place to put your ads might be.

    You might annoy users if ads are easily clickable because they're too close to game controls (advertisers won't like that either!).

Knowing What Tools You Need

When you're building games for Android, you need the following essential tools.

Required

Besides the PC, everything is free:

✔ Development computer

Any PC will do, since the development environment is Java. Faster is better, of course. The Android SDK comes bundled with *emulation* capabilities so you can create virtual Android devices on your PC, but they run extremely slowly.

✔ Java Development Kit (JDK)

✔ An *integrated development environment* (IDE)

✔ Android SDK

Chapter 3 walks you through where and how to download and install all the software you need to get started.

That's all you need to start making games for Android, but there are a number of other items you'll probably want in your toolkit as well.

Recommended

✔ At least one Android device.

Google continues to make improvements to the emulator, but there really is no comparison in testing between an emulated device and a real one:

• You'll save time waiting for the emulator to start up.

• Testing your game with a mouse is very different from playing it on an actual device.

You don't strictly have to own an Android device in order to develop for Android, but it's really not a good idea.

The more devices you can add to your test suite, the better. Especially if you want your game to look and perform well on higher-resolution devices like tablets, you should invest in at least one.

✔ A good graphics program.

- Even if you hire an artist to create the graphics for your game, at some point you will likely need to crop, resize, or otherwise edit them.

- If you don't hire someone, you'll need to create all the graphics on your own, even as placeholders.

GIMP is a free graphics editor with a lot of power, though not very user-friendly. Otherwise, purchasing a good, user-friendly graphics editor will be a sound investment.

✔ Sound-editing software.

Audacity (`audacity.sourceforge.net`) is a wonderful, free piece of sound-editing software that should take care of all your needs, whether you purchase or create your own sound effects and music.

Capitalizing on Your Game

A lot of game developers make games just for fun. If you want to take it one step further — and try to turn your ideas into a business — you will need to think about how you plan to do so.

Chapter 11 is all about monetizing your game, but this section will give an overview of the ways in which you can make money from a game (and potentially help you think of new ways!).

The tried-and-true approaches

The traditional (and obvious) way to make money from your app is to sell it! When you publish to a market, list the price at what you think is a good price point. Most paid games sell between $0.99 and $2.99 USD, but big-budget or high-demand games might ask for even more.

The price point is something you can experiment with as you try to optimize sales. If you're going this route, there are really no particular design decisions that will affect development. Just build a great app! (Simple, right? Maybe so. Just stick with this book.) Realize, however, that paid apps get far fewer downloads than their free counterparts, so if what you're seeking is as wide an audience as possible, asking the players to pay isn't the best option.

You may want to run a sale on your for-pay app periodically, or during holidays. But be aware:

✔ Most markets have a minimum price (usually $0.99 USD).

✔ Some markets (such as Google Play) don't allow you to switch to free and then back to paid!

Another option for making money from games is to give them away. Wait a second . . . how do you make money from a game if you don't charge for it? The so-called *freemium* model has been mastered by the creators of Android.

✔ Google gives away most of its products and services, most of which are incredibly useful and high-quality. How does it make billions of dollars in revenue a year then? Advertising.

You can do the same with your game. Give it away for free and place advertising in the app. You can either

- Try to find your own advertisers.

- Use one of the many ad providers to serve ads in your app.

Typically you'll only get paid when someone clicks one of the ads, but if your game is popular, you can profit quite well from this approach.

If you want to serve ads in your game, some users won't like the ads, and you'll need to be careful about how you place them so they don't interfere with play.

✔ Another freemium model is to give the game away for free, but then charge users to upgrade to a full version, which might include more features or remove ad visibility. This could be either

- A one-shot payment

- A subscription model

Incorporating such a system is a little more complicated than serving ads, so be aware of the technical issues.

✔ In-app purchases offer a rich potential revenue stream. While the game itself could be offered for free, in-game upgrades such as virtual goods or level unlocks can be sold to the player in exchange for real money. Some developers have made a fortune employing this monetization strategy.

Some games are naturally suited to this model, such as

- Simulation

- Role-playing games

In general, you shouldn't try to shove a round peg in a square hole. If your game isn't a good fit with in-app purchases, don't try to force it.

An experiment in game design

In case you were wondering, I did attempt to come up with a new form of monetization. It didn't work for me, but you never know whether it might be worth trying some new approach, and maybe this (ahem) *adventure* will inspire you to invent a whole new way to make money from games.

In 2009, Google announced the second iteration of the Android Developers Challenge, a contest to spur development on the Android platform by offering cash prizes and exposure to developers for creating innovative new apps and games.

For the contest, I developed a game called Relativia, a hybrid puzzle and role-playing game. I also thought it would be interesting to incorporate location-based technology (think GPS), so when the player first starts a game, the world map is generated dynamically, based on their locale

✔ Dungeons and markets in the game would be linked to real-world locations, such as supermarkets or coffee shops.

✔ To enter a dungeon in the game, the players would have to travel physically to specific retail locations, at which point the game would allow them to enter the dungeon and progress.

The idea was to

✔ Give the game away for free

✔ Charge retail locations a sponsorship fee to be mapped to in-game locations.

I thought I had come up with a brilliant new way to make money in the mobile game sector!

Unfortunately, there was a major flaw in this concept. Most people who downloaded and commented on the game said that they enjoyed the game play, but didn't want to have to physically travel to other locations to play the game.

From this experience, I realized that location-based games or apps probably work best if they enrich the player's experience by providing additional value *when the user is already going places* he or she would normally go, rather than compelling the player to go somewhere.

With many of my games, I have used a two-pronged attack, offering most of them as both free *and* paid.

✔ The free versions contain ads and are sometimes feature-limited.

✔ The paid versions have no restrictions.

The free versions point to the paid versions as a form of advertising. I've tried releasing just one version or the other, but this particular strategy has served well.

The moral of the story: Even though my idea didn't pan out, you shouldn't necessarily constrain yourself to existing models. If your game is innovative enough, there just may be a novel way to make money from it, and you just may be hailed as a pioneer in mobile gaming!

Chapter 2

Designing Your Game

....

In This Chapter

▶ Understanding mobile games

▶ Getting into the mind of your audience

▶ Designing user interfaces for games

....

You may already know what kind of games you want to make. Most of the time, game developers work on the kinds of games that they love to play. But not all genres and formats of games fit well on the mobile platform, while some are perfectly suitable for games on the go.

Even though the hardware and software for Android devices continues to get more sophisticated and powerful, bleeding-edge games that strain the limits of these devices' memory and processing power may not be the best way to go. You need to keep in mind that most people won't have the latest and greatest devices, and if you want to target a wide part of the market, your games will need to run on older devices.

In a word, the short answer to the question of what kinds of games are best for mobile is: Short!

Deciding What Kind of Game to Make

Choosing the kind of game you want to make isn't just a matter of deciding what type of game you like to play, or which type of game you think will be the most marketable (although both of these are important).

We consider genre first, though, before moving on to other factors (such as number of players) that affect design.

Genre

Currently Google Play has eight subcategories in Games, each one corresponding to a game *genre*:

- ✔ Arcade & Action: fast-paced games where timing and reflexes are usually important, such as

  - Pac-Man
  - Pinball
  - Fighting games

- ✔ Brain & Puzzle: games you have to think to be good at, such as

  - Crosswords
  - Sudoku
  - Chess

- ✔ Cards & Casino: usually games with dice or cards with a random element, such as

  - Slot simulator
  - Poker
  - Mahjongg

- ✔ Casual: generally easy-to-learn, easy-to-play games for a broad audience, such as

  - Connect the dots
  - Music games

- ✔ Live Wallpaper

  I'm not sure why this category is in Games, but it includes backgrounds for your Home screen that are animated.

- ✔ Racing: cars, motorcycles, that sort of thing

- ✔ Sports Games: football, baseball, and so on

- ✔ Widgets

  Another strange subcategory for games, refers to miniature apps with their own UIs that reside on your Home screen

Discounting Live Wallpaper and Widgets, there are six actual game categories.

One of the first things you should do is browse these categories to get a sense of what games are currently available and which are the most popular. If you haven't already, you'll also want to download and play a few.

One of the upsides to being a game developer is that playing games is considered research!

Market position matters. You're providing a product to users who have many alternatives:

✔ An important consideration is how crowded a particular subcategory is.

Arcade & Action is probably the most fiercely competitive game category on Google Play at the moment. You might consider developing a game that falls into a less competitive genre.

If you want to go up against the toughest competition, you'll need to at least be familiar with it and try to bring something of value that your competitors don't, such as

- Lower cost

- More features

- A better interface

✔ Be mindful about how neatly your game may fall into a particular genre.

If you've just come up with a mind-bending hybrid of a game (say, a racing word game)

- Which category would it fit in better?

- Which category might face less competition and garner more usage?

Category membership is one aspect of your game that you can update dynamically, so just as with choosing a price point, you may want to experiment if your game doesn't fall neatly into one particular category.

Number of players

The number of players for your game may depend on your goals and on the nature of the game.

Single player

Single-player games may be games that are either

✔ Naturally are played alone, like solitaire

✔ Played against a computer version of the usual human opponent

Single-player games a couple of advantages for players and developers:

✔ The virtue of generally not requiring data connectivity to play means the game won't rely on a potentially spotty Internet connection — which means that it can be played anywhere, anytime.

✔ If you're not dealing with data connectivity, the game is also generally going to be less complex, so single-player games are a good idea for the first games you make.

Multiple players

Multiplayer games involve two or more players interacting with one another:

✔ Most often this interaction is via the internet. Players may either

  • Interact in real time, such as a fighting game

  • Play *asynchronously*, making a move at their leisure, which alerts the opponent it's his or her turn to make a move.

  A multiplayer chess game might work this way.

✔ Another form of multiplayer game is *local multiplayer*. Instead of playing someone sight unseen, you play someone sitting in the same room:

  • Devices can still communicate via the Internet.

  • You might also have the option of using a local communication protocol such as Bluetooth or Wi-Fi.

  This multiplayer format is generally less popular than non-local multi-player, but in some cases it may be the perfect format for your game.

✔ Yet another version of multiplayer is *pass-and-play*, where players use a single device, physically handing it off to one another to make plays.

  This form of multiplayer is a bit clunky, but does have the advantage of not requiring device-to-device communication.

  It's probably not a good idea to implement pass-and-play as the only way to play your game, but you might consider it as an additional feature.

Most developers starting out in games aren't members of huge teams with million-dollar budgets, so your best bet is to avoid trying to make a large, complex game right out of the chute. Completing even a simple game can be difficult, but gives you invaluable experience and a sense of accomplishment.

Once you've successfully developed a single-player game, it makes sense to try your hand at multiplayer games, if that's your ultimate goal.

A good intermediary is the asynchronous multiplayer game. Some of the most popular mobile games on the market today fall into this category, in which one player updates the game state locally, then sends those updates to another player.

Asynchronous games have a couple of advantages:

✔ This type of game is less complex and requires less fault tolerance than one that needs to be updated in real time.

If an update to the game state doesn't go through on the first click because of a spotty connection, just allow them to attempt again.

✔ Asynchronous games also allow players to engage with the game at their convenience, rather than having to coordinate a time when both players are available simultaneously.

This format works beautifully for mobile gaming, in which a player can make a move in a game when they have a pause in their busy day, waiting in line at the supermarket or in the dentist's office.

A lot of new game developers overreach. They may love playing MMORPGs (Massively Multiplayer Online Role-Playing Games) and have a dream design for one. Often they underestimate the time, energy, complexity, and resources involved in creating such a game:

✔ Role-playing games, even the simplest ones, usually require a large amount of graphical resources.

Most players of RPGs want to find a variety of armor and weapons, as well as face off against a wide variety of bad guys. You can heavily reuse the same graphics, but then the game becomes monotonous.

✔ MMORPGs or multiplayer FPSs (first-person shooters) are played in real time, which requires sophistication in handling how the game state is updated between players.

Mobile connectivity is generally less reliable than wired data connections, so this can make your game unplayable unless you are really savvy at handling the limitations of mobile technology.

Thinking about how and when people will play your game

Mobile games, as opposed to those played on a console or PC, are generally played

- ✔ On smaller screens
- ✔ On devices with fewer memory and processing resources
- ✔ For shorter periods of time

Some important ramifications of this to your game design are

- ✔ **The duration of game play.** Typically players won't want to stare at and click a small screen for hours at a time.

  Think about how sessions of your game might work as "bite-sized" chunks. As a reference point, most of my games have a median session length of about six minutes.

- ✔ **Fat fingers!** The size of the screen is crucial in mobile game development. Android devices may have a variety of input hardware:

  - • The G1, the first Android device, had a trackball.

  - • Some have hardware keyboards, others don't.

  The most consistent input method for your game will likely be the touchscreen.

  Make buttons for your application

  - • Large enough for easy interactivity

  - • Spaced far enough so that the player does what they want to, when they want to do it

- ✔ **Size of text and graphics.** You'll want to make sure any text is clearly readable, especially on smaller devices.

  The Android SDK lets you scale text according to screen size, but any text embedded in graphics will need to be readable across all resolutions.

One other important design decision that is often overlooked especially by beginning game developers: colorblindness. Up to 10 percent of males can have some form of colorblindness, and if your game relies on color to differentiate between game elements, it may be difficult or unplayable to a significant segment of your market. Not long after I published my puzzle-RPG hybrid *Puzzle Lords*, I received an e-mail from someone who was colorblind, asking if I could add a colorblind mode. The game requires the player to match gems of the same shape by dropping them in a grid. Figure 2-1 shows a sample combat screen without colorblind mode enabled.

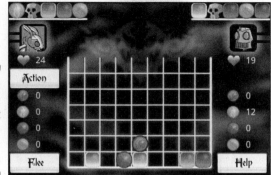

Figure 2-1:
The main
combat
screen
for Puzzle
Lords.

Figure 2-2 is the same combat screen, with colorblind mode enabled. As you can see, I added symbols (X, square, circle, and triangle) to the circular gems:

✔ The circular gems are much more important for matching than the square gems

✔ I determined that adding symbols to all the gems would look overly busy.

This intermediate solution lets players play comfortably in colorblind mode, and the person who originally e-mailed me was happy with the addition.

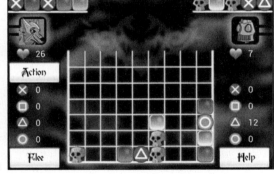

Figure 2-2:
The main
combat
screen for
Puzzle Lords
in colorblind
mode.

No matter what you do, you won't make all of your players happy. Design decisions are often tradeoffs in which you try to

✔ Please the largest number of players.

✔ Reach the widest audience.

Issues such as localization (making your game playable in other countries and locales) and accessibility (making your game playable to those with special needs) often depend on how much time and how many resources you are willing to spend versus keeping your target player base happy.

Identifying Your Target Audience

Android is becoming more and more popular every day, and so the demographics of the users are becoming larger and more varied. As of this writing, the demographics are still skewed in particular directions, possibly enough to impact some of your design decisions. In any case, it never hurts to have more information about the audience for your games.

I'd encourage you to use some form of analytics to learn more about your player base and how they are using your app. Google Play has some built-in analytics, breaking down a lot of useful information about your game and its users, such as

- Downloads versus active installs. Five thousand people may have downloaded your app, but only 500 of those decided to keep it installed.

- You'll want to know what your retention rate is, since it's one good indicator of the quality of your game.

- Google Play also breaks down active installs and downloads for a particular time frame, as well as by

  - OS version

  - Device

  - Country

  - Language

  - App version

  - Carrier

Even though there is a wealth of information through the developer console on Google Play, you may want to install a third-party analytics package or even implement your own.

Some app analytics provide information such as session length and frequency of sessions. Typically user behavior follows a long-tail distribution. That is, you'll usually have

✔ Some small number of users that play your game a lot

✔ A lot of users that don't play your game that much

But keeping an eye on average play length for a given session or average sessions per week will give you some insight into how engaging your game is and how you might update it to make it more appealing to players.

Besides particular information you might gather about the audience for your particular game, there are a number of general demographic trends for Android users that might be of interest.

The Android user base

Because Android was first presented as an open, more technically customizable alternative to iOS, early adopters tended to make up a larger percentage of the user base. These days they still do, but to a lesser extent; with the wide array of devices on every carrier in the US (and many around the world), attracting fans of cutting-edge tech is less of a factor in a game's success.

✔ The Android user base continues to skew slightly more toward males.

- • Their median income tends to be lower than that of iOS users, probably due to the fact that Android offers a wide array of devices, including budget ones.

- • Some research indicates that Android users are less likely to purchase apps or make in-app purchases, but may be more likely to click in-app ads.

This kind of information may guide how you choose to monetize your app.

✔ For some game genres, such as casual game formats like *hidden-object* (where the player tries to find objects in a scene), the demographic for PC players skews slightly toward older and female.

If you decide what kind of game to develop based solely on maximizing your potential audience, you may want to consider the particular makeup of the Android user base. However, a good rule of thumb is to make a game that appeals to a wide spectrum of users.

You can't go too wrong with a game that everyone wants to play!

Casting a wide net or finding a niche

Making a game with widespread appeal might be a strong decision. However, you might find success by targeting a specific demographic that is underserved. As of this writing, Google Play has around 500,000 apps.

When I started developing for Android, I had to contend with only a handful of apps on the market, so competition was far less severe. These days it's difficult to find a segment of the user base that isn't already being served, but it's still possible. And if you can do that, you might find a group of players that will become loyal to you and your brand:

✔ Historically, females are underserved by the video gaming industry. One way you might stand out from your competition is by bucking the demographics and making games specifically for females.

That doesn't necessarily mean filling your game with the first thing you think of that seems "girlish." (Okay, depending on the game, pink unicorns and such might be a good idea! Making hasty assumptions isn't.) More importantly, it means understanding what your audience wants out of a game experience.

A social game focused more on collaboration than competition might be more suited to a female player base. If you can tap in to what makes a particular subset of gamers tick — and give them what they want — they'll come back for more.

✔ Another potential niche is kids' games. More and more smartphones and tablets are being used to either augment kids' early education and development, or at least keep them occupied for a while in the car.

If you can develop games with an educational bent, or that have particular appeal to young children, you just might have a hit on your hands.

✔ Those with special needs, such as the blind, are very underserved by gaming. Designing games without visual input is especially challenging, but it might also flex your creativity in ways you never imagined.

You may choose to find a niche based on something entirely different. For instance, I live in southern Louisiana where a card game called Boo-Ray is fairly popular. Last time I checked, there was no Boo-Ray app on Google Play. Granted, the user base would be small, but possibly highly dedicated if you chose to implement a regional game that has a strong following.

The simultaneous advantage and disadvantage to developing for a niche is that your audience will necessarily be smaller:

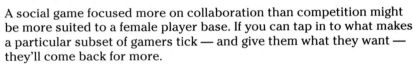

✔ This lets you tailor your app for that user base.

✔ A targeted game may engender more loyalty than a game with widespread appeal, but it may ultimately be too limiting.

Either way, it's a good idea to think hard about what kind of player base you want to develop for.

Targeting Devices

When designing your game, you'll need to determine which devices you are willing to support. This is nearly always a tradeoff between increasing your audience size at the expense of using the latest, greatest features of devices, including enhancements in performance and new features in the OS. Of course, if you do target only the latest devices, eventually the industry will catch up, but it may take some time.

From time to time, the dreaded "F" word rears its head in discussions of Android: *Fragmentation* refers to the proliferation of different Android devices and firmware versions, potentially leading to a disjointed ecosystem where users don't have a consistent experience between Android devices, and developers face the nightmare of developing for way too many different configurations.

iPhone developer advocates like to point out that there are far fewer hardware and software versions to worry about when you're developing for iOS. Okay, technically this is true, but variety is both the boon and the bane of Android. The wide spectrum of OS versions can lead to inconsistent user experiences, but it also entails a rapid release cycle, so innovation marches on at a break-neck pace. The wide spectrum of hardware allows buyers to choose options in all price ranges. You can get a budget Android phone with less power and fewer features, or you can spend more money and get the latest and greatest. The headaches to developers can be mitigated by

✔ Cleverly managing resources

✔ Following Google's guidelines for supporting multiple devices

Meanwhile, offering Android in a variety of shapes, sizes, and costs means that it will penetrate the market at all levels, which means a bigger audience for your games.

In general, I like to try to support as wide a swath of devices as possible, so the examples in this book will follow that principle.

Firmware

The term *firmware* refers to the operating system of a smartphone. The version of Android that a given device runs will determine what features are available, its speed, and many other important factors.

You'll need to think about which versions you want to support:

- ✔ A big part of that decision is what kinds of features you want to use in your game — and the difficulty in making your game compatible with all the versions you want to support.
- ✔ You should test on all supported versions, and that can be a headache, so you'll probably want to try to support a subset of the versions in use.

Android versions

Google maintains a website (`http://developer.android.com/about/dashboards/index.html`) which shows a monthly snapshot of Android versions currently used worldwide.

Historically, the Android ecosystem has had a large number of versions available at any given time:

- ✔ Though two or three versions tend to make up the vast majority (75 percent or more) of the current user base, and those tend to be the more recent versions.
- ✔ Some small percentage of users will still be running much older versions of Android. You would certainly make those users happy if you offered games that ran on those devices, but if development and testing time are at a premium and you have to leave those versions out, the loss is negligible.

When you're making decisions about which OS versions to support, it generally makes sense to prepare for the future, rather than try to cling to the past. You and your user base will be happy if you

- ✔ Avoid using APIs that vary (or are nonexistent) between versions.
- ✔ Keep things simple.
- ✔ Develop in a way that enables your game to play happily regardless of OS version.

Custom ROMs

Because Android is open-source, anyone can take it, modify it, and release a custom version. Manufacturers often "skin" Android to give it a particular look and feel on their particular lines of devices. Some examples include

> ✔ Motorola Blur
>
> ✔ HTC Sense
>
> ✔ Samsung Touchwiz

Though these modifications typically only manipulate the main user interface of the device, rarely the changes made may affect apps run on these devices.

Ideally you would want to test your game across a wide variety of devices, including those that run manufacturers' custom versions. Of course, an indie developer may not be able to afford a test suite of dozens of devices, in which case you may have to make do by downloading emulated versions from manufacturers' websites, or simply crossing your fingers when you release and trying to fix problems after you get feedback from players.

Another, smaller segment of your player base will be those users who have installed custom Read-Only Memory. An avid community of ROM developers is always ready to take the latest builds of Android, modify them, and make them available for anyone who wants to take the risk of rooting their phone and installing a non-factory build of the OS.

There are a surprising number of users with custom ROMs installed, though they can be more difficult to track. Testing for compatibility with custom ROMs is even more difficult than with the normal variety of standard configurations, but be ready for the occasional support e-mail from players using customized ROM.

Hardware

Along with the variety of OS versions, Android is available on a dazzling array of hardware. Before developing and certainly before publishing a game on the platform, you should be mindful of the different types of hardware and how they might affect the way your game looks and plays.

Processors

The first Android device sported a 528-MHz processor and anyone who had one probably remembers the interface being a little sluggish, certainly compared to other smartphones at the time. The hardware has advanced a great deal in a short time, and new devices are now coming with multi-core processors, each in the GHz range.

More powerful devices mean better performance for games, but not without a price. Even playing a relatively simple 2D game can drain the battery pretty quickly, due to

✔ Increased CPU power

✔ Larger, denser displays

Games that use a lot of juice can tend to make a device generate a fair amount of heat as well. So while you *can* make more CPU-intensive games, you might not want to.

Screen sizes

An important distinction to make is between

✔ Screen size (the actual physical measurement of the screen)

✔ Density (which is the number of pixels in a given area).

Current screen sizes are lumped into one of four categories, based on the length of their diagonals, as shown in Figure 2-3.

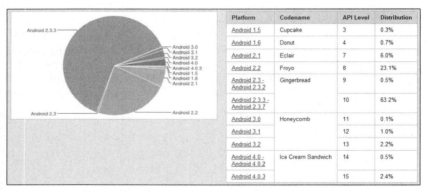

Figure 2-3: Screen sizes for Android devices.

Platform	Codename	API Level	Distribution
Android 1.5	Cupcake	3	0.3%
Android 1.6	Donut	4	0.7%
Android 2.1	Eclair	7	6.0%
Android 2.2	Froyo	8	23.1%
Android 2.3 - Android 2.3.2	Gingerbread	9	0.5%
Android 2.3.3 - Android 2.3.7		10	63.2%
Android 3.0	Honeycomb	11	0.1%
Android 3.1		12	1.0%
Android 3.2		13	2.2%
Android 4.0 - Android 4.0.2	Ice Cream Sandwich	14	0.5%
Android 4.0.3		15	2.4%

The densities of screens are classified in Table 2-1.

Table 2-1	Screen Density	
Name	**Pixels**	**Abbreviation**
Low-density	120	ldpi
Medium-density	160	mdpi
High-density	240	hdpi
Extra-high density	320	xhdpi

As with processors, increased innovation in hardware is resulting in higher density screens with crisper graphics. A good rule to follow when developing across different screen sizes and densities is to

✔ Target the largest screens and make sure your game looks good on those.

✔ Scale down to the smallest screens you're willing to support.

This book lays out the graphical elements so that our games will be playable on every device. Supporting multiple screens can be a daunting and complex subject, though. Google maintains a website specifically for supporting multiple screen sizes:

```
http://developer.android.com/guide/practices/screens_
support.html
```

You should bookmark this page, study it, and refer to it often.

Input types

Along with the variety of Android devices comes a variety of input methods. You can safely bet that most devices will have a touchscreen, but they may include the following forms of input:

✔ Keyboard

✔ Trackball/Trackpad

✔ Microphone

✔ Camera

✔ Accelerometer (senses movement)

✔ GPS (detects location)

You may have an innovative idea for a game that uses one or more of these forms of input. The entire class of *augmented reality* (AR) apps and games generally rely on camera input as they meld real-world images and locations with overlays on the device. Some very popular games use the accelerometer for control inputs, allowing the player to tilt the device to manipulate on-screen elements.

I have a prototype of a game that uses voice input as part of casting spells, which requires a microphone. If the device is a phone (as many Android devices are), that's fine. Just be aware that not all Android devices may have the particular kinds of input your game requires. Luckily, the Android SDK includes ways of letting you specify what hardware is required for your app — and that's covered in

Chapter 4. For now, just be aware that in the planning stages, the less standard your input types are, the more you might be limiting your potential audience. Keep in mind whether this is something your game really requires, and whether or not more than one set of control options might be available. For example, you might make your game use the touchscreen as input by default, but also make it playable via microphone.

Phones

There are dozens of Android phones available now, and they will likely be the primary target for your games for a long time to come.

Accordingly, while designing your game, keep in mind that phones typically have smaller screens than other devices; you'll want to use inputs and graphics that are easily visible and interactive on small screens.

Tablets

Android has not currently penetrated the market for tablets nearly as effectively as it has for smartphones. A notable exception is the Kindle Fire by Amazon, which has sold extremely well.

The most sensible plan for prioritizing for Android devices is to develop for *phone first, then tablet.* If your goal is to try to do well financially, you may have a difficult time targeting tablets as the primary device. However, as the Android tablet market grows, you will definitely want to make sure your game runs and plays well on larger screens.

Tablets have the luxury of large, often very-high-resolution displays. So games will generally be easier to play because game elements will be easier to see and inputs will be easier to interact with.

One potential drawback is that many Android tablets don't have the same auxiliary hardware that many smartphones do. The Kindle Fire doesn't have a camera, microphone, or any location-based services. If your game only uses touch input, that's fine. But take these factors into consideration before you begin to code.

TV and beyond

Google TV, which at its core is Android-powered, has been released in stand-alone set-top boxes as well as integrated into televisions and DVD players. So far it has not caught on, but Google seems intent on continuing to push and support TV as a platform for Android.

While many apps may run on Google TV, the input system is completely different from those of other devices. Currently, Google TV supports input through a remote keyboard device, which has a touchpad. A game designed specifically for touch input would probably have to be modified significantly for use on Google TV, although some games may be more amenable to the format. Right now, if your game doesn't run in that format, the size of the audience doesn't justify putting in the extra developmental effort. But this may change in the future, so it's a good potential market to keep an eye on.

Other — more speculative — markets may include cars. Some major car manufacturers are working on pre-installed Android devices for playing media and navigating via GPS. Of course, you wouldn't want to design a game that the driver would need to interact heavily with, but games for road trips (like I Spy or singing games) could be designed for existing devices, and may port easily over to car systems when they begin to become popular.

And because Android really can run just about anywhere, there are other uses and markets that are likely to arise in the future. Flexible screens will be hitting the market soon, allowing for wearable devices such as armbands! Google's Project Glass is a design in the works for wearable glasses that carry out many smartphone functions. Be ready for thinking about how you might design for such devices.

The more streamlined and intuitive your interface and controls are, the easier it will be to adapt them to future devices. Technology moves rapidly, and if you want to stay in front, you'll need to stay informed and be thinking ahead!

Designing the interface and controls

You've got a lot of important choices to make when it comes to designing how players will change what happens in the game by interacting with it.

Some of the most important factors when considering interface design are to be sure that game elements and controls are

✔ **Intuitive:** After you've completed a workable version of the game, one of the first things you'll want to do is give "The Grandmother Test". This doesn't mean actually giving it to your grandma to play (though that may not be a bad idea if she's up for it). Here "grandmother" refers to someone who is generally not a hardcore game player. The idea is to see how quickly they "get it" when trying to navigate and play your game.

  • If they pick up how to play your game right away, you're doing something right.

- If anything is confusing or frustrating, you'll want to try to ask targeted questions to figure out just what about the interface you need to change.

✔ **Clean:** Make sure that the players can easily see what they need to see and click the things they're trying to click.

If your users can't find their health bar or habitually click one button when they mean to click another, you'll need to think about revision.

✔ **Pretty:** If you want your players to spend a lot of time with your game, you'll want it to look (and sound) good. Nice production values go a long way in making a game popular and keeping it that way.

A big difference between some games that do well and those that don't is often the amount of polish. After coding your game for weeks or months (or even years!), you may not feel like making a lot of cosmetic changes, but the extra effort is often rewarded with happier users who are more willing to play your game — and recommend it to others.

Hardware controls

Depending on the type of game you're planning on implementing, you may want to use hardware, such as the keyboard or trackball/trackpad, for input. If the player is not using the touchscreen for input, there's the added advantage that fingers or thumbs won't be obscuring the screen, leading to a more natural game experience. In practice, this approach isn't always feasible because of the inconsistency among hardware configurations of Android devices.

Prototype your control scheme early in the development process to get a feel for

✔ Whether it's going to work

✔ Whether a wide variety of Android devices will support it

Virtual controls

Sometimes you want to mimic the functionality of hardware controls such as buttons or joysticks when the hardware just isn't available. Virtual controls are emulated versions of hardware controls implemented in software.

For example, you may want your game to use a *directional pad (d-pad)* for moving a character through the game. If you wanted to implement this feature on a phone or tablet that doesn't have a d-pad, you could draw something that looks like a d-pad in one corner of your game, using the touchscreen to capture inputs so that portion of the touchscreen functions *like* a d-pad.

I'll just come right out and say it. I don't like virtual controls. I've never played a game with virtual controls that I like:

- ✔ In general, the response time — not to mention the touch and feel — of virtual controls will be far inferior to what you get from actual hardware.

- ✔ They take up a lot of screen space. Real estate on small screens is at a premium. If you clutter the screen with controls, you have less space to show other elements.

For some games, virtual controls make the most sense. An implementation of Pac-Man without a joystick and buttons, even virtual ones, just wouldn't be the same. They do have the advantage of working on any device with a touchscreen.

Other cultures and languages

App stores are global markets, and Google Play is able to offer your apps in dozens of countries around the world. You might want to consider localizing your game so that players around the world can enjoy it:

- ✔ A number of freelancers and companies will charge you to localize the language in your game.

- ✔ If you have a friend who's a fluent speaker of a particular language with a large demographic, that's even better!

As a general rule, you'll want to maintain the text of all your user interface (UI) elements (such as buttons, titles, and warnings) in a separate file. Chapter 4 will go into more detail about how this is done in practice.

One other thing to consider is cultural differences. Think about how your game might be perceived by particular cultures. If the enemies in your game are WWII Japanese soldiers and they're portrayed very negatively, your game might not go over very well in Japan. You don't need to be overly fussy about political correctness, but your game really *is* going to be available to a global audience as soon as you hit that Publish button.

Players with special needs

Consider players who are blind, deaf, or unable to use traditional modes of input to Android devices. Designing playable games for these types of users can be extremely difficult. But if you specifically target such an underserved demographic, you will probably develop a particularly loyal fanbase.

Tutorials

One way to make your game more playable, especially if it introduces new or unfamiliar concepts, is to include a tutorial.

If your game is novel, you'll want the learning curve to be gentle at first, ramping slowly up in difficulty as you introduce more concepts:

- ✔ A practice mode is one possible way to implement assistance as the player becomes familiar with your game.

- ✔ A dedicated "tips" window can appear when the player enters a new screen.

- ✔ You can display tips on loading screens, a popular practice on many modern games because it works extremely well.

Pay close attention when you give the game to friends or family for the first time, and see how easily they pick it up:

- ✔ If they are having difficulty, it could be an issue with the interface or an inherent problem with the game design.

- ✔ It could be that your game is just new and complex enough that new players need your help to figure out how to engage with it.

  Most beginning game designers don't think of themselves as teachers — they just want to make a cool game! — but sometimes a little teaching goes with the territory.

  Your game may be extremely intuitive to you because you've spent so much time tweaking it in your head. Try to be objective and think about what it's like to see and play your game *for the first time*. Testers will help you with this, of course, but train yourself to think this way as well. When you do, you'll often find that familiar aspects of the game — obvious to you, the maker (of course) — must be pointed out to many of your potential players. That's where tutorials come in.

Finding and/or creating resources (graphics and sound)

Unless you're designing a game that doesn't require graphics or sounds, you're going to need some visual and audible whiz-bang. Even if your game doesn't require graphics, you'll still need an icon and a banner for the market listing. You've really got two choices for these resources: buy them or make them yourself.

Create your own

As a game developer, you're already going to have to wear a lot of hats. If you're an indie, you'll probably have to handle all the business, support, marketing and PR, and any other day-to-day business of running a small game company. Rare is the person who can do all that *and* produce quality art, sound effects, and music.

If your game is not very graphics- or sound-intensive, you might be able to get away with doing everything yourself. If you're working on something like a card game or an abstract physics puzzler, you might be just fine opening up your favorite graphics program and creating resources yourself. But be warned: Some in the game development community have come to refer to bad graphics as "developer art". Even so, a lot of indies don't have the budget to hire an artist, and even making do by themselves they can enjoy a fair amount of success.

If you do tackle your own game art, you should at least invest some time and effort in learning some basics about art and graphic design. Your game is going to be available to millions of people around the world. You want it to look good! Your icon is especially important in making a first impression to prospective players; the appeal of a good-looking icon can't be overstated. Find some books on art and graphic design, and consider taking a course or two at a community college or in continuing education.

Hiring creative contractors

The ideal situation is to hire artists to create wonderful art and music for you. In addition to getting a higher-quality product, you're less likely to stretch yourself thin, giving you more time to develop and make your game more playable and fun.

Even on a relatively small budget, you can take some steps to maximize your return on the money you spend on art and music. The stereotype of the starving artist is, unfortunately, too often true; you can often find students or artists just starting out who are willing to work with you to provide you with affordable art and music for your game.

Art

You'll want nice art in whatever game you develop, but if you're working in a genre like hidden objects or any genre with lush, full-screen art, you'll definitely want to invest in a good artist. If you don't know one personally, you can try to find one either online or in your local community. As with any type of contracting, face time has a lot of value. If you can sit down with your artist over coffee and work through sketches and ideas, meetings can generally be more productive than they'd be over the phone or online:

✔ You might want to consider posting flyers at local colleges, in the mailrooms or cafeterias, and of course wherever art classes are held. You might be surprised at the amount of interest. A lot of aspiring art students may be willing to collaborate just to help build a portfolio.

✔ Online, you can find a great resource for indie game developers in the forums at Indiegamer.com (`http://forums.indiegamer.com/`). A wide range of both artist and music and sound people post samples of their work, as well as posts of availability for projects. You can contact artists via e-mail and ask for hourly or project quotes if you like their work.

✔ Another place to scout out for artists is `deviantART.com`. Amateur and professional artists showcase their work here, and it's a great place to scout them out and approach them with offers to work.

Sound and Music

In many ways, sound and music are generally less prominent for the mobile platform (hint: tiny speakers), but they can still be a key ingredient of a successful game.

Because people will likely be playing your game when they're out in public or otherwise surrounded by other people, often they may be inclined to play your game without sound or music, even if those features are available. (Imagine, say, a user not wanting to wake up the sleeping baby in the next seat on the plane.)

Sound effects or music in your game should be slightly lower on your priority list, and if you do implement them, always offer the option to disable them.

As for finding quality people to generate art and music for you, a lot of the same advice as for finding graphical artists applies: Scout your local colleges for students, as well as the forums at `Indiegamer.com`.

You obviously want great resources for as little money as you want to spend. But everyone values their time and talent, so try to use tact when dealing with creative contractors. I've seen many complaints in game development forums about how many artists are flaky and don't follow through with contract work, but that's probably because you're more likely to hear when something goes wrong than when it goes right. I've personally dealt with a number of creative contractors, and overall I've had very good experiences.

A good policy for contracting work, even for relatively small projects, is to make everything clear in writing up front. A simple contract works well, but at the very least draw up some kind of document that states what is expected of each party, with realistic deadlines. With this approach, there's much less chance of confusion and disagreement down the line.

Treat people with professional courtesy and respect, and they will be much more likely to reciprocate

Chapter 3

Setting Up Your Development Environment

In This Chapter

▶ Getting familiar with the Eclipse development tool

▶ Using the Android SDK

▶ Running your first Android app

*T*he tools for developing Android are freely available for download and use. Even if you've never used an IDE (integrated development environment) like Eclipse, it won't take long for you to get your feet wet.

Starting at the Beginning

Android and all its associated tools run on Java, so the first thing you'll need to do is make sure your development machine meets the supported system requirement. Then you'll need to install the Java Development Kit (JDK).

The following operating systems are currently supported:

✔ Windows XP (32-bit)

✔ Windows Vista (32- or 64-bit)

✔ Windows 7 (32- or 64-bit)

✔ Mac OS X 10.5.8 or later (x86 only)

✔ Linux (tested on Ubuntu Linux and Lucid Lynx)

- Gnu C Library (glibc) 2.7 or later is required

- For Ubuntu Linux, version 8.04 or later is required

- 64-bit distributions must be able to run 32-bit applications

After you've verified that your machine is up to snuff, the next order of business is to install the latest version of the JDK.

Follow these steps:

1. **Point your browser to** www.oracle.com/technetwork/java/
   javase/downloads/index.html

   You should see something like the page in Figure 3-1.

Figure 3-1:
Oracle's
download
page
for Java
products.

2. **Click the download icon for Java Platform (JDK).**

   The page listing downloads for specific platforms appears (See Figure 3-2).

Figure 3-2:
Download
page for
specific
operating
systems.

Java SE Development Kit 7u3

You must accept the Oracle Binary Code License Agreement for Java SE to download this software.

○ Accept License Agreement   ◉ Decline License Agreement

Product / File Description	File Size	Download
Linux x86 (32-bit)	63.65 MB	jdk-7u3-linux-i586.rpm
Linux x86 (32-bit)	78.66 MB	jdk-7u3-linux-i586.tar.gz
Linux x64 (64-bit)	64.53 MB	jdk-7u3-linux-x64.rpm
Linux x64 (64-bit)	77.3 MB	jdk-7u3-linux-x64.tar.gz
Solaris x86 (32-bit)	135.96 MB	jdk-7u3-solaris-i586.tar.Z
Solaris x86 (32-bit)	81.4 MB	jdk-7u3-solaris-i586.tar.gz
Solaris SPARC (32-bit)	138.92 MB	jdk-7u3-solaris-sparc.tar.Z
Solaris SPARC (32-bit)	86.07 MB	jdk-7u3-solaris-sparc.tar.gz
Solaris SPARC (64-bit)	16.14 MB	jdk-7u3-solaris-sparcv9.tar.Z
Solaris SPARC (64-bit)	12.31 MB	jdk-7u3-solaris-sparcv9.tar.gz
Solaris x64 (64-bit)	14.46 MB	jdk-7u3-solaris-x64.tar.Z
Solaris x64 (64-bit)	9.25 MB	jdk-7u3-solaris-x64.tar.gz
Windows x86 (32-bit)	84.12 MB	jdk-7u3-windows-i586.exe
Windows x64 (64-bit)	87.41 MB	jdk-7u3-windows-x64.exe

3. **Click the Accept License Agreement radio button and then click the specific download link for your operating system.**

   For example, the download for Windows 32-bit systems is `jdk-7u3-windows-i586.exe`.

4. **When the file has downloaded, double-click the file to begin the installation process.**

   On Windows, you're prompted by a message such as Do you want to allow the following program to make changes to your computer?

   Click the Yes button to continue with the installation and follow any instructions provided by the installer.

That's it! After the JDK is installed, you can run all the tools required to start building Android games.

The next step is to install Eclipse.

Downloading and Installing Eclipse

Eclipse is an *integrated development environment* (IDE), but what is that exactly? If you've never used an IDE before, it's a piece of software that makes software development a whole lot easier and enjoyable.

If you're an ace programmer with a photographic memory and robotic concentration, all you really need to write code is a simple text editor. Coding in a high-level language like Java is just writing text in a file. But an IDE provides an interface to your projects that makes carrying out simple, repetitive tasks much easier, as well as helping with debugging and troubleshooting.

Android Development Tools (ADT) is a plug-in that integrates with Eclipse to enable Android app development.

Android Development Tools have not always been compatible with the latest version of Eclipse. Double-check here for compatibility before installing Eclipse: `http://developer.android.com/sdk/eclipse-adt.html`.

The recommended version of Eclipse to use with the ADT is Classic. To install Eclipse Classic, follow these steps:

1. **Point your browser to** `www.eclipse.org/downloads`.

   You should see something like the page in Figure 3-3.

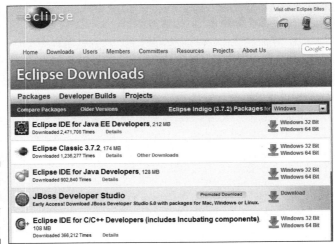

Figure 3-3:
Download
page for
Eclipse.

2. **If you are using Windows, click the appropriate download link (such as "Windows 32-Bit" next to Eclipse Classic 3.7.2).**

   If you are using an OS other than Windows, click the name of the package (such as Eclipse Classic 3.7.2) directly, which opens a page with downloads for other operating systems.

   Eclipse is downloaded as a compressed `.zip` file.

3. **After the file has downloaded, extract the `.zip` file into your desired directory (for example, `c:\Program Files\Eclipse` in Windows).**

4. **Launch Eclipse by double-clicking the eclipse.exe icon.**

   You probably also want to create a shortcut on your desktop or Start menu.

   When you launch Eclipse on Windows, you may be prompted by a message such as `Do you want to allow the following program to make changes to your computer?`

   Click the Yes button to continue with the installation and follow any instructions provided by the installer.

Java is required for Eclipse, so if Java is not properly installed, Eclipse won't work. When Eclipse starts for the first time, you're prompted to select a workspace.

This is the location on your computer where the working files for your project are stored.

Check the "Use this as the default and do not ask again" check box (Figure 3-4) after selecting the location for your desired workspace.

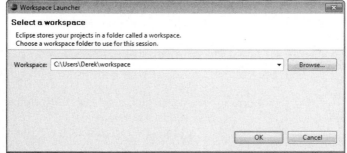

Figure 3-4:
Select a
workspace
in Eclipse.

When you've selected a workspace, the Eclipse welcome screen appears, as shown in Figure 3-5.

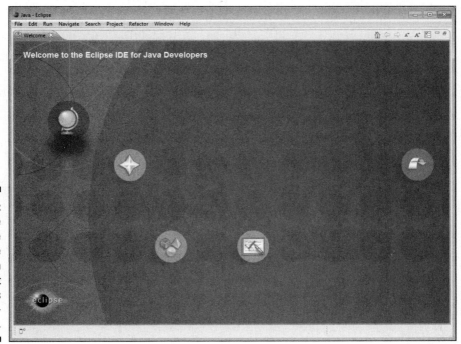

Figure 3-5:
The Eclipse
welcome
screen. The
arrow icon
on the right
launches
the work-
bench view.

Click the arrow icon on the right to launch the workbench view, which should look something like Figure 3-6.

Eclipse is extremely customizable, so you can move views around to organize your workbench however you like. If you're new to Eclipse, though, you'll probably want to leave the default organization in place. This screen is where you'll spend most of your time:

✔ The Package Explorer on the left displays the directory structure for your projects.

At this point, you don't have any projects yet, so there's nothing to display.

✔ The views at the bottom are typically used to analyze problems and output related to your project.

✔ The outline view shows an ordered list of the elements in the currently-selected file.

It can be very useful for navigating the structure of a given file.

✔ The big gray space in the middle is the code view, which is where you'll be entering all your brilliant code!

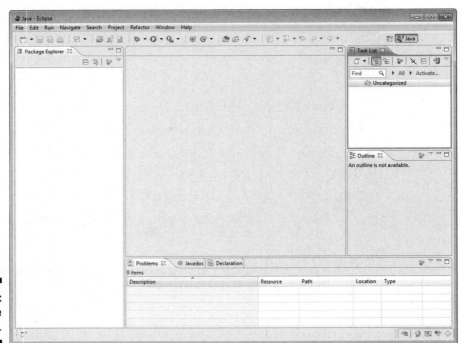

Figure 3-6:
The Eclipse
workbench.

Make line numbers visible in the Eclipse code view:

1. Select Window⇨Preferences.

2. Select General⇨Editors⇨Text Editors.

3. Check the Show line numbers check box.

The Android SDK and ADT still need to be installed before you can develop for Android in Eclipse. Read on to find out how.

Installing the Software

You have to have the Android SDK, which consists of libraries, documentation, and other code, in order to develop Android apps and games.

Note that the Android development tools are updated frequently, so the installation process may vary.

Installing the SDK

Follow these steps to download and install the SDK:

1. Point your browser to `http://developer.android.com/sdk/index.html`**.**

You should see something like the page in Figure 3-7.

2. Click the download link for your platform.

For Windows, Google recommends the installer (`.exe`) download.

3. Double-click the downloaded `.exe` **file.**

Follow the installation wizard instructions.

- If you use the self-extracting installer, at some point during the installation process it will prompt you for a path in which to extract the files.

- If you are not using the installer, but a compression tool to extract the files, you will need to choose a location.

In either case, use `c:\android` (or whatever the root directory on your hard drive is, if you're on another operating system). This will be the default location used throughout this book.

4. Start the SDK Manager.

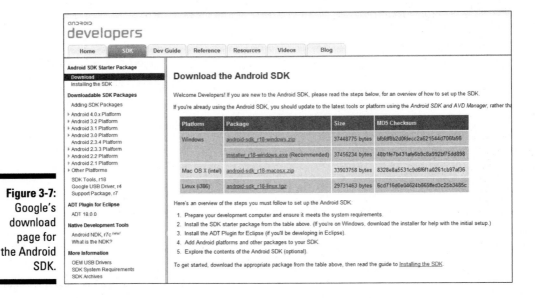

Figure 3-7:
Google's
download
page for
the Android
SDK.

Upon completing the SDK installation, the final screen of the wizard has a check box which reads "Start SDK Manager".

Leave it checked and click Finish.

5. Install the latest Android API (application programming interface).

By default, the SDK Manager will select the packages you need to begin developing with the latest available version of Android. I recommend that you leave the defaults checked, then click Install. A license window will appear.

6. Review the packages to install and their licenses, make sure the Accept radio button is selected, then click Install.

It may take a while to install all the necessary packages.

When the SDK Manager has finished downloading the packages, you may close it.

Installing the ADT

Follow these steps to install the Android Development Tools (ADT) plug-in.

1. Start Eclipse, then select Help⇨Install New Software.

The Install window appears.

2. **Click the Add button.**

   The Add Repository dialog box will appear.

3. **Enter "ADT Plugin" for the name and** `https://dl-ssl.google.com/android/eclipse/` **for the location.**

   The dialog box should look like Figure 3-8. Click OK.

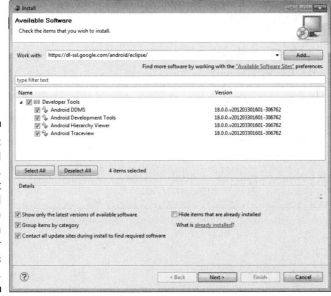

4. **In the Install dialog box, click the check box next to Developer Tools.**

   The dialog box should look something like Figure 3-9.

5. **Click Next.**

   A list of the tools you selected for download appears on the next screen.

6. **Click Next.**

   You're prompted to review the licenses for the software to be installed. You may select the license on the left to read its text in the box on the right.

7. **To accept the license and continue, click the radio button that says** `I accept the terms of the license agreement` **and then click Finish.**

   Upon completion of the installation, you may see a Security Warning dialog box, indicating that you are about to install unsigned content. This sounds scary, though it's perfectly fine. Click OK.

8. **When the installation is complete, you'll need to restart Eclipse.**

   Upon re-launching Eclipse, you should see two new icons in your toolbar, if the ADT was successfully installed in Eclipse. Figure 3-10 shows an example.

Figure 3-10:
The toolbar
in Eclipse
after install-
ing the ADT.

The two new icons launch these parts of the development environment:

   ✔ Android SDK Manager (the icon with the down arrow).

   The Android SDK manager is what you use to update the SDK.

   ✔ Android Virtual Device Manager (AVD).

New versions of the Android SDK are released periodically. These updates may include

   ✔ Bug fixes

   ✔ Enhanced performance for Android tools

   ✔ New functionality

It's a good idea to read blogs or forums related to Android development to stay up to date. Things move fast in the world of Android! These venues usually indicate when any new development tools are available for update. Otherwise you can just launch the tools from within Eclipse every couple of months and check manually.

Connecting Eclipse to the SDK

As it happens, you're not done integrating Android into Eclipse yet. You need to tell Eclipse where you installed the SDK. To do so, follow these steps.

1. **In Eclipse, select Window⇨Preferences.**

   The Preferences window appears.

2. **Select Android from the list in the left panel.**

   Your Android preferences appear, including a text box labeled SDK Location, which should be empty.

3. **For the SDK Location, enter** c:\android **or click Browse and navigate to the location of the SDK.**

4. **Click Apply, then OK.**

Now the Android tools should be successfully integrated into Eclipse. You're ready to create your first virtual device.

The Android Virtual Device (AVD) Manager

This tool allows you to create one or more virtual Android devices that will run on your desktop and behave like actual Android devices.

There are a couple of drawbacks to emulation:

✔ Virtual Android devices are very slow, even though Google has put effort into increasing the performance on emulated devices.

Speed is the major difference between an emulated device and a real one. Performance is worse as the size of the display increases. Trying to test apps or games for devices with very large displays is very difficult.

Invest in a hardware device if you intend to target tablets.

✔ Emulation is a poor test for certain input features.

- Interacting with a virtual device by using a mouse is almost nothing like interacting with the same device using your fingers and/or thumbs. On more than one occasion, I've initially tested an interface on a virtual device, only to realize that UI elements needed to be larger and better-spaced *after* I loaded the UI onto a hardware device.

- If your game uses the accelerometer or some other form of input that is difficult or impossible to emulate, you're better off testing on hardware.

That said, the emulator can come in handy if you're on a budget and can't afford a wide array of test devices.

An AVD is a good first-cut at testing your game. Nothing beats play-testing on an actual device, but if you're testing the initial look and feel of the game, early use of an AVD can be very helpful.

Creating a virtual device

To create a virtual device, follow these steps:

1. **In Eclipse, click the Android Virtual Device Manager icon, or select Window➪AVD Manager.**

   The Android Virtual Device window appears, as shown in Figure 3-11

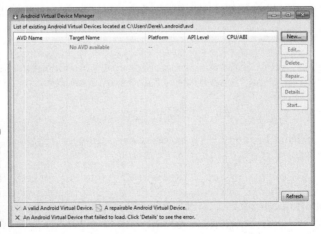

Figure 3-11:
The Android
Virtual
Device
Manager.

2. Click New.

The Create new Android Virtual Device (AVD) window appears, as shown in Figure 3-12.

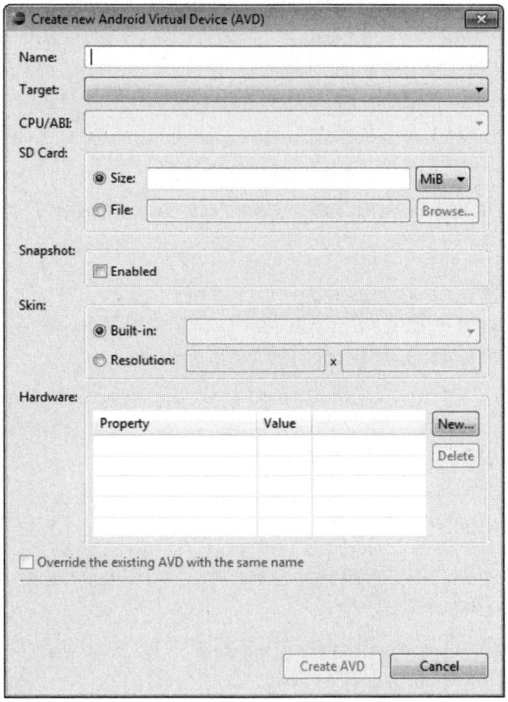

Figure 3-12:
The Create new Android Virtual Device (AVD) window.

3. Enter a name for your new virtual device.

Since you may have a lot of virtual devices, you'll want to use a descriptive name ("AVD1" is a bad idea!). Let's create a device that runs Android 2.1 with an HVGA screen. A good descriptive name for such a device would be "2.1HVGA".

Android naming conventions usually only allow

- Letters *a* through *z* (upper- or lowercase)
- Numbers 0 through 9
- Symbols period (.), dash (–), or underscore (_).

These limitations also apply not only for the names of virtual devices, but also for many names you use throughout Android projects (such as names for resources).

4. **Select an Android version to target from the Target drop-down menu.**

   The versions you selected when installing the SDK will be visible.

   In this case, select Android 2.1 – API Level 7.

5. **Enter a size for the virtual SD card in the Size field.**

   Your game may or may not use the SD card on a device in order to store information like saved games and high scores. There are a number of ways to store information, and not all require the SD card.

   This is optional on virtual devices, but it's a good idea to always implement a virtual SD just in case you need one.

   A good size for a virtual SD card is 1 gigabyte (GB). Enter "1000" in the Size field.

6. **Select a resolution.**

   • Most of the time you'll want to test on the built-in resolutions, available from the Built-in drop-down menu.

   • Occasionally you may want to test for a device with a non-standard display. In that case, you can enter whatever custom values you want.

   In this case, select HVGA. This was the standard resolution for most early Android devices.

   Many devices are being released with higher resolution, but you should still test for HVGA as a baseline.

   Review your settings. They should look like those in Figure 3-13.

   The hardware fields allow you to

   • Further customize the attributes of the devices you're using (such as virtual memory).

   • Provide support for other hardware such as an accelerometer or GPS device.

   Okay, relax. No need to make any adjustments to these settings just now, but as you can see, virtual devices are highly customizable.

7. **Click Create AVD.**

   Your new virtual device will now show up in your list of available virtual devices, as shown in Figure 3-14

You're ready to launch your first virtual device and see it in action!

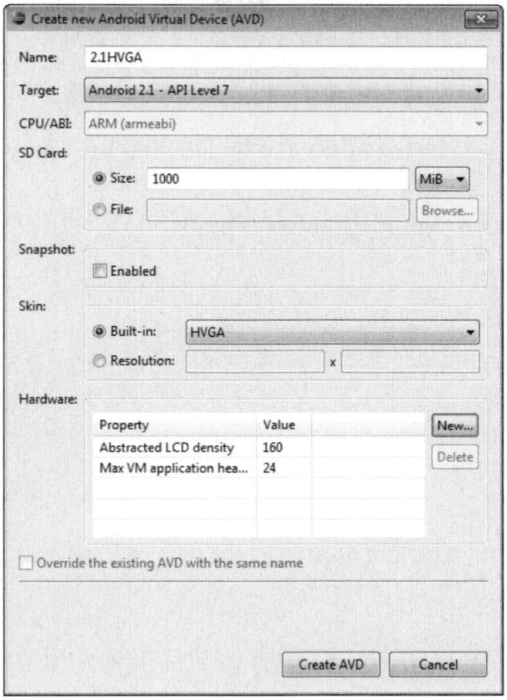

Figure 3-13:
The Create new Android Virtual Device (AVD) window with values filled in.

Figure 3-14:
The AVD with a newly created virtual device.

Launching a virtual device

To launch a virtual device, from the AVD Manager, follow these steps:

1. **Highlight the virtual device in the list by clicking the entry, then click Start.**

   You'll see the Launch Options window (Figure 3-15).

Figure 3-15: The AVD launch options window.

Give it some time. A virtual device typically takes several minutes to completely start up. When the virtual device is finished loading, you should see a home screen similar to that of a hardware device (see Figure 3-16).

If your virtual device has an extremely large display, or you are developing on a smaller screen (like a laptop), you may want to select the *Scale display to real size* check box and enter the display size, in inches, that the virtual device will show you on your monitor.

From this option window, you may also select *Wipe user data*, which clears any saved information related to your game. This is handy and important to use in testing, as you will want to test your game with a clean install, just as if a user were installing the game for the first time.

2. **Click Launch.**

You don't need to re-launch a virtual device every time you run your app. Launching a virtual device usually takes several minutes. When you launch one, leave it running for as long as you intend to test. This is a common mistake of beginning Android developers.

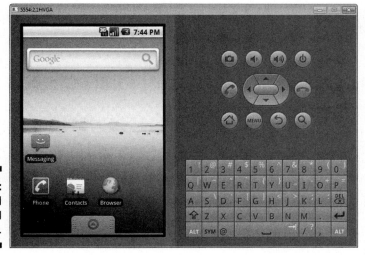

Figure 3-16:
An Android
virtual
device.

The look and feel of a virtual device will depend on the Android version. The one shown in Figure 3-16 is for Android 2.1. Take some time to get familiar with the virtual device by launching sample apps and navigating through the various screens and menus. You'll notice that the interface will probably be slow and laggy compared to what you'd get from the real thing.

Just be patient, and remember: It's a free Android device running on your PC!

Creating an Android Project

When Eclipse is up and running with the Android SDK installed (you'll know it's correctly installed if you've been able to create and run a virtual Android device), you're ready to create your first Android project.

Follow these steps:

1. **In Eclipse, select File⇨New⇨Android Project, or right-click the Package Explorer and select New⇨Android Project.**

   The New Android Project window appears, as shown in Figure 3-17

2. **Enter a name for your project in the Project Name field.**

   For your first project name, enter "Hello World."

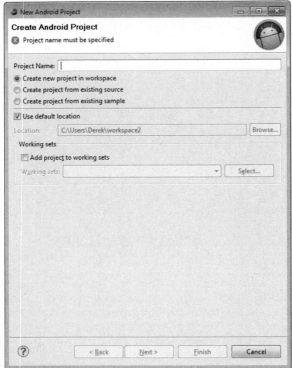

Figure 3-17:
The New
Android
Project
window.

3. **Click Next.**

The New Android Project window prompts you to select a build target, as shown in Figure 3-18.

The *build target* refers to the version of the SDK used to develop the app, not the version of target devices. You'll usually want to select the highest available build target.

If there are no build targets showing in your list of available build targets, try closing and restarting Eclipse before starting another Android project.

4. **Click Next.**

The New Android Project window prompts you to enter application info, as shown in Figure 3-19.

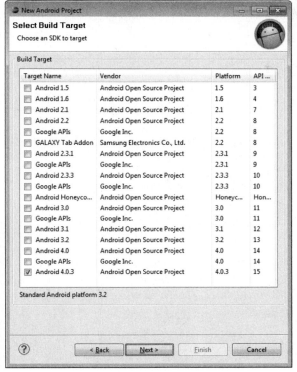

Target Name	Vendor	Platform	API ...
Android 1.5	Android Open Source Project	1.5	3
Android 1.6	Android Open Source Project	1.6	4
Android 2.1	Android Open Source Project	2.1	7
Android 2.2	Android Open Source Project	2.2	8
Google APIs	Google Inc.	2.2	8
GALAXY Tab Addon	Samsung Electronics Co., Ltd.	2.2	8
Android 2.3.1	Android Open Source Project	2.3.1	9
Google APIs	Google Inc.	2.3.1	9
Android 2.3.3	Android Open Source Project	2.3.3	10
Google APIs	Google Inc.	2.3.3	10
Android Honeyco...	Android Open Source Project	Honeyc...	Hon...
Android 3.0	Android Open Source Project	3.0	11
Google APIs	Google Inc.	3.0	11
Android 3.1	Android Open Source Project	3.1	12
Android 3.2	Android Open Source Project	3.2	13
Android 4.0	Android Open Source Project	4.0	14
Google APIs	Google Inc.	4.0	14
✓ Android 4.0.3	Android Open Source Project	4.0.3	15

Figure 3-18:
The New
Android
Project
window,
prompting
for a build
target.

The application name is populated by default with the project name. Just leave that the way it is. You'll need to enter a new package name, though.

A *package name* is a unique identifier with hierarchical structure, typically like a domain name for a website, only in reverse. Package names are always in lowercase to avoid collisions with class names. Throughout this book you'll find it uses the domain agpfd (Android Game Programming for Dummies) — so, for this example, enter com. agpfd.helloworld.

This window also allows you to create an activity by default. Don't make any changes there.

The Minimum SDK drop-down menu allows you to specify the oldest version of Android you want your app to target. Select 4 (Android 1.6) for this example.

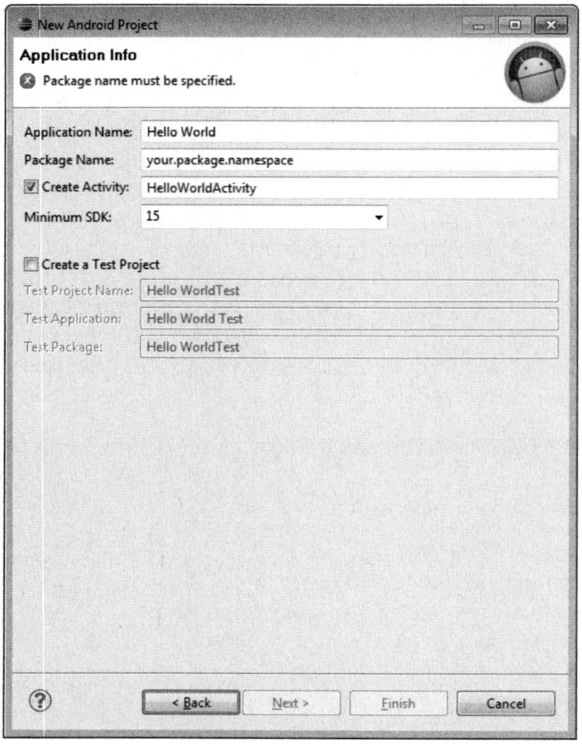

Figure 3-19:
The New
Android
Project
window,
prompting
for applica-
tion info.

5. Click Finish.

Your newly created project should appear in the Package Explorer.

Use the arrows next to each project element to expand or collapse the hierarchy. Your project should look like Figure 3-20, and you should be able to expand the package to see the default activity, `HelloWorldActivity`.

Figure 3-20:
Package
Explorer
view of your
newly cre-
ated project.

Running an Android App

Before you run the app, you'll want to set up your run configurations, which are options for how the app launches.

Your run configuration for a given project can determine whether the app is launched automatically, finding a best match among available devices, or whether you may manually choose a device for launch.

If you leave the default configuration, when you run an app the Android tools will try to find the best match from either your virtual devices or physical devices attached to your computer. If no virtual devices are open, it will launch one.

Manual launch control

I like more fine-grained control over what launches and when, especially since I often have more than one available device that can run the app.

To set up manual launching, follow these steps:

1. **In Eclipse, select Run⇨Run Configurations.**

   The Run Configurations window appears.

2. **Select Android Application, then click the New Launch Configurations button.**

   Configuration options for an Android project appear, as shown in Figure 3-21.

3. **Click Browse, select your Hello World project, then click OK.**

   You should now see the name of your project in the Project field.

   You can enter a custom name for this run configuration if you like, but leaving the default name `New_configuration` is fine.

4. **Select the Target tab.**

   The Automatic option is selected by default. Click the Manual radio button.

   Your window should look something like Figure 3-22.

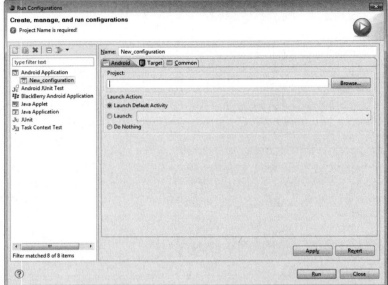

Figure 3-21:
The Run Configurations window.

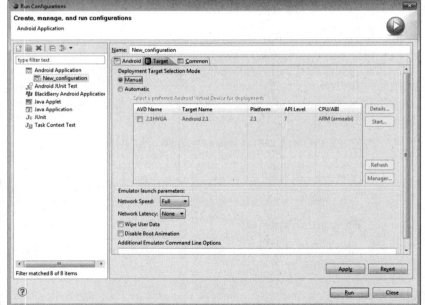

Figure 3-22:
The Target tab in the Run Configurations window.

5. Click Apply, then Close.

Your run configuration is now set up to let you manually select which device you want to upload and launch your game to when you choose to run it.

Starting apps

When you've got a sample project and you've set up the run configuration for that project, you're finally ready to start an app and run it.

Launching an app on a physical device is similar to running one on the emulator. The rest of this chapter shows how to start apps on virtual devices and real devices.

Virtual devices

If you don't have a virtual device running, launch one now by following these steps:

1. Click the AVD button.

2. Select the device, then click Start.

3. Click the Launch button.

When your virtual device is running, follow these steps to launch your Hello World app:

1. Select the project to run, then the Run button in the Eclipse toolbar, or right-click the project name in the Package Explorer and select Run as⇨Android Application.

The Android Device Chooser window appears, as shown in Figure 3-23.

2. Select your virtual device from the list and click OK.

Your app should be running on the virtual device, as shown in Figure 3-24.

Real devices

Testing with a real device requires connection to your device to your development machine; most commonly that's done via USB.

Depending on the device model and your operating system, you may need to install additional drivers. The Android SDK provides a large number of drivers, but there is such a wide array of devices that you may find it necessary to seek out specific drivers for your device. Even with some popular device models, I've had to install additional drivers to get them to work with my development machine.

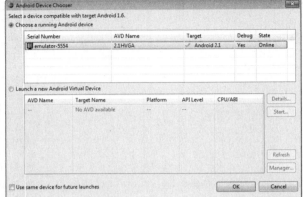

Figure 3-23:
The Android
Device
Chooser
window.

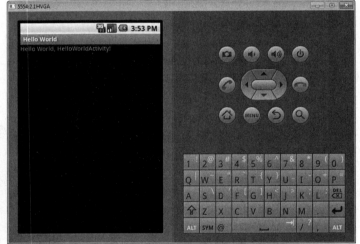

Figure 3-24:
The Hello
World app
running on
a virtual
device.

The installation process for drivers can vary widely depending on your Android device and your development operating system:

✔ In a best-case scenario, you'd just plug your Android device into your development machine via USB and the drivers would be automatically installed.

✔ If the best case is not an option, you might need to visit your Android device manufacturer's website, download the drivers, and follow their installation process.

Apps and games are typically meant to be downloaded and installed from Google Play — so most Android devices are not configured by default to allow apps to be installed from anywhere else. This is a security measure to keep malware from being installed on your Android device without your knowledge. As a developer, you'll want to change this default setting to allow you to install the games you develop from your development machine to your Android device.

To install non-market apps on your device, you'll need to open Settings⇨Application Settings. Two settings are required:

✔ Check the Unknown sources check box.

✔ Click Development, then check the USB debugging check box.

   This allows your computer to read the log output of your device when connected, rather than enabling file transfer by default.

When your device is connected and ready, you can launch your app. The steps to launch your app on a real device are similar to the steps for launching your app on a virtual device:

1. **Click the Run button in the Eclipse toolbar, or right-click the project name in the Package Explorer and select Run as⇨Android Application.**

   When the Android Device Chooser window appears, you should see your device listed, as shown in Figure 3-25.

Figure 3-25: Motorola Droid running Android 2.2.3 is shown as an available device.

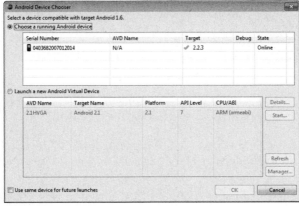

If your device doesn't show up in the list of available devices, you could have a problem with the connection or with the drivers.

2. **Select your device from the list and click OK.**

Your app should be running on the device, as shown in Figure 3-24.

If you tried your app on an emulator, you should see the same output on your device.

You can view the log output of your device from a view within Eclipse, but I prefer to launch a separate command-line window (Windows key + R in Windows). Type **adb logcat** from the command line. Doing so enables the Android Debug Bridge (ADB) and displays the log output from either your virtual or physical device. When debugging, analyzing the log output can be crucial in finding and fixing problems.

Part II
Starting to Program

The 5th Wave   By Rich Tennant

THE FUTURE OF AD PLACEMENT IN VIDEO GAMES

"Watch out for the Necromancer behind the Toyota with the Snapple in his hand."

In this part . . .

Part II gets you started on your development machine, installing and configuring all the tools you need to get started. I walk you through how to install the Eclipse development tool and the Android Software Development Kit (SDK). Then I show you how to create a sample project and give you a closer look at its pieces so you have a foundation for how Android projects are put together and work. Then you get a chance to create a view and start drawing stuff to the screen.

Chapter 4

Dissecting an Android App

. . . .

. . . .

*W*hen you've got your development environment set up, you're ready to start building the next great addictive blockbuster game. This chapter gives you the tools you need to understand how to create a project from the ground up, understand how all the parts fit together, and modify the right settings so that everything works the way it's supposed to.

An Android project is a lot like a standard Java project, but with some important differences. The Android SDK does most of the work for you in building the project structure and adding the necessary files — but as you work on your game, you'll often need to add to this structure and make modifications, so it's important to know where everything is and how it works.

Before you do anything else, you'll have to create a new project, which is really only a few clicks away. So . . . first things first.

Creating a New Project

The Android SDK and Eclipse make it simple to create a new Android project, with a wizard that walks you through the process. Most of the important parts of your game (such as its name and its range of targeted devices) are defined in this creation process.

To create a new project, follow these steps:

1. **Select File⇨New⇨Android Project.**

   The New Android Project Window (Figure 4-1) will display.

   Notice the default location of the workspace. This directory is where all the project files will be located.

2. **In the Project Name field type** Crazy Eights, **and then click Next.**

   The project name is a unique identifier for your project in the Eclipse workspace.

3. **Click Android 4.0 for the Target Name, and then click Next.**

   The New Android Project/Select Build Target window appears, as shown in Figure 4-2.

   The *build target* refers to the SDK level you will be using to develop your game. For example, if you choose a build target of Android 2.2, you can use only the features included in that and earlier levels.

Figure 4-1:
New
Android
Project/
Create
Android
Project
window.

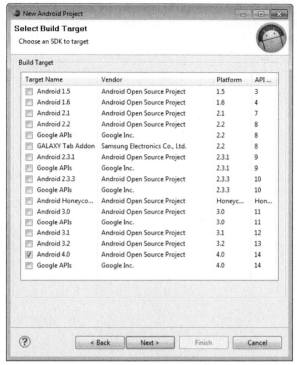

Figure 4-2:
The New
Android
Project/
Select Build
Target
window.

Choose the latest SDK available to develop with. You don't always have to use new features included in the latest SDK, but using the latest version as your build target gives you that option.

4. **In the Package Name field type** com.agpfd.crazyeights, **then click Finish.**

The package name is used to identify the Java package of your app. Once published to the Android Market, two apps cannot have the same package name, so this must be unique.

Package naming for Android follows a general convention established for Java package names:

- Typically, a package name is organized like a reverse URL, with com or org appearing first, followed by the domain name of the authoring organization.

- When you choose a package name for your own apps, you might want to use your company name or website domain (if you have one). Otherwise you can simply choose a domain name that is unique and meaningful to you.

The Minimum SDK option (see Figure 4-3) is the minimum version of Android that a user's device must be running in order to see your app in the market, install it, and run it. In general, you want this option to be set to the lowest possible value to target as many devices as possible.

Figure 4-3:
The New
Android
Project/
Application
Info win-
dow.

Your new project is now created! The package and its associated structure shows up in Eclipse's Package Explorer and should look something like Figure 4-4.

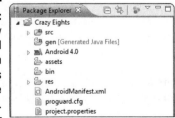

Figure 4-4:
A newly
created
project in
Eclipse's
Package
Explorer.

Taking the Bird's Eye View of a Project

An Android project is organized similar to other Java projects, with a few important exceptions. The Android SDK automatically generates certain features specific to an Android project. As with any other Java project, this one has a *source directory* where all the Java files that handle all the logic of your game are located.

Here are a few other Android-specific aspects of the project, with a brief description of each:

- ✔ **The** R.java **file:** An auto-generated index that assigns unique variables to all the resources in your app. If you open this file, you'll notice a warning saying that you shouldn't manually modify this file.

  Sometimes the R.java file can get out of sync with the actual resources you've declared, causing errors. A quick way to resolve common errors of this type is to

  - Delete the R.java file.

  - Clean the project (Project⇨Clean).

  Doing so regenerates the R.java file and sometimes fixes the problem.

- ✔ **Resources:** The resources directory is where things like graphics, sounds, layouts, and strings are typically located:

  - Graphics are located in one or more drawable subdirectories, typically organized by their intended screen size.

  - XML resources for layouts are located in the layout subdirectory.

  - Strings and styles are in the values subdirectory by default.

- ✔ **The Manifest:** This file, called AndroidManifest.xml, is located in the root directory of the project. The file is where you specify the app name, all activities, permissions, and device targeting.

Editing the Manifest

The manifest is generated automatically when a new Android Project is created.

The New Android Project wizard prompts you for some options that are included in the manifest, but this section demonstrates how to manually edit the manifest file, a useful task that will come up often as you work on your game.

Think of the *manifest* as a specification of everything important about your app. In maritime travel, a ship's manifest describes everything important about that ship: A list of all the crew and passengers, details about the cargo, its country of origin, places it has traveled, and where it is headed. Believe it or not, your app has a lot in common with a ship! When it's ready, you'll be launching it into the high seas of one or more app stores. The manifest will tell everyone what's inside and what devices it is headed for.

View the contents of the manifest by double-clicking the file in the Package Explorer, which will open the file in Eclipse's editor view. Select the `AndroidManifest.xml` tab in the editor view to see the XML, which should look something like the following code:

```xml
<?xml version="1.0" encoding="utf-8"?>
<manifest xmlns:android="http://schemas.android.com/apk/
          res/android"
    package="com.dummies.androidgame.crazyeights"
    android:versionCode="1"
    android:versionName="1.0">
  <uses-sdk android:minSdkVersion="3" />
  <application android:icon="@drawable/icon"
          android:label="@string/app_name">
      <activity android:name=".CrazyEights"
                android:label="@string/app_name">
        <intent-filter>
            <action
            android:name=
            "android.intent.action.MAIN" />
            <category
            android:name=
            "android.intent.category.LAUNCHER" />
        </intent-filter>
      </activity>
  </application>
</manifest>
```

Naming and versioning your game

The `<manifest>` tag has attributes that indicate what the package name, version code, and version name are.

Every time you update your game

- ✔ The package name remains the same.
- ✔ Increment the version code by 1.
- ✔ Change the version name to a higher value.

For example, your second version could be version code "2" with a version name of "1.1".

The Android Market allows apps with the same app name, but not the same package name. If the package name of your app is already in use by an existing app, you'll need to rename your package.

Targeting versions

The `<uses-sdk>` tag indicates the minimum version of the Android OS that can run your game. Currently, Android SDK versions range from 3 (Android 1.5) to 13 (Android 3.2). A lower value for this attribute will allow your app to be visible to Android devices running older versions of the OS.

The wider the range of devices you target, the larger your potential audience, so you'll only want to specify a higher minimum SDK if your game uses features of the SDK that aren't available in older versions.

None of the examples in this book use such features, so you can safely use a value of "3" to target as many devices as possible.

You can designate a target SDK version, to indicate that your game has been extensively tested and is therefore targeted for that version. Add the following attribute to the `<uses-sdk>` tag:

```
android:targetSdkVersion="8"
```

Declaring activities

The `<application>` tag contains attributes indicating the image used for

✔ Your game's icon (`android:icon`), which points to an image in your project's drawable directory

✔ Your game's name (`android:label`), which points to a string in your project's values directory.

All the activities within your application are declared within the `<application>` tag:

✔ When you create a new project, there is only one activity by default.

✔ As you add new activities in your source, you must declare each one in the manifest file, or an error will occur.

For each activity, you can define attributes that control the behavior of the activity. When a device is rotated 90 degrees, by default an app changes orientation to try to match the device.

Often you want to prevent this automatic rotation with games, usually because a game looks and plays well in a specific orientation.

For the Crazy Eights example, edit the main activity so that it will always display in portrait mode, even when the device is rotated, by adding the following attribute to the main activity:

```
android:screenOrientation="portrait"
```

Your edited main activity should look like this:

```
<activity
    android:label="@string/app_name"
    android:name=".CrazyEightsActivity"
    android:screenOrientation="portrait">
    <intent-filter >
        <action
            android:name="android.intent.action.MAIN" />
        <category
            android:name=
            "android.intent.category.LAUNCHER" />
    </intent-filter>
</activity>
```

Each activity may also have an <intent-filter> which further defines what it can and cannot do. By default, the activity created when you make a project from scratch has the action MAIN and the category LAUNCHER. This tells an Android device that this activity should be started when the app is launched.

Setting permissions

Sometimes you may want your app to use certain features that require permissions. For security reasons, some features need to be declared explicitly in the manifest so that upon installation, a user can see that an app is doing certain things behind the scenes. They can then decide whether or not they are comfortable installing such an app.

For example, your game may want to display all the user's contacts so that they can choose a contact to invite to a multiplayer game. If so, the following permission would need to be added to the manifest:

```
<uses-permission
        android:name="android.permission.READ_CONTACTS" />
```

If you don't have this permission declared in your manifest, your game won't work properly. In fact, you'll see a runtime error.

Always check the log output when you run your game to check for errors. You can either

- ✔ View the output in the `LogCat` view in Eclipse.
- ✔ Open a command prompt and type `adb logcat`.

If the error is due to the lack of proper permissions, the log will let you know, and you can then simply add the appropriate permission to fix the problem.

For a full list of permissions see

```
http://developer.android.com/reference/android/Manifest.
        permission.html
```

Targeting different screen sizes

Declarations for the specific screen sizes your game is intended to be played on aren't generated by default. Chapter 2 discusses the wide variety of Android hardware configurations.

Once you decide which screen sizes you want to try to target, a good practice is to explicitly declare that information in your manifest.

The following is an example of using the `<supports-screens>` tag:

```
<supports-screens
                android:smallScreens="false"
                android:normalScreens="true"
                android:largeScreens="true"
                android:xlargeScreens="true"
                android:anyDensity="true"
</supports-screens>
```

- ✔ Small screens generally refer to devices such as QVGA, which are generally 320x240.
- ✔ Normal screens are most often HVGA, with a screen size of 480x320.

✔ Large screens are WVGA, and are most typically 800x600 or 854x600.

✔ X-large screens are typically XWVGA, usually tablet-size.

The following website is the official Android resource for developing for multiple screen sizes:

```
http://developer.android.com/guide/practices/screens_
                support.html
```

And that's it! You can either

✔ Edit parts of the manifest by clicking the appropriate tabs at the bottom of the editor view (as shown in Figure 4-5).

✔ Edit the XML directly, which is what we do throughout this book as needed.

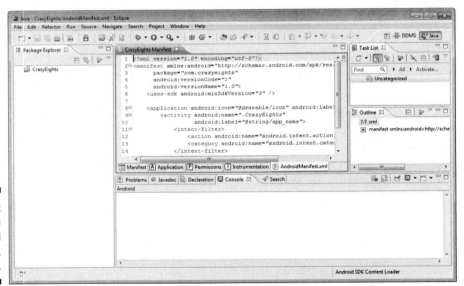

Figure 4-5: Viewing the Android Manifest. xml.

Organizing Resources

The resources directory of a project is where all images and sounds are located, along with files that modify the look and feel of your game. The directory is abbreviated `res` and is located in the root directory of your project.

Figure 4-6 shows the resources directory expanded, with each of its subdirectories.

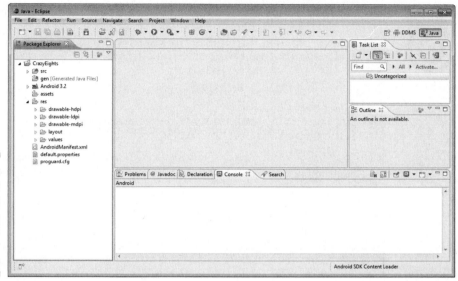

Figure 4-6:
The
resources
directory,
expanded
to view sub-
directories.

Depending on the SDK version you used to create your project, your resources directory might look a little different. But the basic structure should be the same.

Drawables

There should be at least one drawable subdirectory in the `/res` directory. This is where all images, including your game's icon, should be placed.

In the preceding example, three subdirectories were automatically generated:

- ✔ `drawable-hdpi` will hold images for high-density screens.
- ✔ `drawable-ldpi` will hold images for low-density screens.
- ✔ `drawable-mdpi` will hold images for medium-density screens.

If your directory structure is set up the same way, you'll notice that the Android SDK placed the default Android app icon of the appropriate size in each directory:

✔ The `ldpi` icon is 36x36.

✔ The `mdpi` icon is 48x48.

✔ The `hdpi` icon is 72x72.

If you want to target tablets and other very high-resolution devices, you should create another directory at the same level as the three just mentioned (`ldpi`, `mdpi`, and `hdpi`):

1. **Right-click the** `res` **directory.**

2. **Select New⇨Folder.**

3. **Type** `"drawable-xhdpi"` **as the Folder name.**

4. **Click Finish.**

   The dimensions for an extra-high-density icon should be 96x96.

The first thing you'll want to do with regard to drawables is create your own icons and replace the default ones.

For the Crazy Eights example, I've provided a sample icon in four different sizes for you to use (as shown in Figure 4-7). However, I'd encourage you to create your own, using your favorite graphics software.

Figure 4-7:
Sample icon
for Crazy
Eights.

Once you have your new icons, place them in the appropriate drawable directory. Delete the icons provided by the SDK and rename each of your icons `"icon.png"`.

When you design your game, one of the first decisions you need to make is the range of device hardware you want to target. If you want to target as wide a range as possible in order to maximize your audience size, you'll need to develop your game so that it explicitly supports specific screen sizes, or so that it scales automatically to whatever screen sizes you want to support.

Render graphics to the screen in a relative way, so that no matter what the screen size, the game will have a consistent look and feel:

✔ Include images that look good on the highest-resolution device you want to support.

✔ Scale the images down when they're viewed on lower-resolution devices.

Layouts

A *layout file* is an XML document that defines how a given view looks. The layout

✔ Specifies all the elements that will be displayed, such as

- Text
- Images
- Input fields

✔ Determines how they are laid out with respect to each other.

You're not going to be using layouts in game development as much as an Android developer who is building other types of apps, since you're going to be creating your own custom view and directly drawing text and images to the screen. But you will be using layouts for some things, like the layouts of dialog boxes, so you'll need to know how they work.

In the `res/layout` directory of your project, you'll see that there is a file called `main.xml,`. as shown in Figure 4-8. This file was automatically generated when you created the project. Double-click the file in the Package Explorer to view it in Eclipse.

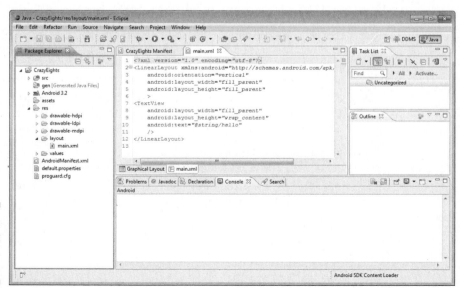

Figure 4-8: The layout file for main. xml.

When you open a layout file, there are two tabs at the bottom of the file in the editor view in Eclipse. One is the Graphical Layout, which lets you view and modify the layout in a graphical mode, allowing you to drag and drop different interface elements to and from your layout. If you click the tab with the filename, you'll see the XML code itself (Figure 4-8).

 Get used to modifying things like your manifest and your layout files directly in XML. With layouts, you can preview them using the Graphical Layout tab, but editing the XML directly will give you a better understanding of how the code actually works.

In the case of the `default main.xml` layout file, you should only see two elements: `LinearLayout` and `TextView`. The different types of layouts are

- ✔ **FrameLayout.** Generally for holding a single element, like an image.
- ✔ **LinearLayout.** Aligns elements in one direction, either horizontally or vertically.
- ✔ **TableLayout.** Arranges elements according to a table configuration, with rows and columns.
- ✔ **RelativeLayout.** Gives the most flexibility, allowing you to align specific elements relative to one another.

`LinearLayout` is sufficient for most simple cases, but if you're interested in learning more about other layouts, check out:

```
http://developer.android.com/guide/topics/ui/
            layout-objects.html
```

In the case of the default XML generated for `main.xml`, the `LinearLayout` element includes an orientation attribute, which can be either horizontal or vertical for linear layouts. In your case, it should be vertical by default. This means that all the elements inside the `LinearLayout` tag will be displayed vertically down the screen next to each other.

The `LinearLayout` also includes attributes determining its width and height, both of which are "fill_parent". This means that this layout will stretch itself to fit the height and width of whatever screen it is displayed on.

The layout only has one child element, a `TextView`, which also has width and height attributes. The width is `"fill_parent"`, but the height is `"wrap_content"`, which means that this element will only fill up as much vertical space as its contents, in this case the text it is displaying. The text attribute references a string called `"hello"`.

You'll see where that string is stored in the next section, but for now, try making some small changes to this file and either previewing it in the Graphical Layout tab of the editor view, or running it on a device or emulator.

Some suggested changes include these:

- ✔ Copy the `TextView` and paste a copy just below the current one, so that you have two exact copies of the same `TextView`.
- ✔ Change the orientation attribute of the `LinearLayout` tag from `"vertical"` to `"horizontal"`.
- ✔ Use the `android:textColor` attribute for the `TextView` to change the default color of the text.

Strings

All the text that appears in your game that is not part of an image, from button text to tutorials, can be specified in the `strings.xml` file located by default in the `res/values` directory.

You can hard-code the text into either your Java or layout files, and this is usually okay as long as you don't intend to reuse text much or target more than one language. Hard-coding text is generally not a recommended practice, though you'll still find a lot of apps and games that do it.

The recommended practice is to keep all text in the `strings.xml` file, giving each string a unique name, then referencing the strings from your code. By default, two strings are generated when you create a new app:

```
hello

app_name
```

For the example, open the `strings.xml` file in your new Crazy Eights project under `res/values`. You should see something like Figure 4-9.

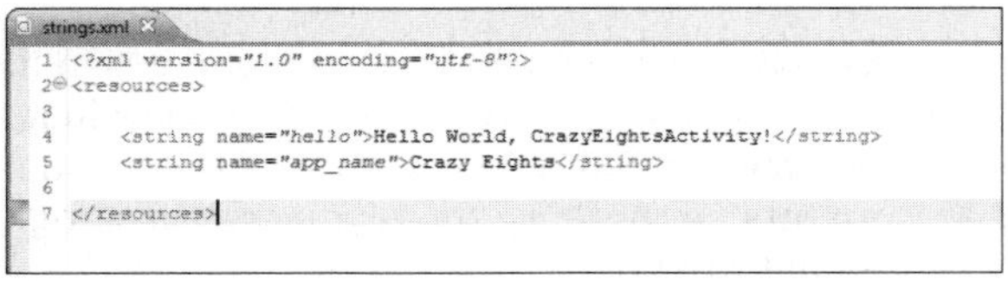

Figure 4-9:
Default
contents of
strings.
xml.

```
strings.xml
1  <?xml version="1.0" encoding="utf-8"?>
2  <resources>
3
4      <string name="hello">Hello World, CrazyEightsActivity!</string>
5      <string name="app_name">Crazy Eights</string>
6
7  </resources>
```

The "hello" string is used to display sample text when an app is first run. The "app_name" string is used to display the name of the app under the icon in the launcher.

Any time you want to add new text to your game, add another entry into this file, which can then be referenced from your code.

If you reuse the same text in multiple places in your game, you only have to change it once in the strings.xml file. This organization also makes localizing your game a lot easier. For each other language, you add a new values directory appended with the country code for that locale. For example, if you wanted to add support for Spanish, you would create a new directory in res/ called values-es (for Español). You would need a file called strings.xml in that directory, with the same string names, though the contents would be in Spanish. For example:

```
<string name="app_name">Los Ochos Locos</string>
```

If a player on a device has its locale settings set to ES, then when they play your game, all the text will be populated from the contents of the values-es directory. You can add support for as many languages as Android supports, and as many as you want to get translations for.

Check supported locales in the Android documentation on their website before you invest in a translator.

Styles

Styles allow you to apply a particular look and feel throughout your app. Styles are applied to views, and work a lot like cascading stylesheets (CSS) in web design. You define styles in XML, and they reside in the res/values directory of your project. You then reference them from other views to apply the style to that view.

Themes

A theme is just a broader use of styles, applying them across an entire activity or application. If you apply a style as a theme, every view in an activity will have that style automatically applied to it.

We won't be using styles or themes in this book, but if your game takes a different tack from the one covered here you might want to explore this topic more on your own. See the official Android documentation on Styles and Themes at

```
http://developer.android.com/guide/topics/ui/themes.html
```

Sounds

You may or may not want to include sound effects and music in your game. A lot of games work fine without them, especially on the mobile platform where players often play games in public areas where they may not want to be heard. If you do use sounds in your game, by default they should be located in the res/raw directory. If it doesn't exist, you'll need to create it.

You can find a list of supported media types at

```
http://developer.android.com/guide/appendix/media-
           formats.html
```

For sounds, I always use Ogg Vorbis (.ogg), which is an open audio-compression format. The compression and quality are excellent, and .ogg files are supported by a large number of sound-editing software programs.

Organizing the Source Directory

The source directory (/src) contains the Java files where you will write all the logic that makes your games go. Source files reside in a package. When you create an Android project, a default package is created, but you can add as many new packages as you like. If your game is particularly complicated, you may want to separate your source files into logical groupings, such as files that handle persisting data, sounds, or other subcategories.

To create a new package in Eclipse

1. **Right-click the /src directory.**

2. **Select New⇨Package.**

   The New Java Package dialog box will appear, as shown in Figure 4-10.

Just enter a name for the package with the same domain name as your other packages, with the new extension name — here's an example:

```
"com.agpfd.crazyeights.sound"
```

New Java Package

Java Package
Create a new Java package.

Creates folders corresponding to packages.

Source folder: Crazy Eights/src   Browse...

Name:

? | Finish | Cancel

Figure 4-10:
The New
Java
Package
dialog box.

You can then add or move source files to this new package. The games we work on in this book won't be that complex, so we'll keep all the source files in one package. But if your project starts piling up Java files, you can save yourself a lot of headache by organizing them in a logical, easy-to-find way. Anyone else who looks through your code will appreciate the effort as well!

Below the source directory (see Figure 4-11), you may have also noticed the /gen directory. This directory contains files automatically generated for you by the Android SDK.

Figure 4-11:
The source
directory of
an Android
project.

```
▲ 📁 Crazy Eights
  ▲ 📁 src
    ▲ 🏢 com.dummies.androidgame.crazyeights
      ▷ 🗋 CrazyEightsActivity.java
  ▲ 📁 gen [Generated Java Files]
    ▲ 🏢 com.dummies.androidgame.crazyeights
      ▷ 🗋 BuildConfig.java
      ▷ 🗋 R.java
```

✔ The BuildConfig.java file contains settings for build configurations. You shouldn't encounter any issues with this file and you should never have to look at it.

✔ The R.java file contains references to all your resources (layouts, images, etc.). Every time you add a new resource it is automatically added to this file, assigning a unique identifier to the resource. The R.java file acts as a master index for your resources.

Don't modify the contents of generated files yourself. Doing so can often lead to nasty bugs if these files get out of sync with your project. You may encounter problems with the R.java file in particular. Although you don't want to modify it manually, sometimes a good practice is to delete it and clean your project (Project⇨Clean), which causes the file to be generated again.

Understanding Activities

An *activity* is a running process within an application. One of the first big decisions you'll make as an Android developer is how to design how your game will handle transitions — for example, moving from the title screen to the main play screen, or to a new level after completing the previous one. Your game will always have at least one activity, the one that is the first to start when your game launches.

If you look in the AndroidManifest.xml of one of your apps, you'll see this XML nested inside one activity:

```
<intent-filter >
   <action android:name=
       "android.intent.action.MAIN" />
   <category android:name=
       "android.intent.category.LAUNCHER" />
</intent-filter>
```

This XML designates that activity as the main activity, the first one to be started when the app is launched. You can have multiple activities in your game, but only one main activity.

Every activity in your game must be declared in the manifest. If you don't declare one of your activities in the manifest, you'll get a runtime error.

✔ A new activity can be launched from within the main activity, and another after that, so that you can have a stack of activities running in your game.

✔ Another option is to only have one activity, while transitioning between views. This is the approach we'll take in this book, but it doesn't mean it's the only (or the best) way of doing things.

The lifecycle of an activity

Each activity has its own lifecycle as it is created, started, used, then killed. Figure 4-12 shows this lifecycle and when transitions are made between states.

It's important to understand what happens when with activities, since they're the backbone of any Android app or game. Figure 4-12 shows when each method within an activity is called (for example, onCreate is called when the activity is launched).

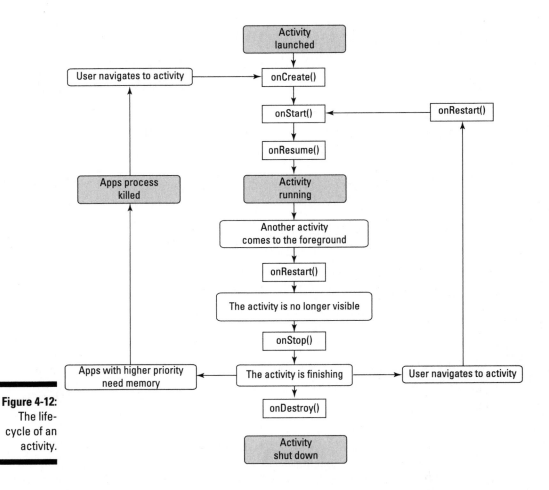

Figure 4-12: The life-cycle of an activity.

An activity can be running in the background, still using system resources even though the user can't see it. If too many activities are running in the background, and the system runs out of memory, Android will prioritize them and kill off the less important ones.

You'll want to consider the kinds of cases a player may encounter when playing your game. Since many Android devices are phones, they may get a phone call while playing your game. In this case, the phone activity will get priority, become visible to the user, and your game and all its activities will be put in the background. How will your game handle this? You'll want to strongly consider

✔ Saving the game state when onPause() is called

✔ Restoring the game state in one of the early methods, such as onResume().

Get familiar with the lifecycle of activities, and when you test, make sure you think about what kind of scenarios your game needs to handle. When someone is playing your game on a mobile device, they're using that device for lots of other things besides playing games!

Creating an activity

Whenever you make a new Android project in Eclipse, the main activity will be generated with a single class with a single method, onCreate(), as shown in Figure 4-13.

Figure 4-13:
Default contents of the main activity of a new Android project.

```
J CrazyEightsActivity.java ⊠
  1  package com.dummies.androidgame.crazyeights;
  2
  3⊕ import android.app.Activity;⬚
  4
  5
  6  public class CrazyEightsActivity extends Activity {
  7      /** Called when the activity is first created. */
  8⊖     @Override
  9      public void onCreate(Bundle savedInstanceState) {
 10          super.onCreate(savedInstanceState);
 11          setContentView(R.layout.main);
 12      }
 13  }
```

The onCreate() method takes a Bundle as input.

A *Bundle* is an object that maps string values to parcelable types. Basically it's a way for you to store certain types of information to pass between activities.

The `onCreate()` method is where the content view is set, which determines what the user sees on the screen. In this case, this is done by the line:

```
setContentView(R.layout.main);
```

This sets the content of the current view to the `main.xml` file in the `res/layout` directory.

> ✔ For games, we'll be creating our own custom views and setting the content view to those.
>
> ✔ Because `onCreate()` is the first method called in any activity, it's the place where you'll want to initialize variables used throughout this activity.

Resuming an activity

Suppose someone is playing your game and gets a phone call. Follow the flow in Figure 4-12, starting with `Activity Running`. Your game will call `onPause()`, which is typically where you'll want to store any information (such as the game state).

When someone opens or closes a hardware keyboard or reorients a device, this action causes a configuration change that also interrupts your application. Make sure you test your game to handle these cases.

If the user finishes a phone call and then navigates back to your game, note that

> ✔ `onRestart()`, `onStart()`, and `onResume()` are all called before the activity actually starts again. Any code that restores saved information could be placed in one of these methods.
>
> ✔ `onStart()` and `onResume()` are called whenever the activity is started from scratch.

You'll want to be careful about when and how you try to restore the game state.

If this all seems overwhelming, don't worry. In the case of Crazy Eights, I show you how to handle your game state in the context of the activity lifecycle. For now, just make sure you're familiar with the basic flow in Figure 4-12.

Destroying an activity

The `onDestroy()` method is called when the activity is finished and ready to shut down.

This can happen in a number of instances, such as when your game is not visible, running in the background, and the Android OS runs out of memory and kills your activity:

- ✔ If the player is playing your game and presses the Home button on their device, this will not actually kill your activity; instead, it displays the Home screen.
- ✔ If the player presses the Back button, doing so kills the current activity.

In most game-development environments, the developer customarily includes menu items to allow the user to quit the game to return to the Home screen of whatever platform the game is being played on.

This question is sometimes asked in forums by beginning game developers new to mobile platforms. While you can include a UI element that kills the activity, such as a Quit button, this approach is not recommended by the Android development guidelines.

Android apps and games should be developed to work similarly; the default behavior should be to leave an activity running in the background by pressing the Home button on the device and to kill the activity by pressing the Back button. Thus you don't need to explicitly include a Quit menu item or button in your game.

Using Views

The View object in Android is the basic class for drawing and handling input.

Views can be defined using XML, but for our games, we're going to implement our own custom views so that we can have more control over what is drawn and how the player interacts with our game.

Differences between View and SurfaceView

The View object is the simplest way to handle drawing and user interaction in Android, and the official documentation recommends using it if you're implementing a game without heavy animation.

For simplicity's sake, we're going to use the `View` object for the first full game we implement, Crazy Eights. The game does not require significant animation, so it should be well-suited to the simplest case. In the `View` object, the drawing is handled in the same thread as all other processing, which is not particularly efficient.

The `SurfaceView` is a special type of view that handles drawing in a dedicated thread, so that it can draw whatever is on the Canvas concurrently with other things happening. This makes `SurfaceView` more efficient than `View`, and better at handling heavy drawing demands, such as in a real-time arcade-style game. Using the `SurfaceView` is also more complicated than using a normal view, so consider the tradeoff when implementing your own game.

We'll be using `SurfaceView` for the second game covered in this book, Whack-a-Mole.

Instantiating a custom view

Okay, let's get back to developing your game. To create a custom view, all you need to do is create a new class and have it extend `View`.

1. **Right-click the package (`com.agpfd.crazyeights`) in which you want to create the new view.**

2. **Select New➪Class.**

3. **Enter a name, such as `MyView` and then click Finish.**

   Naming conventions for classes in Java use uppercase for each word, with no spaces.

Listing 4-1:   Starting Custom View for Crazy Eights

```
package com.agpfd.crazyeights

import android.content.Context;
import android.view.View;

public class CrazyEightsView extends View {

    public CrazyEightsView(Context context) {
        super(context);
        // TODO Auto-generated constructor stub
    }
}
```

4. Next to the class name in the code view, add extends View.

You'll need to add

- Imports for both Context and View

- A constructor

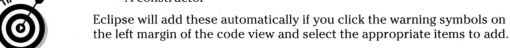

Eclipse will add these automatically if you click the warning symbols on the left margin of the code view and select the appropriate items to add.

Your bare-bones custom view should look something like the one in Listing 4-1.

Drawing in a view

Once we have a custom view, to draw what we want in it, all we need to do is override the onDraw() method. We're going to modify our custom view to draw a red circle.

To do so, add the code from Listing 4-2 to your custom view.

Listing 4-2: Custom View Modified to Draw a Red Circle

```
package com.agpfd.crazyeights

import android.content.Context;                      →3
import android.graphics.Canvas;
import android.graphics.Color;
import android.graphics.Paint;
import android.view.View;

public class CrazyEightsView extends View {

    private Paint redPaint;                          →11
    private int circleX;                             →12
    private int circleY;
    private float radius;

    public CrazyEightsView(Context context) {
        super(context);
        redPaint = new Paint();                      →18
        redPaint.setAntiAlias(true);
        redPaint.setColor(Color.RED);
        circleX = 100;
        circleY = 100;
        radius = 30;
    }
```

(continued)

Listing 4-2 *(continued)*

```
    @Override
    protected void onDraw(Canvas canvas) {
        canvas.drawCircle(circleX, circleY, radius,
            redPaint);                                      →28
    }
}
```

Lines 3-7: These are the imports you need for the various classes from the Android graphics package we'll be using.

Line 11: We need a `Paint` object that defines the attributes of how our circle will be painted on the canvas.

Lines 12-14: Variable declarations for the size and location of the circle.

Lines 18-23: In the `onCreate()` method we're going to initialize our variables with the desired values. The coordinate system in Android places the origin (0,0) in the upper-left corner. These values will draw our circle 100 pixels to the right and 100 pixels down from the upper left corner of the screen, with a radius of 30 pixels.

Line 28 actually draws the circle. The `drawCircle()` method takes in the *x* and *y* coordinates, the radius, and the `Paint` object.

The last thing we need to do is modify our main activity to set our custom view as the content view. Modify the contents of your main activity to look like Listing 4-3.

Listing 4-3:   Main Activity Setting the Content View to a Custom View

```
package com.agpfd.crazyeights;

import android.app.Activity;
import android.os.Bundle;

public class CrazyEightsActivity extends Activity {
    /** Called when the activity is first created. */
    @Override
    public void onCreate(Bundle savedInstanceState) {
        super.onCreate(savedInstanceState);
        CrazyEightsView myView = new
            CrazyEightsView(this);                          →11
        setContentView(myView);                             →12
    }
```

Line 11 creates a custom view, passing in the main activity as context. Line 12 sets the content view to our custom view. And that's it! Run this app, either in an emulator or on an Android device, and you should see something like the screenshot in Figure 4-14.

Figure 4-14: Screenshot of a Galaxy Nexus running the "red circle" app.

Your results may vary. We're not controlling for screen sizes or densities at all, so your circle may look smaller or larger relative to the display properties of the device you're using. But this simple example shows the basics of how something is drawn to the screen. When we begin handling user input and changing the state of the screen in response to the input, we're well on our way to making a game!

Handling input

There are many potential input methods for Android devices. The touchscreen is the most common and reliable method for input for games. So while it's possible to use the keyboard, accelerometer, trackball, and such for input, we're going to keep things simple and focus on the touchscreen for our games.

You can always refer to the official Android site (`developer.android.com`) for insight into how to implement other input methods, but let's look at how to use the touchscreen for input.

Add the code from Listing 4-4 to `CrazyEightsView.java`, just after the `onDraw()` method.

Listing 4-4:   Bare-bones Method for Handling Touch Events

```
public boolean onTouchEvent(MotionEvent event) {
        int eventaction = event.getAction();                →2
        int X = (int)event.getX();                          →3
        int Y = (int)event.getY();

        switch (eventaction ) {                             →6

        case MotionEvent.ACTION_DOWN:
           break;

        case MotionEvent.ACTION_MOVE:
           break;

        case MotionEvent.ACTION_UP:
           break;
        }
        invalidate();                                       →17
        return true;

}
```

Line 2: Gets an integer associated with whatever action the user is taking (for example, pressing down on the screen).

Lines 3-4: These lines get the *x* and *y* coordinates on the screen for where the event is happening.

Lines: 6-15: We're using a switch to handle three possible cases, when the user

Puts a fingertip down on the screen (ACTION_DOWN)

Drags the fingertip across the screen (ACTION_MOVE)

Removes the finger from the screen (ACTION_UP)

Line 17: Invalidate is the command to the view to tell it that a change has occurred and that the canvas needs to be redrawn.

Let's add some logic that will change the location of our red circle when the user touches the screen. Modify your ACTION_UP case to look like the following:

```
case MotionEvent.ACTION_UP:
    circleX = X;
    circleY = Y;
    break;
```

What these two lines do is assign the coordinates for the center of our circle to the point on the screen where you lifted your finger. After adding this code, save your project, then run it and see the results. If you're using an emulator, wherever you click the screen, the dot should move. With a real device, wherever you touch the screen, the dot should move. Cool, huh?

You might find that you'll want to make changes based on ACTION_UP, because if you make them on ACTION_DOWN the finger can obscure what's being displayed on the screen at that point. You can always experiment and see what feels the most intuitive to you.

Try moving the logic we just added to the ACTION_MOVE case and see how the app behaves as you drag your finger across the screen. Get familiar with this logic; it gets a lot of use in our games.

Part III
Making Your First Game: Crazy Eights

The 5th Wave   By Rich Tennant

"This program's really helped me learn a new language. It's so buggy I'm constantly talking with overseas service reps."

In this part . . .

Part III gets you to start building your first game! I show you how to configure a view to behave the way you want it, and then how to load and render all the necessary images. You get the word on how to handle user interactivity to launch the play screen, and then you build all the working pieces of a functioning single-player card game. I even show you how to code a halfway decent computer opponent. In the end, voilá — you have your first complete Android game.

Chapter 5

Creating a Simple Title Screen

In This Chapter

▶ Handling graphics for backgrounds

▶ Making functional buttons

▶ Transitioning between screens

*W*hat will be the first thing your game's players see when they launch your game? Some games go straight into play mode, but most commonly the player sees a title screen or *splash page*. Sometimes the game shows credits preceding a title screen, or credits listed right on the title page. Either way, almost all games (including the very first video games) have some sort of initial screen that gives the player a place to start a new game, resume an old game, change options, and/or view high scores.

This common feature of games — including mobile games — is a logical place to start building your own version of Crazy Eights. You'll want a screen that looks good on as many different devices as possible, displays the name of the game, and includes buttons for starting or resuming a game.

You can download sample files for this chapter at www.dummies.com/go/androidgameprogramming.

Creating a Custom View

The title screen needs a custom view. To create that view, first you create a new class that extends view:

1. **Right-click the package name in your Crazy Eights project and select New⇨Class.**

2. **Name the new class** TitleView **and click Finish.**

3. **Modify the contents of the new file so that it matches the code in Listing 5-1.**

Listing 5-1:   The Initial Custom View for the Title Screen

```
package com.agpfd.crazyeights;
import android.content.Context;
import android.graphics.Canvas;
import android.view.MotionEvent;
import android.view.View;

public class TitleView extends View {                          →8

    public TitleView(Context context) {
        super(context);
    }

    @Override
    protected void onDraw(Canvas canvas) {                      →15

    }

    public boolean onTouchEvent(MotionEvent event) { →19
        int eventaction = event.getAction();
        int X = (int)event.getX();
        int Y = (int)event.getY();

        switch (eventaction ) {

        case MotionEvent.ACTION_DOWN:
            break;

        case MotionEvent.ACTION_MOVE:
            break;

        case MotionEvent.ACTION_UP:
            break;
        }
        invalidate();
        return true;
    }
}
```

Here is a brief explanation of what the various lines do:

→8   The class has to extend `View` because you're making your own custom view.

→**15**   Here you override the onDraw() method. That's because you'll
be adding the logic to draw your title graphic and buttons a little
later on.

→**19**   This logic is for handling cases where the player touches the
screen. It's empty for now, but you add some logic later on to
handle interactions with the button.

Before loading and drawing any graphics to the screen, you need to add a
couple of other important pieces of logic to your fledgling game:

✔ How the game handles screen orientations

✔ How the game handles idle time (that is, what happens if the player
doesn't interact with the device for a while)

You also see how to make your game full-screen to maximize space.

Loading the Title Graphic

You'll have to load and draw graphics, and to do that you need some images!
You can make your own, of course. But I've provided some default images
for you.

The res directory of your project might or might not have a default drawable directory. If it doesn't, add one:

1. **Right-click the res directory.**

2. **Select New⇨Folder.**

3. **Name the new folder drawable.**

    Put your graphical resources there.

A common problem with loading and drawing bitmaps in Android is the
dreaded Out of memory error, which occurs while an app is running on a
device or emulator. If you make any number of games for Android, you will
probably encounter this error at some point, especially if you're attempting
to load and draw very large images, draw a lot of images, or both. There are
many potential solutions to this problem, but it's best to try to prevent it in
the first place by not going overboard with your graphical resources. Try to
load and draw only what you need at the time.

Figure 5-1 shows the graphic that appears on the title screen.

Figure 5-1:
Graphic for
title screen
for Crazy
Eights.

Now modify your `TitleView` file to look like Listing 5-2.

Listing 5-2:   Loading a Bitmap

```
import android.graphics.BitmapFactory;
import android.graphics.Bitmap;

public class TitleView extends View {

    private Bitmap titleGraphic;                              →6

    public TitleView(Context context) {

        super(context);
        titleGraphic =
            BitmapFactory.decodeResource(getResources(),→10
            R.drawable.title_graphic);
    }
```

Here is a brief explanation of what the various lines do:

→**6**   Here you declare the bitmap object for your title graphic.

→**10**   This line actually loads the bitmap into memory so that you can
          draw it to the screen. You're loading it in the constructor for the
          view. `BitmapFactory` creates bitmaps from various sources. In
          this case, the bitmap is being decoded from the file you just put in
          your `drawable` directory.

Keep in mind that you're not supposed to touch the `R.java` file (described
earlier) that's automatically generated by the Android SDK. Whenever you
place a file in one of your resource directories, when the project is built, it
looks in those directories and creates references to your resources. That's
how you can pass in the parameter that tells `BitmapFactory` which image
to load — namely, `R.drawable.title_graphic`.

Because you're only loading a few images in this view, you load them all in the constructor. Games often have lots of graphical resources, so you might end up writing a separate method or class to handle the loading.

Drawing the Title Graphic

Here's where you draw the graphic to the screen; it works much like drawing a circle to the screen (described in Chapter 4), except what you're drawing this time is your loaded bitmap.

Modify your onDraw() method to look like Listing 5-3.

Listing 5-3:   Drawing a Bitmap to the Screen

```
@Override
protected void onDraw(Canvas canvas) {
        canvas.drawBitmap(titleGraphic, (0, 0, null);
}
```

The coordinate system in Android places the origin in the upper-left corner of the screen. For now, all you draw is the graphic with x and y coordinates (0,0) — which places it in the upper-left corner.

✔ Edit the CrazyEightsActivity.java to replace the lines:

```
CrazyEightsView myView = new CrazyEightsView(this);
```

with:

```
TitleView tView = new TitleView(this);
```

✔ Replace:

```
SetContentView(myView);
```

With:

```
SetContentView(tView);
```

Once you've modified your TitleView and CrazyEightsActivity based on the previous two sections of this chapter, launch the game in an emulator or on a device.

What you see onscreen should look something like Figure 5-2.

Figure 5-2:
Title graphic
drawn in the
upper-left
corner of
the screen.

Okay, this doesn't look all that great, but don't worry — you'll get to improve
it in a minute. First you center the graphic horizontally. Then, in the next few
sections of the chapter, you make sure the screen appears in your preferred
orientation, maximize the screen space by making the game full-screen, and
(eventually) update the game with your own custom icon. For now, you've
got a handle on loading and drawing your own images to the screen.

The first item of business is to figure out how to center the graphic horizontally on the screen. If you were using one of Android's default views, of course, the SDK would provide some built-in functionality for centering elements onscreen. Because this is your own custom view, however, you get to wrestle those elements into place on your own.

Okay, get a grip: Modify your `TitleView` to look like Listing 5-4.

Listing 5-4: Determining the Screen Dimensions and Centering the Graphic

```
public class TitleView extends View {

    private Bitmap titleGraphic;
    private int screenW;                                           →4
    private int screenH;

    public TitleView(Context context) {
        super(context);
        titleGraphic =
            BitmapFactory.decodeResource(getResources(),
                R.drawable.title_graphic);
    }

    @Override
    public void onSizeChanged (int w, int h, int oldw,
            int oldh){                                             →14
        super.onSizeChanged(w, h, oldw, oldh);
        screenW = w;
        screenH = h;
    }

    @Override
    protected void onDraw(Canvas canvas) {
            canvas.drawBitmap(titleGraphic,                       →22
            (screenW-titleGraphic.getWidth())/2, 0, null);
    }
```

Here is a brief explanation of what the various lines do:

→**4**   These lines add variable declarations to keep track of the width and height of the screen.

→**14**   Here you're overriding the `onSizeChanged` method, which is called by a view after the constructor but before anything is drawn. All you're doing is grabbing the values of the width and height of the screen. Don't use the height yet; just grab it for future reference anyway.

→22 Now, when you draw your graphic, you replace the *x* position with a little math. First, you subtract the width of the graphic from the screen width, to find out how much space is available. Then you divide that by two to put equal amounts of space on either side of your graphic.

Run the game again. This time it should look something like Figure 5-3.

Figure 5-3:
Title graphic
drawn on
the screen,
centered
horizontally.

Getting better. At least now the graphic is centered horizontally.

For practice, you might want to figure out how to center the graphic vertically on the screen. Just make sure you change it back before you add the buttons later in the chapter!

Handling Screen Orientation

Because the vast majority of Android devices are handheld, they can be easily reoriented by the player (either on purpose or accidentally!). You need to think about how your game will handle this. The two orientations are

- ✔ Portrait (the longer edge of the screen is vertical)
- ✔ Landscape (the shorter edge is vertical)

One approach is to make your game compatible with both orientations, which involves adding logic for laying out UI elements for both orientations. Also, when the screen orientation changes in Android, the current activity is destroyed and restarted — requiring additional logic to handle those tasks.

Right now your game allows the screen orientation to change when the device is rotated. Launch the game on either a device or emulator and rotate the device (whether in hand or onscreen).

You can switch between orientations in the emulator by pressing Ctrl+F11 (on a PC) or Ctrl+Fn+F11 (on a Mac).

When you rotate the device, you should see the title graphic displayed upright to be consistent with the new orientation. But if you did allow this orientation to occur, if UI elements were laid out below the title graphic, you'd need to provide logic to draw them to the right of the title graphic or they wouldn't be visible.

Often games have their best playability in a particular orientation. Handling orientation changes makes your code more complex and might even be more frustrating and confusing for your users. So to keep things as simple as possible for your first game, you add logic that specifies a particular screen orientation and disables the ability to change it.

Crazy Eights will be *fixed* in portrait orientation, so that when the player rotates the device, no orientation changes occur. Okay, equal time here: You get to design the second game in this book (Whack-a-Mole) in landscape mode.

You can accomplish what you want with only two lines of code. Open the `AndroidManifest.xml` file and modify it to look like the code in Listing 5-5.

Listing 5-5: Manifest Modified for Portrait Orientation

```xml
<?xml version="1.0" encoding="utf-8"?>
<manifest xmlns:android="http://schemas.android.com/apk/
          res/android"
    package="com.agpfd.crazyeights"
    android:versionCode="1"
    android:versionName="1.0" >

    <uses-sdk android:minSdkVersion="5" />

    <application
        android:icon="@drawable/ic_launcher"
        android:label="@string/app_name" >
        <activity
            android:label="@string/app_name"
            android:name=".CrazyEightsActivity"
            android:screenOrientation="portrait"          →15
            android:configChanges=
                    "orientation|keyboardHidden"          →16
            >
            <intent-filter >
                <action android:name=
                    "android.intent.action.MAIN" />
                <category android:name=
                    "android.intent.category.LAUNCHER" />
            </intent-filter>
        </activity>
    </application>

</manifest>
```

Two lines added in this code — 15 and 16 — keep the game in portrait orientation:

- Line 15 specifies the screen orientation for the app.
- Line 16 makes sure that screen orientations do not occur when either
  - The hardware keyboard is slid open or closed on a device
  - The software keyboard is enabled or disabled.

Android devices with hardware keyboards typically treat the opening or closing of the keyboard the same as an orientation change. With these two lines of code, you're cementing your game in portrait mode no matter what the users do with their devices.

Once you've made these changes to your game's manifest file, launch the game once more and rotate the screen. This time you should notice that the title graphic launches in portrait orientation, and stays in that orientation no matter which way you orient the device. Cool, huh?

Controlling Screen Timeout

If you own an Android device, you may have noticed that after a certain period of inactivity, the screen times out and the device goes to sleep. The interval for this timeout is modifiable in the OS settings.

Many of the people who play your games might not even be aware that the timeout interval is something they can change. What they will care about is the hassle if they're concentrating on making a play or in the middle of an exciting point in your game and the screen goes dark because they haven't touched it lately.

This little surprise happened with my word game WordWise. Players would be studying the tiles in their rack, trying to think up a great word to play, and the screen would go dark. The default setting for my own device is five minutes (I was annoyed at the small default interval of time, so I changed it). In testing, this was something I overlooked, since my own timeout interval was so large.

This isn't as big an issue with games where the player is constantly interacting with the screen, but it can be annoying when the screen darkens in the middle of a game, so you'll want to mull your options.

Luckily, the Android SDK gives us the option of toggling whether or not the screen timeout kicks in. One line of code and two new imports will do it.

Modify your `CrazyEightsActivity` file to look like Listing 5-6.

Listing 5-6: Disabling Screen Timeout for a View

```
package com.agpfd.crazyeights;

import android.app.Activity;
import android.os.Bundle;
import android.view.Window;
import android.view.WindowManager;

public class CrazyEightsActivity extends Activity {
    /** Called when the activity is first created. */
    @Override
    public void onCreate(Bundle savedInstanceState) {
        super.onCreate(savedInstanceState);
        TitleView tView = new TitleView(this);
        tView.setKeepScreenOn(true);                    →14
        setContentView(tView);
    }
}
```

Line 14 toggles the `KeepScreenOn` setting for a particular view. In this case, you're setting `KeepScreenOn` to `true` for your title view. You can go ahead and delete the `CrazyEightsView`. You won't need it anymore. Just right-click the file name and select Delete.

Try it out with and without this line of code by launching the app and waiting for the screen to time out. Set your screen time out to something low like 30 seconds (Settings⇨Display⇨Sleep). If the screen stays active after your time-out setting, you know it's working.

This approach has its tradeoffs, of course. For a lot of people, the display is what uses up the most battery life. When you disable the timeout for an app, you're also effectively draining the user's battery faster. No matter how you design and develop your game, you're likely to get some negative feedback. You can't please all the people all the time. Sometimes you just need to do what you think is best and what will generate the fewest negative e-mails.

Making the Game Full-Screen

Games designed for consoles and PCs have the luxury of space. Most are played on large displays with either keyboards and mice or game controllers with fine-grained controls. Most games on Android devices are played on a very small screen, using fingers or thumbs (not very fine-grained) for input. Space is at a premium in mobile games, so I try to maximize available screen space by making most games full-screen. As with the timeout issue, some players won't be happy, but most probably will, and many won't even notice.

If you decide to make your game full-screen, here's how you do it. Modifying the code of your `CrazyEightsActivity` to look like Listing 5-7.

Listing 5-7:   Making a View Display Full-Screen

```
package com.dummies.androidgame.crazyeights;

import android.app.Activity;
import android.os.Bundle;
import android.view.Window;
import android.view.WindowManager;

public class CrazyEightsActivity extends Activity {
    /** Called when the activity is first created. */
    @Override
    public void onCreate(Bundle savedInstanceState) {
        super.onCreate(savedInstanceState);
        TitleView tView = new TitleView(this);
        tView.setKeepScreenOn(true);
        requestWindowFeature(Window.FEATURE_NO_TITLE);  →15
        getWindow().setFlags
            (WindowManager.LayoutParams.FLAG_FULLSCREEN,  →16
            WindowManager.LayoutParams.FLAG_FULLSCREEN);  →17
        setContentView(tView);
    }
```

Line 15 tells the activity not to show the title of the app, and lines 16-17 set the window to full-screen. After you make these changes, launch the game. It should look something like Figure 5-4.

Figure 5-4:
Title screen
without app
title, set to
full-screen.

Adding buttons

Displaying non-interactive graphics is great and all, but at some point you need to let the player actually click the screen and do things. So here's the drill on how to add a button to your title screen. There are three important tasks:

✔ Draw the button where you want it to be.

✔ Handle the *down* state when the user touches it.

The *up* state is when the button is not being interacted with; the *down* state is what the button looks like while it is being pressed.

Websites often have an *over* state as well, but that's not generally relevant for a touchscreen.

✔ Actually perform a relevant function when touched. In this case, launch another view where the game will be played.

Figure 5-5 shows the default state of the button you use.

Figure 5-5:
Default state of the Play button for the title screen.

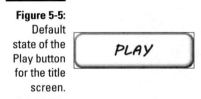

The steps to load and draw the button graphics are similar to those you take for loading and drawing the title graphic:

1. **Add the following line along with your other variable declarations in** `TitleView`:

```
private Bitmap playButtonUp;
```

2. **Load the bitmap by adding the following line in the** `TitleView` **constructor:**

```
playButtonUp =
        BitmapFactory.decodeResource(getResources(),
        R.drawable.play_button_up);
```

3. **Draw the button on the screen by adding the following line of code to your** `onDraw()` **method:**

```
canvas.drawBitmap(playButtonUp,
        (screenW-playButtonUp.getWidth())/2,
        (int)(screenH*0.7), null);
```

Here you used the same logic as you did when drawing the title image to center the image horizontally. With the height, you draw the top of the image at a height that is 70 percent of the screen height, so no matter what display you're using, the button will always be about three quarters from the top of the screen.

When you run the game, it should now resemble Figure 5-6.

Figure 5-6:
Title screen
with the
Play button
added.

Throughout this book, you use relative placement for graphics like this one. If you place graphics by hard-coding pixel values (for example, 500 pixels from the top of the screen), you'll get radically different results on different devices. If you don't like where you've placed the button, feel free to experiment by modifying the percentage value. For example, try 0.6 or 0.8 instead of 0.7. Just remember to always try to use relative positioning.

Handling Button States

A good practice in UI design is to provide the users with feedback when they are interacting with a UI element.

You've got the button where you want it, but right now it doesn't do anything.

In the case of a button, you'd like the users to know they've successfully touched the button by providing an alternate state when the button is pressed. That's what you'll do here.

Figure 5-7 shows the graphic for the down state of the button you'll be using.

Figure 5-7:
Down state
of the Play
button.

The steps that load the graphic for the down state of the button are similar to those for loading the up state:

1. **Add the following line along with your other variable declarations to** TitleView.

```
private Bitmap playButtonDown;
```

2. **Load the bitmap by adding the following line to the** TitleView **constructor.**

```
playButtonDown =
        BitmapFactory.decodeResource(getResources(),
        R.drawable.play_button_down);
```

Now you've got the bitmap loaded and you're ready to draw it, and you know where you want to draw it. But you only want to draw this state when the user is actually clicking the button. Here's how to do that:

1. **Add in a** `boolean` **variable to keep track of whether the button is currently being pressed. Add the following line along with your other variable declarations:**

   ```
   private boolean playButtonPressed;
   ```

2. **In the** `onTouchEvent()` **method, modify the case of** `MotionEvent.ACTION_DOWN` **to look like Listing 5-8.**

Listing 5-8:   Detecting a Button Press

```
case MotionEvent.ACTION_DOWN:
        if (X > (screenW-playButtonUp.getWidth())/2 &&
            X < ((screenW-playButtonUp.getWidth())/2) +
                    playButtonUp.getWidth()) &&
            Y > (int)(screenH*0.7) &&
            Y < (int)(screenH*0.7) +
            playButtonUp.getHeight()) {
              playButtonPressed = true;
            }

    break;
```

The conditional checks to see whether the player is touching the screen within the bounds of the Play-button graphic

- The first two conditions check for the horizontal bounds.

- The last two conditionals check for the vertical bounds.

If you determine that the touch event is within the bounds of the graphic, you set your boolean to `true`.

3. **Set the same boolean to** `false` **when the user lifts the fingertip from the screen. Add the following line to the** `MotionEvent.ACTION_UP` **case:**

   ```
   playButtonPressed = false;
   ```

4. **Draw the up state if the boolean is** `false` **and the down state if the boolean is** `true`**. Modify your** `onDraw()` **method to look like Listing 5-9.**

Listing 5-9:   Drawing Button States

```
@Override
protected void onDraw(Canvas canvas) {
    canvas.drawBitmap(titleGraphic, (screenW-
    titleGraphic.getWidth())/2, 0, null);
     if (playButtonPressed) {
        canvas.drawBitmap(playButtonDown,
        (screenW-playButtonUp.getWidth())/2,
        (int)(screenH*0.7), null);
     } else {
        canvas.drawBitmap(playButtonUp,
        (screenW-playButtonUp.getWidth())/2,
        (int)(screenH*0.7), null);
     }
            }
```

Here you're drawing both graphics in the same location, but which one you draw depends on whether the button is being pressed.

Now launch the game and try out your new button! It still doesn't do much when pressed, but it should at least change states.

Launching the Play Screen

If you want the Play button on your title screen to launch the play screen, you need a game screen to launch! So before you add functionality to your button, create an empty game screen:

1. **Create a new class by right-clicking the package and selecting New⇨Class.**

2. **Enter** `GameView` **for the name, then click Finished.**

3. **Modify the contents of this new class to match Listing 5-10.**

   You need all the same methods here as in your `TitleView`, but for now they won't do anything meaningful. Without anything to draw, this view displays a blank screen — which is fine as a placeholder for now.

Listing 5-10:   The Initial Custom View for the Game Screen

```
package com.agpfd.crazyeights;
import android.content.Context;
import android.graphics.Canvas;
import android.view.MotionEvent;
import android.view.View;

public class GameView extends View {                      →8
```

(continued)

Listing 5-10 *(continued)*

```
public GameView (Context context) {
    super(context);
}

@Override
protected void onDraw(Canvas canvas) {                    →15

}

public boolean onTouchEvent(MotionEvent event) {  →19
        int eventaction = event.getAction();
        int X = (int)event.getX();
        int Y = (int)event.getY();

        switch (eventaction ) {

        case MotionEvent.ACTION_DOWN:
            break;

        case MotionEvent.ACTION_MOVE:
            break;

        case MotionEvent.ACTION_UP:
            break;
        }
        invalidate();
          return true;
    }
}
```

You have a couple of choices about how you display this view:

✔ Replace the current content view with the GameView instead of the TitleView

✔ Launch a new activity for the game.

What's the difference? If you launch a new activity, it will go on a stack above the main activity. If the player is in a game, when they hit the back button on their device, instead of the game closing, the game activity will be destroyed. But since the main activity is still running, the player will simply return to the title screen. You'll go with this implementation to show you how to launch multiple activities within your game.

There's almost always more than one way to do things.

If you're going to launch a new activity, you have to create it first:

1. **Right-click the package.**
2. **Select New⇨Class.**
3. **Enter "GameActivity" as the name of the new class**
4. **Click Finished.**

Modify the contents of this class to look like Listing 5-11.

Listing 5-11:   The Initial Game Activity

```
package com.agpfd.crazyeights;

import android.app.Activity;
import android.os.Bundle;
import android.view.Window;
import android.view.WindowManager;

public class GameActivity extends Activity {
    /** Called when the activity is first created. */
    @Override
    public void onCreate(Bundle savedInstanceState) {
        super.onCreate(savedInstanceState);
        GameView gView = new GameView(this);
        gView.setKeepScreenOn(true);
        requestWindowFeature(Window.FEATURE_NO_TITLE);
        getWindow().setFlags
            (WindowManager.LayoutParams.FLAG_FULLSCREEN,
            WindowManager.LayoutParams.FLAG_FULLSCREEN);
        setContentView(gView);
    }
}
```

This should look familiar. The contents are almost the same as your main activity, but instead of creating a `TitleView` and setting it as the content view, you're creating a `GameView` and setting that as the content view instead. You've also got the logic here for keeping the screen on and setting the view to full-screen.

Every activity in your app must be declared in the manifest; if you tried to launch this activity now, you'd get an error. So open the `AndroidManifest.xml` file for your game and add the declaration for the new activity, as seen in Listing 5-12.

Listing 5-12:   AndroidManifest.xml Declaring GameActivity

```xml
<?xml version="1.0" encoding="utf-8"?>
<manifest xmlns:android="http://schemas.android.com/apk/
          res/android"
    package="com.agpfd.crazyeights"
    android:versionCode="1"
    android:versionName="1.0" >

    <uses-sdk android:minSdkVersion="5" />

    <application
        android:icon="@drawable/ic_launcher"
        android:label="@string/app_name" >
        <activity
            android:label="@string/app_name"
            android:name=".CrazyEightsActivity"
            android:screenOrientation="portrait"
            android:configChanges=
                    "orientation|keyboardHidden"
            >
            <intent-filter>
                <action android:name=
                    "android.intent.action.MAIN" />
                <category android:name=
                    "android.intent.category.LAUNCHER" />
            </intent-filter>
                    </activity>
        <activity

                                                      →23

            android:label="@string/app_name"
            android:name=".GameActivity"
            android:screenOrientation="portrait"
            android:configChanges=
                    "orientation|keyboardHidden"
            >
        </activity>
    </application>

</manifest>
```

Lines 23 – 29 are the declaration for your new activity. Notice that you've added the proper lines for fixing the orientation in portrait mode. You'll need to do this for each activity you add.

When you've got a new GameView and GameActivity, and the manifest is squared away, you're ready to launch your new activity when the Play button is clicked.

Intents

An *intent* is a request from an app to the Android system to perform an operation. It's most commonly used to launch a new activity, which is what you'll be using them for.

An intent takes in the current context as a parameter, so you'll need to store a copy of the context in `TitleView`:

1. **Add the following declaration to your variable declarations:**

   ```
   private Context myContext;
   ```

2. **Modify the constructor of** `TitleView` **to assign the context to your new local copy, so that it looks like Listing 5-13.**

Listing 5-13:   Holding a Reference to Context

```
public TitleView(Context context) {
    super(context);
    myContext = context;
    titleGraphic =
            BitmapFactory.decodeResource(getResources(),
            R.drawable.title_graphic);
    playButtonUp =
            BitmapFactory.decodeResource(getResources(),
            R.drawable.play_button_up);
    playButtonDown =
            BitmapFactory.decodeResource(getResources(),
            R.drawable.play_button_down);
}
```

Now that you have a copy of the context, you can create and fire your intent to start a new activity. You want to do that when the player has clicked the Play button, so modify the `ACTION_UP` case of your `onTouch()` method to look like Listing 5-14.

Listing 5-14:   ACTION_UP Case Launching a New Activity

```
case MotionEvent.ACTION_UP:
if (playButtonPressed) {
      Intent gameIntent = new Intent(myContext,
        GameActivity.class);                          →69
    myContext.startActivity(gameIntent);             →70
  }
  playButtonPressed = false;
  break;
```

Lines 69-70 are only executed if the Play button has been determined to have been pressed in the ACTION_DOWN case:

- ✔ Line 69 creates the new intent, passing in the local copy of the context and the class name of the activity you want to launch (GameActivity. class).
- ✔ Line 70 calls startActivity() and passes in the intent you just created, which will launch the new activity.

After adding these lines, you'll need a new import along with the others in this file; it looks like this:

```
import android.content.Intent;
```

When you've made these changes, launch the game and click the Play button. When you let your finger up from the button, you should be taken to a new blank screen: your empty GameView. It's blank because you haven't put anything there yet! Click the back button on whatever devices you're using and you should be returned to the title screen.

Now you've got a functional title page that launches a new activity holding the view where all of game play will take place. In the next chapter, you build the interface for playing the game; first, however, here's a quick word about bundles and their relationship to intents.

Bundles

When you launched your new activity and its associated view, you didn't pass any information between the old activity and the new one; you can do that when you need to:

- ✔ Before you launch the new activity, you can simply call the putExtras() method on the new intent and pass in a key-value pair.
- ✔ When the new activity is created, you can then call getExtras() to extract the information.

It isn't time yet to use this technique, since you have no need to pass information between your title screen and game screen, but it's worth mentioning because at some point you will probably want to do this. Consult the official Android documentation for examples and more information if you find that this technique is something you need to do.

Chapter 6

Creating a Basic Play Screen

• •

In This Chapter

▶ Loading multiple images

▶ Handling logic, taking turns, and advancing the game

▶ Making a simple computer opponent

• •

A fter the title screen is functional, it's time to build the meat of the game — the play screen. You need images for each of the cards in the deck. I've provided the images for you in the digital resources. You can see how to load them in bulk, shuffle, and deal.

Picking up, moving, and dropping cards in the right spots are all important tasks, as is displaying the current game state. You'll also implement a random AI to test against initially, and then refine it later to provide more of a challenge to players.

You can download sample files for this chapter at

www.dummies.com/go/androidgameprogramming

Displaying Cards

To make your game realistic, players need to see the cards in their own hands and in the discard pile. This requires several steps of programming.

Loading the card images

Before you load the card images, you have to create a new class for cards. Follow these steps:

1. **Right-click the package and then select New⇨Class.**

2. **Name the new class** `Card` **and click Finish.**

3. **Modify the contents of the new class to look like Listing 6-1.**

Listing 6-1: The New Card Class

```
package com.agpfd.crazyeights;

import android.graphics.Bitmap;

public class Card {

    private int id;
    private Bitmap bmp;

    public Card(int newId) {                            →10
        id = newId;
    }

    public void setBitmap(Bitmap newBitmap) {           →14
        bmp = newBitmap;
    }

    public Bitmap getBitmap() {
        return bmp;
    }

    public int getId() {                                →22
        return id;
    }
}
```

Here's a brief explanation of various lines of code in this listing:

→**10–12** The constructor takes in the unique `id` for the card.

Suits are ranked in order by suit, and the numbering system for card `id`s consists of a base value for the suit plus the value of the rank of each card, as shown in this list:

* Diamonds (100)

* Clubs (200)

* Hearts (300)

* Spades (400)

The cards are ranked from 2 to 14, from the deuce to the ace (high): The id for the deuce of diamonds is 102, the three of diamonds is 103, the ace of spades is 414, and so on.

When you name your own image files, follow this convention: card102.png. You're using the prefix "card" because Android doesn't allow only numeric values for the names of resource files.

→**14–20** You have set and get methods for the bitmap image for a particular card.

→**22–25** These lines return the id of the card.

The Card class becomes a little more complex later in this chapter. All you need to do now is pass in the id when you create a card to be able to set/get the bitmap associated with it.

Now you're ready to add the logic to create a deck and load all cards with their associated images in GameView. You can start by adding new variable declarations (as shown in Listing 6-2).

Listing 6-2:   New Variable Declarations for GameView

```
private Context myContext;
private List<Card> deck = new ArrayList<Card>();
private int scaledCardW;
private int scaledCardH;
```

Here are the functions of Listing 6-2:

✔ The first line is a local copy of the context, which you need in order to load bitmaps.

✔ The second line is a list of Card objects that will hold your deck.

✔ The last two lines are variables for the scaled width and height for each card.

The card images that are provided are rather large. You scale them to fit the game display size.

To store a local copy of the context, add the following line to the GameView constructor:

```
myContext = context;
```

Now you're ready to create a new method in GameView that creates a deck of 52 playing cards and loads their associated images. Add the method in Listing 6-3 to your GameView.

Listing 6-3: Initializing a 52-Card Deck

```
private void initCards() {
    for (int i = 0; i < 4; i++) {                              →2
        for (int j = 102; j < 115; j++) {
            int tempId = j + (i*100);                          →4
            Card tempCard = new Card(tempId);                  →5
            int resourceId = getResources().getIdentifier
                ("card"+ tempId, "drawable",
                myContext.getPackageName());                   →6
            Bitmap tempBitmap = BitmapFactory.
                decodeResource(myContext.getResources(),
                resourceId);
            scaledCardW = (int) (screenW/8);                   →10
            scaledCardH = (int) (scaledCardW*1.28);
            Bitmap scaledBitmap = Bitmap.
                createScaledBitmap(tempBitmap,
                scaledCardW, scaledCardH, false);
            tempCard.setBitmap(scaledBitmap);
            deck.add(tempCard);                                →15
        }
    }
}
```

Here's a brief explanation of various lines in this listing:

→2 The outer loop cycles through the four suits (diamonds, clubs, hearts, spades), and the inner loop cycles through each of the card ranks (deuce through ace).

→4 You get the id for a particular card based on the convention mentioned earlier in this section.

→5 You create a new card and pass in its id.

→6 You get the resource id of your image based on the filename and then load the bitmap.

→10 The scaled width is ⅛ the screen width, allowing seven cards to fit comfortably side by side horizontally.

   The height of each card is 1.28 times the width. You use these scaled values to create a scaled bitmap and then set that bitmap for your card.

→15 Finally, you add the newly created card to your deck.

You'll also need to add the following imports:

```
import android.graphics.Bitmap;
import android.graphics.BitmapFactory;
```

This code cycles through all 52 cards, loads their images, and adds them to the deck.

If the cycling is processor-intensive on your test device, use smaller images to reduce the load time. (On higher-resolution devices, the images may not be as clear.)

Call your new method by adding the following line to your `onSizeChanged()` method:

```
initCards();
```

To test whether the cards are loaded correctly, you can temporarily add the following line to the `onDraw()` method:

```
canvas.drawBitmap(deck.get(0).getBitmap(), 0, 0, null);
```

The `get()` method on an `ArrayList` retrieves the object at that index, so you can load any of the 52 cards by passing an index value of 0 through 51. The preceding line loads the deuce of diamonds and draws it in the upper left corner of the screen. Give it a try, but delete this line of code before you move on.

Dealing the cards

After the deck is initialized, you're ready to deal the cards to each player's hand and draw the cards to the screen. You create two new `ArrayLists`, one for each player's hand.

Add the following variable declarations to `GameView`:

```
private List<Card> myHand = new ArrayList<Card>();
private List<Card> oppHand = new ArrayList<Card>();
Private List<Card> discardPile = new ArrayList<Card>();
```

In the preceding declarations

- ✔ The first declaration is used to hold the human player's cards.
- ✔ The second declaration is for the computer opponent's hand.
- ✔ The third declaration is for the discard pile.

Now you add two new methods to GameView, each with its own task:

- ✔ A method that deals the first seven cards to each player
- ✔ A reusable method for drawing a single card from the deck and adding it to the hand

Add the two methods shown in Listing 6-4 to GameView.

Listing 6-4: Methods for Dealing and Drawing Cards

```
private void drawCard(List<Card> handToDraw) {                    →1
    handToDraw.add(0, deck.get(0));
    deck.remove(0);
    if (deck.isEmpty()) {                                          →4
        for (int i = discardPile.size()-1; i > 0 ; i--) {
            deck.add(discardPile.get(i));
            discardPile.remove(i);
            Collections.shuffle(deck,new Random());
        }
    }
}

private void dealCards() {
    Collections.shuffle(deck,new Random());                        →14
    for (int i = 0; i < 7; i++) {                                  →15
        drawCard(myHand);
        drawCard(oppHand);
    }
}
```

Here's a brief explanation of various lines in this listing:

→1   This is the method for drawing a single card from the deck and adding it to a particular list of cards. The method passes in the hand to which the card will be added. The card at index 0 of the deck is then added to the hand in line 92 and removed from the deck in line 93.

→4   In Crazy Eights, when the draw pile is empty, you shuffle back into it all cards of the discard pile, except for the top one. If the deck is empty after a draw, you loop through all cards except the first one in the discard pile, add the first one to the deck, and then remove it from the discard pile.

→**14**   Java provides a utility function for collections to randomize the order of a list, so you're using this function to shuffle the deck.

→**15**   You loop seven times to add a card to each player's hand, calling the method you just created.

You'll also need the following import:

```
import java.util.Random;
```

Call your new method by added the following line to your `onSizeChanged()` method:

```
dealCards();
```

Each player's opening hand now has seven cards, though you can't see them.

Next, you display the state of the game and then handle control interactions.

Displaying the game state

Chapter 1 presents a mock-up of the play screen. Figure 6-1 revisits that screen as a starting point.

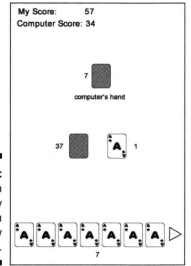

Figure 6-1: Mock-up of the play screen for Crazy Eights.

Keep the background black for now. Rather than display both scores at the top, orient the scores with the top and bottom of the screen so that the opponent's score is at the top and your score is at the bottom.

Before you display the scores, you have to add in another variable to help scale the UI elements. Add the following variable declaration to your `GameView`:

```
private float scale;
```

This variable lets you scale elements on the screen, such as the text size. You can set the value in your constructor by using this line:

```
scale = myContext.getResources().getDisplayMetrics().
        density;
```

This line sets the scaling factor to the density settings you've chosen for whatever device the game appears on. You use this line to scale such onscreen elements as text size.

First things first: Draw some text on your canvas. You need a `Paint` object, which defines the properties for drawing the text to the screen:

✔ Add the following variable declaration to `GameView`:

```
private Paint whitePaint;
```

✔ You'll also need the following import:

```
import android.graphics.Paint;
```

Next, in your constructor, you have to define the properties of the `Paint` object. Modify your `GameView` constructor to look like Listing 6-5.

Listing 6-5: Designating the Properties of `Paint`

```
public GameView(Context context) {
    super(context);
    myContext = context;
    scale =
            myContext.getResources().getDisplayMetrics().density;
    whitePaint = new Paint();                                        →5
    whitePaint.setAntiAlias(true);                                   →6
    whitePaint.setColor(Color.WHITE);
    whitePaint.setStyle(Paint.Style.STROKE);
    whitePaint.setTextAlign(Paint.Align.LEFT);
    whitePaint.setTextSize(scale*15);                               →10
}
```

Here's a brief explanation of various lines in this listing:

→**5**   This line creates the new `Paint` object.

→**6-9**   Anti-aliasing attempts to make the text look smoother. You're setting the color to white and aligning it to the left of wherever you start drawing the text.

→**10**   This is the line where you use your scale variable. You set the text size to 15 times the scaling factor. On displays with a density of 1, the font appears in size 15. When the density changes, so does the font size, to maintain a consistent look across devices.

You'll also need to add the following import:

```
import android.graphics.color
```

Now you add the code for drawing the scores to the screen:

✔ Add declarations for the variables to hold scores:

```
private int oppScore;
private int myScore;
```

✔ Modify the `onDraw()` method to include the code in Listing 6-6.

Listing 6-6:   Drawing Scores to the Screen

```
@Override
protected void onDraw(Canvas canvas) {
    canvas.drawText("Computer Score: " +
            Integer.toString(oppScore), 10,
            whitePaint.getTextSize()+10, whitePaint);
    canvas.drawText("My Score: " +
            Integer.toString(myScore), 10,
            screenH-whitePaint.getTextSize()-10,
            whitePaint);
```

You use the `drawText()` method of `canvas` to draw text, passing in the parameters you want to use:

✔ In the case of the computer's score, you're drawing it 10 pixels from the left of the screen and 10 pixels from the top, which you get by adding the size of the text to 10.

✔ You pass in the `Paint` object that you defined in your constructor.

With your score, everything is much the same as *drawing the opponent's score,* except that you're drawing on the bottom of the screen and subtracting the text size and 10 pixels from the height of the screen.

After you add the code in this section, run the game to see how it appears. It should look similar to Figure 6-2.

Figure 6-2:
The game screen displays players' scores.

You've started displaying the game state on your screen, so now you display the respective hands. Modify the onDraw() method to include the code in Listing 6-7.

Listing 6-7:   Drawing Cards in a Hand

```
for (int i = 0; i < myHand.size(); i++) {
    if (i < 7) {
        canvas.drawBitmap(myHand.get(i).getBitmap(),
                i*(scaledCardW+5),
                screenH-scaledCardH-
                whitePaint.getTextSize()-(50*scale),
                null);
    }
}
```

These lines display your hand. Loop through the first seven cards, and lay them out horizontally, 5 pixels apart. The *y* position of each card subtracts

✔ The height of the card

✔ The height of your score text

✔ 50 scaled pixels from the bottom edge of the screen

Run the game. It should look similar to Figure 6-3.

Now you display the computer opponent's hand. Because the game's player can't see an opponent's cards, there's no need to lay out those cards in the same way. You can let them overlap much more than the player's cards do, because the player sees only the backs of the opponent's cards.

First, you load the graphical image for the back of the card. Create a local Bitmap variable in GameView by adding the following line to your variable declarations:

```
private Bitmap cardBack;
```

You load this bitmap in the onSizeChanged() method to take advantage of the screen width and height information updated at run time.

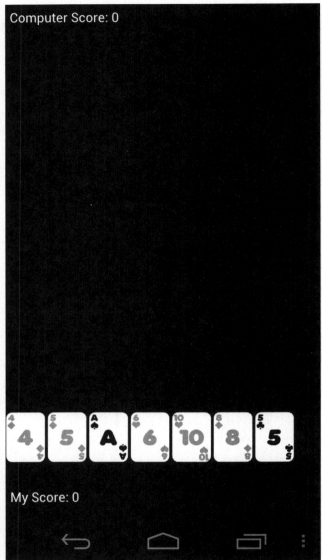

Figure 6-3:
The game
screen
displays
the player's
hand.

Modify the onSizeChanged() method to include the code in Listing 6-8.

Listing 6-8:   Loading the Card Back Graphic

```
Bitmap tempBitmap =
          BitmapFactory.decodeResource
          (myContext.getResources(),
          R.drawable.card_back);
scaledCardW = (int) (screenW/8);
scaledCardH = (int) (scaledCardW*1.28);
cardBack = Bitmap.createScaledBitmap
          (tempBitmap, scaledCardW,
          scaledCardH,false);
```

Just as you load the original graphic for each card front and scale it based on the dimensions of the current screen, you load and scale it for the card-back graphic.

Now modify the onDraw() method to include the code in Listing 6-9.

Listing 6-9:   Drawing the Opponent's Hand

```
for (int i = 0; i < oppHand.size(); i++) {
    canvas.drawBitmap(cardBack,
            i*(scale*5),
            whitePaint.getTextSize()+(50*scale),
            null);
}
```

You add these lines to draw the card-back graphic for each card in the opponent's hand:

✔ You space them only 5 pixels apart so that they overlap.

✔ You draw them at the height of your text plus 50 pixels from the top of the screen.

When you run the game, it should look like Figure 6-4.

Next, you show the draw and discard piles. You can represent the draw pile with a single card-back image. Simply add the following line to your onDraw() method:

```
canvas.drawBitmap(cardBack,
          (screenW/2)-cardBack.getWidth()-10,
          (screenH/2)-(cardBack.getHeight()/2), null);
```

You're drawing the draw pile roughly centered on the screen, so the x position starts with half the screen width, minus the width of the card and another slight offset of 10 pixels.

You're doing this because you want to draw the discard pile next to the draw pile with a little space between them. The *y* coordinate is half the screen height minus half the height of the card image.

When you run the game, it should look like Figure 6-5.

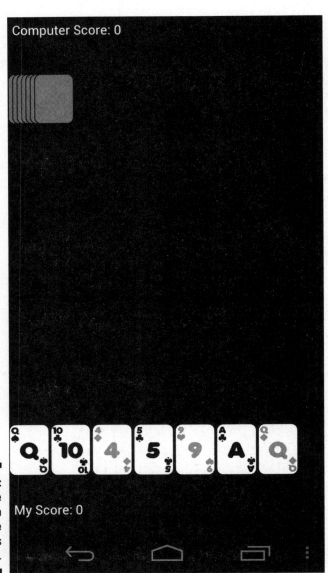

Figure 6-4:
The game screen displays the opponent's hand.

Figure 6-5:
The game
screen
displays the
draw pile.

Drawing the discard pile is slightly trickier. Add the lines in Listing 6-10 to your `onDraw()` method.

Listing 6-10:   Drawing the Discard Pile

```
if (!discardPile.isEmpty()) {
    canvas.drawBitmap(discardPile.get(0).getBitmap(),
        (screenW/2)+10,
        (screenH/2)-(cardBack.getHeight()/2),
        null);
}
```

You're checking to see whether the discard pile contains cards. If it does, you display the top card (index 0) slightly to the right of the draw pile and at the same height.

If you were to run this code now, you wouldn't see anything, because you haven't added cards to the discard pile. In Crazy Eights, you start the discard pile by adding the top card from the draw pile, after both players have been dealt their cards.

To add a card to the discard pile, you can reuse the method for drawing cards. You deal both players their cards in the `onSizeChanged()` method. After the `dealCards()` call, add this line:

```
drawCard(discardPile);
```

This line moves the top card from the draw pile to the discard pile. When you run the game now, you should see a screen similar to Figure 6-6.

Figure 6-6:
The game
screen
displays the
discard pile.

Taking Your Turn

After you display the vital game elements displayed on the play screen (both scores, both hands, the draw pile, and the discard pile), you can move on to handling the game logic, such as determining who plays first and how to alternate turns.

Handling turns

To handle turns, you

- Add a `boolean` variable to `GameView` that keeps track of the player's turn.
- Enable or disable certain logic based on the value of that `boolean`.

Add the following declaration to your other variable declarations:

```
private boolean myTurn;
```

Then, in the constructor, add this line:

```
myTurn = new Random().nextBoolean();
```

This value randomly decides who goes first — the computer opponent or the player. You toggle this value every time either player makes a valid play.

The next couple of sections show you how to

- Enable players to draw and pick up cards to make valid plays.
- Enable the computer opponent to make valid plays.

Crazy Eights has only two valid plays:

- Play a card that matches either the suit or rank of the card on top of the discard pile (or an eight).
- Draw a card.

Before you move on, make a simple computer opponent that returns legal moves. Later in this chapter, I show you how to make the opponent more sophisticated.

Because you need to get both the rank and suit from a card to evaluate valid plays, you need to modify the Card class. Modify its code to look like Listing 6-11.

Listing 6-11:   Handling Ranks and Suits

```
package com.agpfd.crazyeights;

import android.graphics.Bitmap;

public class Card {

    private int id;
    private int suit;
    private int rank;
    private Bitmap bmp;

    public Card(int newId) {
        id = newId;
        suit = Math.round((id/100) * 100);          →14
        rank = id - suit;                           →15
    }

    public void setBitmap(Bitmap newBitmap) {
        bmp = newBitmap;
    }

    public Bitmap getBitmap() {
        return bmp;
    }

    public int getId() {
        return id;
    }

    public int getSuit() {
        return suit;
    }

    public int getRank() {
        return rank;
    }

}
```

In Listing 6-11, you've added

- ✔ Integer variables to hold both the rank and suit
- ✔ Logic to determine the values of these variables from the `id` of the card

The value of the card is calculated from the `id`:

- ✔ Line 14 rounds the `id` to the nearest hundred to get the suit.

  For example, if the card `id` were 309 (the nine of hearts), line 14 would round it to 300 to get the suit (hearts, in this case).

- ✔ Line 15 subtracts the rounded value from the `id` to get the rank.

  If the card `id` were 309, Line 15 would subtract the suit value from the `id` (309–300) to get the rank value of 9.

You've also added a `getSuit()` and `getRank()` method to return these values.

When you have the right logic in the `Card` class, you're ready to create the computer player. Here's how:

1. **Right-click the package in Eclipse and select New⇨Class.**

2. **Enter** `ComputerPlayer` **for the class name and click OK.**

3. **Modify the contents of your newly created class to match Listing 6-12.**

Listing 6-12: A Simple Computer Opponent

```
package com.agpfd.crazyeights;

import java.util.List;

public class ComputerPlayer {

    public int makePlay(List<Card> hand, int suit,
            int rank) {
        int play = 0;
        for (int i = 0; i < hand.size(); i++) {          →9
            int tempId = hand.get(i).getId();            →10
            int tempRank = hand.get(i).getRank();
            int tempSuit = hand.get(i).getSuit();
            if (rank == 8) {
                if (suit == tempSuit) {
                    play = tempId;
```

```
                }
            } else if (suit == tempSuit ||                    →17
                    rank == tempRank ||
                    tempId == 108 || tempId == 208 ||
                    tempId == 308 || tempId == 408) {
                play = tempId;
            }
        }
        return play;
    }

    public int chooseSuit(List<Card> hand) {
        int suit = 100;
        return suit;
    }
}
```

You have only two methods for now:

✔ makePlay():

- Takes in the computer player's hand and the valid suit and/or rank to play

- Returns the id for a valid play from its hand

 ✔ chooseSuit(): Is called only if the computer opponent plays an 8.

Eights are wild. When one is played, its owner gets to name a suit that the opponent also must then play.

Lines 9–21 loop through each card in the computer player's hand:

1. Lines 10–12 determine the rank and suit of each card.

2. Line 13 checks to see whether the rank of the top card of the discard pile is an 8.

   If so, it checks for the suit to be played. If a card in the computer player's hand matches the valid suit, the id of that card is set as the card to be played.

3. If the top card isn't an 8, lines 17–20 check to see whether each card in the computer player's hand matches either the rank or suit of the card that's played.

   If it matches, that card's id is set to return as the one to play.

4. If none of the conditions in either loop is met, there's no valid play among the cards in the computer opponent's hand.

By setting the default value of the play variable to 0, when a valid play isn't found, 0 is returned when this method is called, indicating that a card must be drawn.

For the `chooseSuit()` method, for now you always return 100 (diamonds). This value is sufficient only to produce a playable computer opponent. In Chapter 7, you can see how to analyze the game state and make the computer player a little more sophisticated — and challenging.

Now your game has a playable opponent. Before you begin alternating plays between the player and the opponent, you must ensure that you've handled all logic for the human player interacting with cards and making valid plays, as explained in the following three sections.

Picking up cards

Because you're working on the human side of the game's turns while you implement and test this code, you set the `myTurn` variable to `true` rather than let it be set randomly:

✔ Comment out the following line (the following sidebar shows you how):

```
myTurn = new Random().nextBoolean();
```

✔ Insert the following line:

```
myTurn = true;
```

It ensures that the game screen always starts with the human player's turn active.

Now the game should detect whether the user touches the screen in an area that contains a playable card. First you add a few more variables to draw the card as it's being moved across the screen. Add the following lines to your variable declarations in `GameView`:

```
private int movingCardIdx = -1;
private int movingX;
private int movingY;
```

The preceding code has these functions:

✔ The first variable keeps track of the index of the card that's being moved.

✔ The other two variables

• Keep track of the user's finger on the screen.

• Make that information available to all methods in GameView.

Now modify the onTouchEvent() method to look like Listing 6-13.

Listing 6-13: Picking Up and Moving Cards

```
public boolean onTouchEvent(MotionEvent event) {
    int eventaction = event.getAction();
    int X = (int)event.getX();
    int Y = (int)event.getY();

    switch (eventaction ) {

    case MotionEvent.ACTION_DOWN:
        if (myTurn) {                                    →8
        for (int i = 0; i < 7; i++) {                    →9
            if (X > i*(scaledCardW+5) &&
                X < i*(scaledCardW+5)
                + scaledCardW &&
                Y > screenH-scaledCardH-
                whitePaint.getTextSize()-
                (50*scale)) {
                movingCardIdx = i;
                movingX = X;
                movingY = Y;
            }
        }
        }
        break;

        case MotionEvent.ACTION_MOVE:
         movingX = X;                                    →24
         movingY = Y;
         break;

        case MotionEvent.ACTION_UP:
        movingCardIdx = -1;                              →29
         break;
        }
        invalidate();
        return true;
    }
```

REMEMBER

Commenting code

In most programming languages, *comments* allow programmers to include text that isn't live code within a program file. Usually, these are messages about the file as a whole, or specific lines or sections of code, helping to make the code more understandable. A special character may begin or end the comment. However, the same commenting function can allow you to disable lines and sections of code while you develop.

Commenting and uncommenting code throughout the development process is a routine, helpful practice that lets you enable and disable logic, depending on what you're testing or working on.

Use double forward slashes (//) to comment out a single line of code, like this:

```
//myTurn =
    new Random()nextBoolean();
```

Use the combination forward-slash-and-asterisk (/*) to comment out blocks of code, letting it open the block to be commented out. Use the reverse combination — the asterisk-and-slash (*/) — to close the block:

```
/*
myTurn =
    new Random()nextBoolean();
System.out.println("hello");
*/
```

Here's a brief explanation of various lines in this listing:

→8   A player should be able to pick up and move cards only on their turn.

→9   Loop through the first seven cards in the player's hand (the ones being displayed), and check to see whether the player has touched the screen on a card that's being displayed. If so, you assign the index of that card to `movingCardIdx` as well as to the current *x* and *y* positions to the `movingX` and `movingY` variables.

→24   As the player moves his or her finger across the screen, you keep track of the *x* and *y*. You use this information when drawing the bitmap for the card being moved.

→29   When the player lifts the finger from the screen, you reset the `movingCardIdx` to indicate that no cards are being moved.

The previous logic keeps track of picked-up and moving cards, but has no visual impact until you update the `onDraw()` method. Modify this method to look like Listing 6-14.

Listing 6-14: Drawing Moving Cards

```
@Override
protected void onDraw(Canvas canvas) {
    canvas.drawText("Computer Score: " +
            Integer.toString(oppScore), 10,
            whitePaint.getTextSize()+10, whitePaint);
    canvas.drawText("My Score: " +
            Integer.toString(myScore), 10,
            screenH-whitePaint.getTextSize()-10,
            whitePaint);
    for (int i = 0; i < oppHand.size(); i++) {
        canvas.drawBitmap(cardBack,
            i*(scale*5),
            whitePaint.getTextSize()+(50*scale),
            null);
    }
    canvas.drawBitmap(cardBack,
            (screenW/2)-cardBack.getWidth()-10,
            (screenH/2)-(cardBack.getHeight()/2), null);
    if (!discardPile.isEmpty()) {
        canvas.drawBitmap(discardPile.get(0).getBitmap(),
                    (screenW/2)+10,
                    (screenH/2)-(cardBack.getHeight()/2),
                    null);
    }
    for (int i = 0; i < myHand.size(); i++) {
        if (i == movingCardIdx) {                         →22
            canvas.drawBitmap(myHand.get(i).getBitmap(),
                    movingX,
                    movingY,
                    null);
        } else {                                          →27
                canvas.drawBitmap
                        (myHand.get(i).getBitmap(),
                        i*(scaledCardW+5),
                        screenH-scaledCardH-
                        whitePaint.getTextSize()-
                        (50*scale), null);
        }
    }
    invalidate();
}
```

Note that you've moved to the end of the method the code for drawing your own hand. Why? Because the order in which items are drawn in this method determines whether they're drawn above or below other items. The reason didn't matter when you weren't moving elements around, but now that you're moving a card that you've picked up, you want it to appear above all other elements on the screen. In other words, you don't want a card that you're dragging across the screen to appear underneath the draw pile. Experiment with the order in which items are drawn to get a feel for what I'm talking about. Trust me — this particular ordering works best.

Here's a brief description of a couple of lines in this listing:

→22   You check to see whether the index of a given card in your hand matches the `movingCardIdx`. If so, you draw the card at the current *x* and *y* position of the player's finger.

→27   If the `movingCardIdx` doesn't match any index values for cards in your hand (for example, when it's –1), you draw the rest of your hand as you did before.

Run the game, and try picking up and moving cards around the screen. You'll probably notice that the picked-up card is drawn with the upper left corner of the card at the position where your finger is touching the screen. So the card is drawn under your finger, obscuring it.

This is an issue when displaying UI elements in a touchscreen environment. You can improve this aspect of the UI by modifying the `movingX` and `movingY` values. Though you can center the bitmap on the point where the player is touching the screen, I like for the element offset to appear above and to the left of the point that's touched.

Test on a real device. Testing your game only on an emulator can give you a false sense of screen interaction using touch:

✔ When you run a game on an emulator, you interact with the UI elements using your mouse and the pointer icon, which is much smaller and finer-grained than interacting with a screen using your finger.

✔ When you're picking up and moving UI elements, the mouse pointer typically doesn't obscure whatever element you're moving, and your finger does.

Have a look at Listing 6-15, where I've added offsets to the *x* and *y* positions for the card being picked up and moved.

Listing 6-15:   Adding an Offset to Moving Cards

```
public boolean onTouchEvent(MotionEvent event) {
    int eventaction = event.getAction();
    int X = (int)event.getX();
    int Y = (int)event.getY();

    switch (eventaction ) {
```

```
case MotionEvent.ACTION_DOWN:
        if (myTurn) {
            for (int i = 0; i < 7; i++) {
                if (X > i*(scaledCardW+5) &&
                        X < i*(scaledCardW+5)
                        + scaledCardW &&
                        Y > screenH-scaledCardH-
                        whitePaint.getTextSize()-
                        (50*scale)) {
                    movingCardIdx = i;
                    movingX = X-(int)(30*scale);    →16
                    movingY = Y-(int)(70*scale);    →17
                }
            }
        }
        break;

case MotionEvent.ACTION_MOVE:
        movingX = X-(int)(30*scale);                →24
        movingY = Y-(int)(70*scale);                →25
        break;
```

I've only modified four lines here, 16–17 and 24–25. I've added a 30-pixel offset to the left and a 70-pixel offset up. This way, the card is generally

✔ Centered horizontally at the point of touch

✔ Offset vertically so that the user can see the rank and suit of the card as it moves

You can use different offset values, but do *not* draw the card completely under the player's finger as the card moves. Experiment with offset values that you like until they feel intuitive and user-friendly to you. Then you can move on to handling the logic for playing valid cards on the discard pile.

Playing cards

Before allowing a dragged card to be played on the discard pile, you need to know whether it's a valid play.

To keep track of valid plays, add these two variables to your variable declarations.

```
private int validRank = 8;
private int validSuit = 0;
```

You initialize the valid rank as an 8 because an 8 is always legal to play. These values are updated every time a card is played. You get the initial values from the first card that's placed face-up in the discard pile, which is done with the initialization of the deck and hands in the onSizeChanged() method. Modify that method to look like Listing 6-16.

Listing 6-16: Getting Valid Suit and Rank Values

```
@Override
public void onSizeChanged (int w, int h, int oldw,
            int oldh){
    super.onSizeChanged(w, h, oldw, oldh);
    screenW = w;
    screenH = h;
    Bitmap tempBitmap = BitmapFactory.
            decodeResource(myContext.getResources(),
            R.drawable.card_back);
    scaledCardW = (int) (screenW/8);
    scaledCardH = (int) (scaledCardW*1.28);
    cardBack = Bitmap.createScaledBitmap(tempBitmap,
            scaledCardW, scaledCardH, false);
    initCards();
    dealCards();
    drawCard(discardPile);
    validSuit = discardPile.get(0).getSuit();          →15
    validRank = discardPile.get(0).getRank();          →16
}
```

Lines 15–16 get the suit and rank of the first card placed on the discard pile. With that information in hand, you're ready to see whether a dragged card is a valid play:

✔ **A valid play:** Add it to the discard pile.

✔ **Not a valid play:** Do nothing, "returning" it to the player's hand.

You check in the ACTION_UP case of onTouchEvent(). Modify the ACTION_UP case to look like Listing 6-17.

Listing 6-17:   Checking for Valid Plays

```
case MotionEvent.ACTION_UP:
    if (movingCardIdx > -1 &&                              →2
        X > (screenW/2)-(100*scale) &&                     →3
        X < (screenW/2)+(100*scale) &&
        Y > (screenH/2)-(100*scale) &&
        Y < (screenH/2)+(100*scale) &&
        (myHand.get(movingCardIdx).getRank() == 8 ||
        myHand.get(movingCardIdx).getRank() ==             →8
            validRank ||
        myHand.get(movingCardIdx).getSuit() ==             →9
            validSuit)) {
                validRank = myHand.get                     →10
                    (movingCardIdx).getRank();
                validSuit = myHand.get                     →11
                    (movingCardIdx).getSuit();
                discardPile.add(0, myHand.                 →12
                get(movingCardIdx));
                myHand.remove(movingCardIdx);              →13
            }
        movingCardIdx = -1;
                                                           break;
```

Here's a brief explanation of various lines in this listing:

→**2** This line checks to see whether a card is being moved.

→**3–6** The only action the player can take with a card in hand is to play it on the discard pile, so you don't have to worry about accuracy. You're simply verifying that the player has dropped the card within an area of 200 x 200 pixels in the center of the screen. If you want to adjust the drop area by changing these values, go for it.

→**8–9** These lines check to see whether the card being dragged is a valid rank or suit.

→**10–11** If the dragged card meets the right conditions, you get the rank and suit of the card and set the current valid values.

→**12–13** Then you add the dragged card to the discard pile at index 0 and remove it from the player's hand.

Try it out. You should be able to

✔ Drag cards that match either the suit or the rank of the top card in the discard pile.

✔ Drop cards in the middle of the screen, adding them to the discard pile.

Playing an 8 requires special handling because you get to choose the valid suit. You can set the valid rank as 8 because it's always playable, but you need a way for the player to choose a particular valid suit: the dialog box.

Showing dialog boxes (and toasts)

The *dialog box* (also known as a *dialog*) is an onscreen element that offers choices to the user; it's among the most common and widely used UI elements in games.

In your game, you use dialog boxes to

✓ Display end-of-hand and end-of-game states

✓ Let players choose the suit when an 8 is played, which is what you're using one for now

The dialog box will contain three elements:

✓ Some text

✓ A *spinner* (or *drop-down menu,* in Android),

The spinner is populated with four values — strings for the four suits.

✓ A button

Before you do anything else, create a new file in your resource folder from which you can reference the names of the suits. They're held in a string array, so you need to create a new file for it.

1. **Right-click the `res>values` folder in your project and select New⇨File.**

2. **Name the new file `arrays.xml`.**

3. **Click Finished.**

Modify the contents of your newly created file to match Listing 6-18.

Listing 6-18:   The `arrays.xml` File

```
<resources>
<string-array name="suits">
    <item>Diamonds</item>
    <item>Clubs</item>
    <item>Hearts</item>
    <item>Spades</item>
</string-array>
</resources>
```

This file is straightforward. You're naming the array "suits," and each item is the name of a suit.

The next file you need to create is a layout file for the dialog box:

1. **Right-click the `res>layout` folder.**

2. **Choose New⇨File.**

3. **Name the new file `choose_suit_dialog.xml`.**

4. **Click Finished.**

Modify the contents of the new file to match Listing 6-19.

Listing 6-19: The `choose_suits_dialog.xml` File

```xml
<?xml version="1.0" encoding="utf-8"?>
<LinearLayout
android:id="@+id/chooseSuitLayout"
android:layout_width="275dp"
android:layout_height="wrap_content"
android:orientation="vertical"
android:layout_gravity="top"
xmlns:android="http://schemas.android.com/apk/res/android"
>
<TextView
android:id="@+id/chooseSuitText"
android:layout_width="wrap_content"
android:layout_height="wrap_content"
android:text="Choose a suit."
android:textSize="16sp"
android:layout_marginLeft="5dp"
android:textColor="#FFFFFF"
>
</TextView>
<Spinner
android:id="@+id/suitSpinner"
android:layout_width="fill_parent"
android:layout_height="wrap_content"
android:drawSelectorOnTop="true"
/>
<Button
android:id="@+id/okButton"
android:layout_width="125dp"
android:layout_height="wrap_content"
android:text="OK"
>
</Button>
</LinearLayout>
```

As mentioned, the layout contains three UI elements: text, spinner, and button. All three are contained in a `LinearLayout` (the simplest layout format in Android), which lays out elements in a straight line. In this case, you've set the orientation for the layout as `"vertical"`, so the elements are laid out from top to bottom.

Note that each element has an `id`, which is how you reference them from the Java files. Also note the use of `dp` for pixel dimensions and `sp` for text size. These density-independent units scale with the size of the display. You can preview a layout on the Graphical Layout tab. Yours should look similar to Figure 6-7.

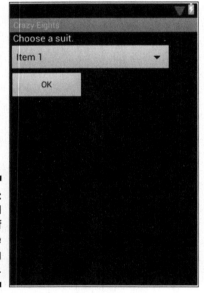

Figure 6-7:
Graphical
preview of
the Choose
Suits dialog
box.

Though you can customize dialog boxes, don't do anything fancy with this one. For your own game, experiment with themes and styles to make your dialog boxes more visually appealing. For now, simply implement the basics so that you can get a playable game up and running.

When you have the proper resource files, you can add code to display your dialog box at the right time (when the human player plays an 8). In your `GameView`, add the new method `showChooseSuitDialog()` with the content shown in Listing 6-20.

Listing 6-20: The `showChooseSuitsDialog()` Method

```
private void showChooseSuitDialog() {
    final Dialog chooseSuitDialog =                         →2
        new Dialog(myContext);
    chooseSuitDialog.requestWindowFeature
        (Window.FEATURE_NO_TITLE);
    chooseSuitDialog.setContentView
        (R.layout.choose_suit_dialog);
    final Spinner suitSpinner = (Spinner)                   →5
        chooseSuitDialog.findViewById(R.id.suitSpinner);
    ArrayAdapter<CharSequence> adapter =                    →7
            ArrayAdapter.createFromResource(
            myContext, R.array.suits,
            android.R.layout.simple_spinner_item);
adapter.setDropDownViewResource
        (android.R.layout.simple_spinner_dropdown_item);
    suitSpinner.setAdapter(adapter);
    Button okButton =                                       →11
            (Button) chooseSuitDialog.findViewById
            (R.id.okButton);
    okButton.setOnClickListener
            (new View.OnClickListener(){
        public void onClick(View view){
            validSuit = (suitSpinner.
                getSelectedItemPosition()+1)*100;
            String suitText = "";
            if (validSuit == 100) {
                suitText = "Diamonds";
            } else if (validSuit == 200) {
                suitText = "Clubs";
            } else if (validSuit == 300) {
                suitText = "Hearts";
            } else if (validSuit == 400) {
                suitText = "Spades";
            }
            chooseSuitDialog.dismiss();
            Toast.makeText(myContext,                        →27
                "You chose " + suitText,
                Toast.LENGTH_SHORT).show();
        }
    });
    chooseSuitDialog.show();
}
```

Here's a brief explanation of various lines in this listing:

→2   First you create a final instance of a dialog box. Then you set the attribute of having no title before setting the content view to the `choose_suit_dialog.xml` file you just created.

→**5**   This line creates a final instance of a spinner, referencing the `id` of the spinner in your layout file.

→**7**   An `ArrayAdapter` supplies data to a view and determines its format. This line creates an `ArrayAdapter` using the suits array in your resource directory. You use default layout parameters for spinner items (how items are displayed when the spinner hasn't been clicked) and for spinner drop-down items (how items are displayed when the spinner has been clicked). Then you set this new adapter as the one for your spinner.

→**11**   You reference the button in your layout file and set an `onClick-Listener()`, which performs whatever logic you designate when `onClick()` is called by the user clicking the button. Line 168 sets the `validSuit` by getting the index of the selected spinner item, adding 1, and multiplying by 100. This provides the proper value for the suit based on the selected item. The suit names in the suit array must be in the proper order, or else this process doesn't work correctly.

→**27**   To reinforce the player's choice, a *Toast* (a brief system message) flashes on the screen. You can use a Toast to display certain types of information that require neither a dedicated dialog box nor a player's selection.

In this case, you display the chosen suit:

- ✔ The lines immediately preceding line 27 declare a text variable to hold the text for the chosen suit. The `if` statements

  - Check the `validSuit` variable.

  - Assign the proper text to the `suitText` variable.

- ✔ Line 26 dismisses the dialog box. You can control the display time of the Toast by using the last parameter. In this case, the Toast flashes on the screen for a couple of seconds.

You'll also need the following import statements:

```
import android.widget.ArrayAdapter;
import android.widget.button;
```

You should show the dialog box only when the player has just played an 8 and needs to choose which suit the opponent must play. To do so, modify the ACTION_UP case of onTouchEvent() (see Listing 6-21).

Listing 6-21: Launching the Choose Suits Dialog box

```
case MotionEvent.ACTION_UP:
    if (movingCardIdx > -1 &&
        X > (screenW/2)-(100*scale) &&
        X < (screenW/2)+(100*scale) &&
        Y > (screenH/2)-(100*scale) &&
        Y < (screenH/2)+(100*scale) &&
        (myHand.get(movingCardIdx).getRank() == 8 ||
         myHand.get(movingCardIdx).getRank() ==
           validRank ||
         myHand.get(movingCardIdx).getSuit() ==
             validSuit)) {
            validRank =
                    myHand.get(movingCardIdx).getRank();
            validSuit =
                    myHand.get(movingCardIdx).getSuit();
            discardPile.add(0,
            myHand.get(movingCardIdx));
            myHand.remove(movingCardIdx);
            if (validRank == 8) {                      →14
            showChooseSuitDialog();                }
    }
    movingCardIdx = -1;
    break;
```

You've added lines 14–16. If an 8 has been played, call your new method for displaying the Choose Suits dialog box. As always, give it a try. The dialog box, when launched, should look similar to Figure 6-8.

When you click the spinner, the list of items should open, as shown in Figure 6-9.

If you want to test without having to play an 8, simply comment out that condition so that the dialog box displays for all valid plays. In the following section, you handle an important case: a player who cannot make a valid play having to draw until a valid play is possible.

Figure 6-8:
Displaying
the Choose
a Suit dialog
box.

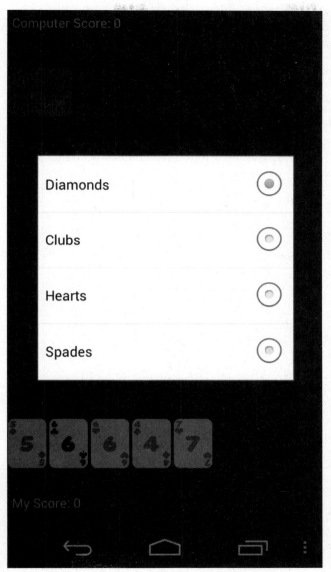

Figure 6-9:
List items for
the Choose
a Suit
spinner.

Taking cards from the draw pile

Adding a card from the draw pile to the human player's hand is simple enough. After all, you already have a simple `drawCard()` method. But you have a number of other issues to consider in addition to adding a card to the player's hand.

In Crazy Eights, a player who can't make a valid play must continue drawing until they can make one — which means that the player may have seven cards or more. In your initial game screen mock-up, you use an arrow key to rotate through the hand, displaying only seven cards at a time. From a UI perspective, you can handle this task in many different ways; in this instance, you implement an arrow key.

Add the following bitmap to your variable declarations:

```
private Bitmap nextCardButton;
```

Now you need to load it, so add the following line of code to the `onSizeChanged()` method:

```
nextCardButton = BitmapFactory.decodeResources()
        (getResources(),
R.drawable.arrow_next);
```

Now you need to modify the part of the `onDraw()` method that draws your hand. Replace the code that draws your hand with the contents of Listing 6-22.

Listing 6-22:   Drawing a Hand with More than Seven Cards

```
if (myHand.size() > 7) {                                     →1
    canvas.drawBitmap(nextCardButton,
            screenW-nextCardButton.getWidth()-(30*scale),
            screenH-nextCardButton.getHeight()-
            scaledCardH-(90*scale),
            null);
}
for (int i = 0; i < myHand.size(); i++) {                    →7
    if (i == movingCardIdx) {
        canvas.drawBitmap(myHand.get(i).getBitmap(),
                movingX,
                movingY,
                null);
    } else {
        if (i < 7) {                                         →14
```

```
            canvas.drawBitmap(myHand.get(i).getBitmap(),
                i*(scaledCardW+5),
                screenH-scaledCardH-
                whitePaint.getTextSize()-(50*scale),
                null);
        }
    }
}
```

Here's a brief explanation of most of the lines in this listing:

→**1–6**   This block of code draws the next button, but only if your hand size is greater than 7.

→**7–12** Loop through all cards in your hand. If the index value matches the moving card index, you draw that moving card.

→**14–19** Otherwise, the card is drawn in its normal position in the hand, but only if its index value is one of the first seven cards.

Now you can visually handle a hand holding more than seven cards. Before you enable the drawing functionality, however, you need a way to determine whether the player should be allowed to draw a card.

In your `GameView`, add the method shown in Listing 6-23.

Listing 6-23:   Checking for Valid Draws

```
private boolean checkForValidDraw() {
    boolean canDraw = true;
    for (int i = 0; i < myHand.size(); i++) {
        int tempId = myHand.get(i).getId();
        int tempRank = myHand.get(i).getRank();
        int tempSuit = myHand.get(i).getSuit();
        if (validSuit == tempSuit || validRank == tempRank
            ||
            tempId == 108 || tempId == 208 ||
            tempId == 308 || tempId == 408) {
            canDraw = false;
        }
    }
    return canDraw;
}
```

This chunk of code should look familiar — similar logic is used in your simple computer opponent to check for valid plays. This method is checking to see whether the player's hand contains a card that either matches the current rank or suit or contains an 8:

✔ If so, it returns true.

✔ If not, it returns false.

Now add the code, shown in Listing 6-24, for drawing a card to the `ACTION_UP` case of your `onTouchEvent()` method.

Listing 6-24:   Drawing a Card Into a Hand

```
if (movingCardIdx == -1 && myTurn &&
        X > (screenW/2)-(100*scale) &&
        X < (screenW/2)+(100*scale) &&
        Y > (screenH/2)-(100*scale) &&
        Y < (screenH/2)+(100*scale)) {
            if (checkForValidDraw()) {
                drawCard(myHand);
            } else {
                Toast.makeText(myContext, "You have a
                valid play.", Toast.LENGTH_SHORT).show();
            }
}
```

If the player has no card in hand, they click the draw pile (or anywhere near it). As with playing, you're detecting only whether the player clicks in the middle of the screen, near the draw pile:

✔ When they do, you call your `checkForValidDraw()` method

✔ If it returns true, you draw a card and add it to the hand.

✔ If the player has a valid play, you inform them with a Toast.

Finally, you add the logic for rotating the cards displayed in the player's hand if it contains more than seven cards. Luckily, Collections in Java provide a built-in method for rotating lists. You call this method when the player holds more than seven cards and clicks the Next Card button.

Add the code in Listing 6-25 to the `ACTION_UP` case of your `onTouchEvent()` method.

Listing 6-25:   Cycling Through Cards in a Large Hand

```
if (myHand.size() > 7 &&
    X > screenW-nextCardButton.getWidth()-(30*scale) &&
    Y > screenH-nextCardButton.getHeight()-scaledCardH-
        (90*scale) &&
    Y < screenH-nextCardButton.getHeight()-scaledCardH-
        (60*scale)) {
        Collections.rotate(myHand, 1);
}
```

The conditional statement determines whether the player has more than seven cards and is clicking the button.

If so, the indices of the cards are shifted upward by 1, and the last card in the list is moved to the front. Try it out. You should now be able to make valid plays, and when you can't, you should be able to draw. When your hand size is larger than seven, you should be able to use the Next button to cycle through the cards.

In previous sections, you leave the turn toggled to the human player while you implement all possible actions they can take. After you have that logic implemented, you can see in the following section how to alternate turns so that you can feel like you're playing an actual game.

Advancing play

Though earlier sections show you how to work on the functionality for playing and drawing cards for the human player, you've left the myTurn variable toggled to true. It's time to return it to initialize randomly. You handle the initialization in the onSizeChanged() method — the same place you initialize nearly everything else.

Modify your onSizeChanged() method to match the contents of Listing 6-26.

Listing 6-26: Initializing Player Turns

```
@Override
public void onSizeChanged
          (int w, int h, int oldw, int oldh){
    super.onSizeChanged(w, h, oldw, oldh);
    screenW = w;
    screenH = h;
    Bitmap tempBitmap = BitmapFactory.
          decodeResource(myContext.getResources(),
          R.drawable.card_back);
    scaledCardW = (int) (screenW/8);
    scaledCardH = (int) (scaledCardW*1.28);
    cardBack = Bitmap.createScaledBitmap(tempBitmap,
          scaledCardW, scaledCardH, false);
    nextCardButton = BitmapFactory.
          decodeResource(getResources(),
          R.drawable.arrow_next);
    initCards();
    dealCards();
    drawCard(discardPile);
```

(continued)

Listing 6-26 *(continued)*

```
    validSuit = discardPile.get(0).getSuit();
    validRank = discardPile.get(0).getRank();
    myTurn = new Random().nextBoolean();            →19
    if (!myTurn) {
        makeComputerPlay();
    }
}
```

You see in line 19 that you've returned to randomizing the `myTurn` variable:

 ✔ If that value is false, you call the new method `makeComputerPlay()`.

 ✔ If the value is true, you simply wait for user input.

We commented out the line initializing `myTurn` in the constructor. To keep the code clean, you can delete that commented line from the constructor.

To implement the new method for making computer plays, you add the method in Listing 6-27 to your `GameView`. First you'll need to add a variable for the computer player along with your other variable declarations at the top of the file:

```
private ComputerPlayer computerPlayer = new
        ComputerPlayer();
```

Listing 6-27:   Handling Computer Opponent Plays

```
private void makeComputerPlay() {
    int tempPlay = 0;                                       →2
    while (tempPlay == 0) {                                 →3
        tempPlay = computerPlayer.makePlay(oppHand,
            validSuit, validRank);
        if (tempPlay == 0) {
            drawCard(oppHand);
        }
    }
    if (tempPlay == 108 || tempPlay == 208 ||
            tempPlay == 308 || tempPlay == 408) {
        validRank = 8;
        validSuit =                                         →12
            computerPlayer.chooseSuit(oppHand);
        String suitText = "";
        if (validSuit == 100) {
```

```
            suitText = "Diamonds";
        } else if (validSuit == 200) {
            suitText = "Clubs";
        } else if (validSuit == 300) {
            suitText = "Hearts";
        } else if (validSuit == 400) {
            suitText = "Spades";
        }
        Toast.makeText(myContext, "Computer chose " +
            suitText, Toast.LENGTH_SHORT).show();
    } else {
        validSuit = Math.round((tempPlay/100) * 100);  →26
        validRank = tempPlay - validSuit;
    }
    for (int i = 0; i < oppHand.size(); i++) {              →29
        Card tempCard = oppHand.get(i);
        if (tempPlay == tempCard.getId()) {
            discardPile.add(0, oppHand.get(i));
            oppHand.remove(i);
        }
    }
    myTurn = true;                                         →36
}
```

Here's a brief explanation of various lines in this listing:

→**2**   You initialize a temporary variable to hold the id of the played card.

→**3**   A value of 0 for the id indicates no matching cards. The computer player needs to draw a card, so you set up a while loop. As long as the computer player indicates that it needs to draw, you draw a card into its hand. A valid id for a card to be played escapes the loop.

→**12**   If the computer chooses to play an 8, you call its chooseSuit() method, which for now is set to always return diamonds. You then notify the user of the chosen suit via a Toast. Though you may want to always display the current valid suit on the screen, for now, stick with a temporary notification.

→**26–27** If the computer player doesn't play an 8, you simply reset the valid rank and valid suit to whatever the played cards' values are.

→**29**   Loop through the opponent's hand, adding the played card to the discard pile and removing it from their hand.

→**36**   Finally, you toggle the turn back to the human player.

You need to add a last bit of code before turns are properly alternated throughout a game. When the human player makes a move, you call the method you just made. The human player makes a move after dropping a card on the discard pile; that's what you need to modify.

Modify the section of code in the ACTION_UP case of onTouchEvent(va), as shown in Listing 6-28.

Listing 6-28:   Passing the Turn to the Computer Opponent

```
case MotionEvent.ACTION_UP:
    if (movingCardIdx > -1 &&
        X > (screenW/2)-(100*scale) &&
        X < (screenW/2)+(100*scale) &&
        Y > (screenH/2)-(100*scale) &&
        Y < (screenH/2)+(100*scale) &&
        (myHand.get(movingCardIdx).getRank() == 8 ||
         myHand.get(movingCardIdx).getRank() == validRank
         ||
         myHand.get(movingCardIdx).getSuit() ==
         validSuit)) {
            validRank =
          myHand.get(movingCardIdx).getRank();
            validSuit =
          myHand.get(movingCardIdx).getSuit();
            discardPile.add(0, myHand.get(movingCardIdx));
            myHand.remove(movingCardIdx);
            if (myHand.isEmpty()) {
                //handle end of hand
            } else {
                if (validRank == 8) {                    →17
                    showChooseSuitDialog();
                } else {
                    myTurn = false;
                    makeComputerPlay();
                }
            }
        }
    }
```

In Lines 17–19, you simply check to see whether the player played an 8.

 ✔ If so, you call the showChooseSuitsDialog() method.

 ✔ If not, you toggle the turn variable and call the method for the computer to play.

If the human player plays an 8 and the Choose Suits dialog box is displayed, the computer should play only after the dialog box is dismissed, so you need to update the showChooseSuitsDialog() method.

Modify your `showChooseSuitsDialog()` method to match Listing 6-29.

Listing 6-29:   Passing the Turn After Choosing a New Suit

```
private void showChooseSuitDialog() {
    final Dialog chooseSuitDialog = new Dialog(myContext);
    chooseSuitDialog.requestWindowFeature
            (Window.FEATURE_NO_TITLE);
    chooseSuitDialog.setContentView
            (R.layout.choose_suit_dialog);
    final Spinner suitSpinner = (Spinner)
chooseSuitDialog.findViewById(R.id.suitSpinner);
    ArrayAdapter<CharSequence> adapter =
            ArrayAdapter.createFromResource(
                myContext, R.array.suits,
android.R.layout.simple_spinner_item);
    adapter.setDropDownViewResource
            (android.R.layout.simple_spinner_dropdown_item);
    suitSpinner.setAdapter(adapter);
    Button okButton = (Button)
            chooseSuitDialog.findViewById(R.id.okButton);
    okButton.setOnClickListener(new View.OnClickListener()
            {
        public void onClick(View view){
            validSuit =
            (suitSpinner.getSelectedItemPosition()+1)*100;
            String suitText = "";
            if (validSuit == 100) {
                suitText = "Diamonds";
            } else if (validSuit == 200) {
                suitText = "Clubs";
            } else if (validSuit == 300) {
                suitText = "Hearts";
            } else if (validSuit == 400) {
                suitText = "Spades";
            }
            chooseSuitDialog.dismiss();
            Toast.makeText(myContext, "You chose " +
            suitText, Toast.LENGTH_SHORT).show();
            myTurn = false;                              →30
            makeComputerPlay();                          →31
        }
    });
    chooseSuitDialog.show();
}
```

Lines 30–31 are added, toggling the turn variable and making the computer play.

Now, whenever you launch the game screen, the player who goes first is chosen randomly, and you can make plays with the computer player responding. You may notice that the opponent plays instantly after the human player makes a move. Of course, computers are fast, so they don't need much time to think about plays (especially your rather unsophisticated player). Because it doesn't feel much like players' turns are alternating when the computer responds so quickly, consider implementing either

- ✔ A Toast indicating the played card
- ✔ A delay between the human player's play and the computer's play

Also, you're not handling the case of either player running out of cards, in which case the hand should end. I tell you how to handle this task, and how to improve your computer opponent and scoring, in Chapter 7.

Chapter 7

Finishing Your First Game

. . . .

In This Chapter

▶ Handling the end of a hand and the end of a game

▶ Developing a more sophisticated player AI

▶ Using your own launcher icon

. . . .

After you have every core element that enables you to represent the game state and make plays from both hands, your only remaining tasks are to handle the ends of hands and games — and to make a few improvements. You're almost finished with your first game!

You can download sample files for this chapter at

www.dummies.com/go/androidgameprogramming

Ending Hands and Games

You've got all the logic for making plays within a game, but hands and games can't go on forever, right? You need to make sure the game can recognize states when the hand or game should come to an end so that scores can be tallied so the game can either

▸ Progress to the next hand

▸ Determine who won and who lost

Ending a hand

The hand should end when either player plays their last card. But then these three things should happen:

   ✔ Update the scores.

   ✔ Display a dialog indicating that the hand is over.

   ✔ Start a new hand.

To handle the scoring first, you add a new variable to keep track of how many points were earned by a given player for the hand. You reset this variable after each hand. Add the following line to your variable declarations in `GameView`:

```
private int scoreThisHand = 0;
```

To handle the scoring value for each card, you update the Card object. Open the `Card` class and add the following variable declaration along with the others:

```
private int scoreValue = 0;
```

Now modify the constructor of Card to match Listing 7-1, and add the new getScoreValue() method.

Listing 7-1:   Tracking the Score Values of Cards

```
public Card(int newId) {
    id = newId;
    suit = Math.round((id/100) * 100);
    rank = id - suit;
    if (rank == 8)                                          →5
       scoreValue = 50;
    } else if (rank == 14) {
       scoreValue = 1;
    } else if (rank > 9 && rank < 14) {
       scoreValue = 10;
    } else {
       scoreValue = rank;
    }
}

public int getScoreValue() {                                →16
    return scoreValue;
}
```

Here's a brief explanation of what the various lines do:

→**5–10**   These lines check the rank of the card and assign a score value to your variable when the card is created. In Crazy Eights, eights that remain in a player's hand at the end of the game are worth 50 points to the opponent. Face cards are worth 10 points; aces, 1 point; and all other cards, their face values. There are other scoring conventions, so feel free to use your own, though you'll stick with this standard one for now.

→**16**   You then need a method to get the score value when you tally the scores.

Next, you add the new method `updateScores()` to your `GameView` with the contents of Listing 7-2.

Listing 7-2:   The New `updateScores()` Method

```
private void updateScores() {
   for (int i = 0; i < myHand.size(); i++) {
      oppScore += myHand.get(i).getScoreValue();
      scoreThisHand += myHand.get(i).getScoreValue();
   }
   for (int i = 0; i < oppHand.size(); i++) {
      myScore += oppHand.get(i).getScoreValue();
      scoreThisHand += oppHand.get(i).getScoreValue();
   }
}
```

This listing loops through the hand that still has cards:

✔ One hand is empty, so only one of these loops even does anything. If your hand is empty, you increment the score with the value of each card in your opponent's hand.

✔ You also increment the `scoreThisHand` variable, which you use to inform the player of how many points were earned from this hand.

✔ Likewise, when your opponent's hand is empty, they get the point value of each card in your hand.

Now that the scores are updated, you display a new dialog to indicate that the hand has ended. It needs

✔ Text to tell the player who ran out of cards and how many points were awarded

✔ A button to dismiss the dialog and advance to the next hand

If you're making a new dialog with different UI elements, you need a new layout. Follow these steps:

1. **Right-click the res/layout folder and select New⇨File.**

2. **Name the file** end_hand_dialog.xml **and click OK.**

3. **Modify the contents to match Listing 7-3.**

Listing 7-3:   The `end_hand_dialog.xml` File

```xml
<?xml version="1.0" encoding="utf-8"?>
<LinearLayout
android:id="@+id/endHandLayout"
android:layout_width="275dp"
android:layout_height="wrap_content"
android:orientation="vertical"
android:layout_gravity="top"
xmlns:android="http://schemas.android.com/apk/res/android"
>
<TextView
android:id="@+id/endHandText"
android:layout_width="wrap_content"
android:layout_height="wrap_content"
android:text=""
android:textSize="16sp"
android:layout_marginLeft="5dp"
android:textColor="#FFFFFF"
>
</TextView>
<Button
android:id="@+id/nextHandButton"
android:layout_width="125dp"
android:layout_height="wrap_content"
android:text="Next Hand"
>
</Button>
</LinearLayout>
```

This listing is an even simpler version of the Choose Suit dialog layout. Again, you're using a `LinearLayout` to align the elements vertically within the dialog, and you have only two elements:

✔ `TextView`

You leave the default text for the `TextView` empty for now because you'll modify it by informing the player who ran out of cards on a given hand and how many points they earned from their opponent's remaining cards.

✔ `Button`.

The button has the default text `Next Hand`.

Now you add the method that gets called when a given hand is finished. Add the method shown in Listing 7-4 to your `GameView`.

Listing 7-4:   The `endHand()` Method

```
private void endHand() {
   final Dialog endHandDialog = new Dialog(myContext);
   endHandDialog.requestWindowFeature
            (Window.FEATURE_NO_TITLE);
   endHandDialog.setContentView(R.layout.end_hand_dialog);
   updateScores();                                              →5
   TextView endHandText = (TextView)                            →6
           endHandDialog.findViewById(R.id.endHandText);
   if (myHand.isEmpty()) {
      endHandText.setText("You went out and got " +
         scoreThisHand + " points!");
   } else if (oppHand.isEmpty()) {
      endHandText.setText("The computer went out and got "
           + scoreThisHand + " points.");
   }
   Button nextHandButton = (Button)                             →15
         endHandDialog.findViewById(R.id.nextHandButton);
   if (oppScore >= 300 || myScore >= 300) {
      nextHandButton.setText("New Game");
   }
   nextHandButton.setOnClickListener
           (new View.OnClickListener(){
      public void onClick(View view){
          initNewHand();
          endHandDialog.dismiss();
      }
   });
   endHandDialog.show();
}
```

This listing is similar to the method that displays the Choose Suits dialog. It follows this process of events:

1. You create a new dialog, ensure that it doesn't display a title, and then set the content to the new layout file.

2. You then call the `updateScores()` method in line 5 to display the scoring information in the dialog. Line 6 creates a reference to the `TextView`, and then the next few lines set the text, depending on who ran out of cards and how many points were earned.

3. Reference the button (starting with line 25), and set the onClickLis-
tener() and its associated logic. You call a new method, initNe-
wHand(), which you haven't written yet, and then dismiss the dialog.

You'll also need the import:

```
import android.widget.TextView;
```

Now put in the initNewHand() method. Add the code in Listing 7-5 to your
GameView.

Listing 7-5:   The initNewHand() Method

```
private void initNewHand() {
    scoreThisHand = 0;                                          →2
    if (myHand.isEmpty()) {                                     →3
        myTurn = true;
    } else if (oppHand.isEmpty()) {
        myTurn = false;
    }
    deck.addAll(discardPile);                                   →8
    deck.addAll(myHand);
    deck.addAll(oppHand);
    discardPile.clear();
    myHand.clear();
    oppHand.clear();
    dealCards();                                                →14
    drawCard(discardPile);
    validSuit = discardPile.get(0).getSuit();
    validRank = discardPile.get(0).getRank();
    if (!myTurn) {                                              →18
        makeComputerPlay();
    }
}
```

Here's a brief explanation of the lines in the listing:

→2   Reset the points earned for the hand.

→3–7   Determine who will play first in the next hand. The player who
        goes out gets to play first in the next hand, so you check to see
        whose hand is empty and set the myTurn variable accordingly.

→**8–13** These lines add the discard pile and both players' hands back to the deck, and then clear the lists for the hands and the discard pile. You're essentially putting all cards back into the deck.

→**14–17** Deal the cards and add the top card to the discard pile, setting the valid suit and rank based on that card.

→**18–20** Finally, if it isn't the human player's turn, you instruct the computer to play. Otherwise, the game simply waits for play input from the player.

Now that you have all the associated logic to handle the end of a hand, you need to call it when either player runs out of cards. Check in the two places where the human and computer make their play — for the human, in the `ACTION_UP` case of `onTouchEvent()`.

Modify the relevant code in `ACTION_UP` that handles dropping a card onto the discard pile to match the code in Listing 7-6.

Listing 7-6:   Checking for End-of-Hand on the Human's Turn

```
case MotionEvent.ACTION_UP:
   if (movingCardIdx > -1 &&
       X > (screenW/2)-(100*scale) &&
       X < (screenW/2)+(100*scale) &&
       Y > (screenH/2)-(100*scale) &&
       Y < (screenH/2)+(100*scale) &&
       (myHand.get(movingCardIdx).getRank() == 8 ||
           myHand.get(movingCardIdx).getRank() ==
               validRank ||
           myHand.get(movingCardIdx).getSuit() ==
               validSuit)) {
       validRank = myHand.get(movingCardIdx).getRank();
       validSuit = myHand.get(movingCardIdx).getSuit();
       discardPile.add(0, myHand.get(movingCardIdx));
       myHand.remove(movingCardIdx);
       if (myHand.isEmpty()) {                        →14
           endHand();
       } else {
          if (validRank == 8) {
              showChooseSuitDialog();
```

(continued)

Listing 7-6 *(continued)*

```
        } else {
            myTurn = false;
            makeComputerPlay();
        }
    }
}
```

Starting with line 14, you simply add a check to see whether the player's hand is empty:

- ✔ If the player's hand is empty, you call the endHand() method.

- ✔ Otherwise, you continue the game by either calling the Choose Suits dialog or passing the turn to the computer.

What about the computer player? Find your makeComputerPlay() method in GameView and modify it to match Listing 7-7.

Listing 7-7: Checking for End-of-Hand on the Computer's Turn

```
private void makeComputerPlay() {
    int tempPlay = 0;
    while (tempPlay == 0) {
        tempPlay = computerPlayer.makePlay(oppHand,
            validSuit, validRank);
        if (tempPlay == 0) {
            drawCard(oppHand);
        }
    }
    if (tempPlay == 108 || tempPlay == 208 || tempPlay ==
            308 || tempPlay == 408) {
        validRank = 8;
        validSuit = computerPlayer.chooseSuit(oppHand);
        String suitText = "";
        if (validSuit == 100) {
            suitText = "Diamonds";
        } else if (validSuit == 200) {
            suitText = "Clubs";
        } else if (validSuit == 300) {
            suitText = "Hearts";
        } else if (validSuit == 400) {
            suitText = "Spades";
        }
```

```
      Toast.makeText(myContext, "Computer chose " +
          suitText, Toast.LENGTH_SHORT).show();
   } else {
      validSuit = Math.round((tempPlay/100) * 100);
      validRank = tempPlay - validSuit;
   }
   for (int i = 0; i < oppHand.size(); i++) {
      Card tempCard = oppHand.get(i);
      if (tempPlay == tempCard.getId()) {
         discardPile.add(0, oppHand.get(i));
         oppHand.remove(i);
      }
   }
   if (oppHand.isEmpty()) {                              →35
      endHand();
   }
   myTurn = true;
}
```

You've added a check from line 35 after playing a card, to see whether the opponent's hand is empty. If so, you call the `endHand()` method. You should be able to launch the game and play out a real-life hand of Crazy Eights!

If you go out first, you should see a dialog similar to the one in Figure 7-1.

In this case, the human player ran out of cards first and earned 46 points from the opponent's hand. Note also that the scores displayed at the top and bottom of the screen have been updated. At this point, you can play endless rounds of Crazy Eights, with the scores updating after every hand. But there's no way for the game to end. Typically, a game ends when one player's score reaches a predetermined goal. In this case, you use 300 points.

Ending a game

If you end the game when one player reaches or exceeds 300 points, you don't need to do much other than modify the `endHand()` method. Points are accumulated only at the conclusion of a hand, so you simply need to add some additional logic to detect end-of-game conditions and display different information in your existing End Hand dialog.

Figure 7-1:
Displaying
the end-of-
hand dialog.

Modify your `endHand()` method to match Listing 7-8.

Listing 7-8: **Handling the End of the Game**

```
private void endHand() {
    final Dialog endHandDialog = new Dialog(myContext);
    endHandDialog.requestWindowFeature
            (Window.FEATURE_NO_TITLE);
    endHandDialog.setContentView(R.layout.end_hand_dialog);
    updateScores();
    TextView endHandText = (TextView)
        endHandDialog.findViewById(R.id.endHandText);
    if (myHand.isEmpty()) {
        if (myScore >= 300) {                                    →9
            endHandText.setText("You reached " + myScore +
                " points. You won! Would you like to play again?");
        } else {
            endHandText.setText("You went out and got " +
                    scoreThisHand + " points!");
        }
    } else if (oppHand.isEmpty()) {
        if (oppScore >= 300) {
            endHandText.setText("The computer reached " +
                oppScore + " points. Sorry, you lost. Would you
                like to play again?");
        } else {
            endHandText.setText("The computer went out and
                got " + scoreThisHand + " points.");
        }
    }
    Button nextHandButton = (Button)
        endHandDialog.findViewById(R.id.nextHandButton);
    if (oppScore >= 300 || myScore >= 300) {                     →27
        nextHandButton.setText("New Game");
    }
    nextHandButton.setOnClickListener
            (new View.OnClickListener()
            {public void onClick(View view){
            if (oppScore >= 300 || myScore >= 300) {             →32
                myScore = 0;
                oppScore = 0;
            }
            initNewHand();
            endHandDialog.dismiss();
        }
    });
    endHandDialog.show();
}
```

Here's a brief explanation of various lines in the listing:

→**9–24** You've added conditionals to check whether either score equals or exceeds 300. If so, you display a different message, indicating that the game is over and who won, and asking whether the player wants to play another game.

→**27** Detect whether either score exceeds 300, and if so, set the text on the button to New Game instead of the default Next Hand.

→**32–35** The only other modification is zeroing out both players' scores if the game is over before initializing a new hand.

Wrapping Up the Game

After you have all the necessary logic for playing not just one game but also starting new games, all the essential nuts and bolts are in place. However, the computer player is still not a capable opponent.

You'll make improvements to make the game more competitive before updating the launcher icon and wrapping everything up.

Coding the opponent AI

You aren't doing anything particularly sophisticated to the AI. Crazy Eights is a simple game, and its strategy, accordingly, isn't complicated. Some games warrant different levels of strength for computer players, but that's not necessary here. You simply want the computer player to provide a decent challenge.

There's no need to make the game play optimally, because it's a relatively simple game. Your players may not appreciate a computer that plays better than they do!

When I first released my Dominoes game, I coded a fairly simple AI. All it does is look for the highest possible point gain on its turn. If it can't score on its turn, it plays a random legal move. I thought that this difficulty level was reasonable for an AI because it doesn't play defensively or consider the remaining point totals if the human player runs out of cards first. But I still received complaints that the game was too difficult to play against. One user wrote that he had played it dozens of times and simply couldn't beat it. He might simply have been unlucky, but the moral of the story is that you need to find a reasonable balance for your computer opponents, and not worry about how well they're playing. You'll likely get complaints that your computer players are both too good and not good enough.

In the case of the Crazy Eights player, you make only two significant changes to improve it, which should make it suitable for average play. Both have to do with playing an 8:

✔ Ensure that the computer plays an 8 only when it has no other legal play.

✔ Be smart about which suit the computer chooses when it plays an 8.

Open your `ComputerPlayer` class and modify the `makePlay()` method to match Listing 7-9.

Listing 7-9:   Updated `makePlay()` Method for the Computer Player

```
public int makePlay(List<Card> hand, int suit, int rank) {
    int play = 0;
    for (int i = 0; i < hand.size(); i++) {                    →3
        int tempId = hand.get(i).getId();
        int tempRank = hand.get(i).getRank();
        int tempSuit = hand.get(i).getSuit();
        if (tempRank != 8) {
            if (rank == 8) {
                if (suit == tempSuit) {
                    play = tempId;
                }
            } else if (suit == tempSuit || rank == tempRank)
            {
                play = tempId;
            }
        }
    }
    if (play == 0) {                                           →17
        for (int i = 0; i < hand.size(); i++) {
            int tempId = hand.get(i).getId();
            if (tempId == 108 || tempId == 208 || tempId ==
                308 || tempId == 408) {
                play = tempId;
            }
        }
    }
    return play;
}
```

In the previous version of this method, you loop through the computer player's hand, and if a given card is a legal play, set it as the play to make and then return it. Here, you separate out the logic for playing an 8 and a non-8:

✔ Lines 3–16 loop through the computer's hand the first time, determining whether each card that isn't an 8 is a legal move.

If a legal non-8 move is found, it's set to the current play.

✔ Lines 17–25 are executed only if a non-8 legal play is found. If not, this loop looks for an 8 in the computer player's hand, and if one is found, it's set to the current play.

✔ If no legal play is found, 0 is returned, indicating that the computer must draw a card.

This change means that the computer player is holding its 8 cards longer and playing them only when necessary, which is generally a smart way to play.

Next, you modify the `chooseSuit()` method, as shown in Listing 7-10.

Listing 7-10: Updated `chooseSuits()` Method for the Computer Opponent

```
public int chooseSuit(List<Card> hand) {
    int suit = 100;
    int numDiamonds = 0;                                    →3
    int numClubs = 0;
    int numHearts = 0;
    int numSpades = 0;
    for (int i = 0; i < hand.size(); i++) {                 →7
        int tempRank = hand.get(i).getRank();
        int tempSuit = hand.get(i).getSuit();
        if (tempRank != 8) {
            if (tempSuit == 100) {
                numDiamonds++;
            } else if (tempSuit == 200) {
                numClubs++;
            } else if (tempSuit == 300) {
                numHearts++;
            } else if (tempSuit == 400) {
                numSpades++;
            }
        }
    }
    if (numClubs > numDiamonds &&                           →22
```

```
        numClubs > numHearts &&
        numClubs > numSpades) {
      suit = 200;
   } else if (numHearts > numDiamonds && numHearts >
          numClubs && numHearts > numSpades) {
      suit = 300;
   } else if (numSpades > numDiamonds && numSpades >
          numClubs && numSpades > numHearts) {
      suit = 400;
   }
   return suit;
}
```

When the computer player plays an 8 and chooses a suit, it should choose the suit that is most prevalent in its hand. Before, it always picked diamonds (which isn't an effective strategy).

Follow the steps below to improve the suit choice when the computer player plays an 8:

1. Add four variables to track the number of each suit (lines 3–6).

2. In Lines 7–21, loop through the computer player's hand and count the number of each suit.

3. From line 22 on, check to see which suit count is greater than all the others.

   • If it's greater, set it to the suit to be returned.

   • Otherwise, the default of diamonds is returned.

Give it a shot. You should find that this version of the computer player is a reasonably good challenge.

You could continue to make improvements, but as I mention earlier in this chapter, be careful — the more casual the game, the less likely your players will want to face a difficult challenge. If you're designing a chess app, use strong AI and give a number of different skill levels to your computer opponents. But with Crazy Eights, a modestly good computer player works well.

Making your own launcher icon

After the game is finished, you still haven't updated the launcher icon from the default. Designing good-looking icons is harder than you might think.

Your launcher icon should be simple, visually appealing, and instantly recognizable. If you have money in the budget, consider hiring a graphic designer to make your icon.

The icon should look good at different sizes because you'll provide a resized icon for the four current screen densities. Figure 7-2 shows the Crazy Eights icon at each of the four generalized screen densities.

Figure 7-2:
The Crazy
Eights icon
for each
screen
density.

From left to right, the icons are for

✔ xhdpi (96 x 96)

✔ hdpi (72 x 72)

✔ mdpi (48 x 48)

✔ ldpi (36 x 36)

The icon graphic has to be located in the proper `res/drawable` folder, and each file must have the same name. The default launcher is named `ic_launcher`, so I typically replace that graphic with my own and name it the same as the old default graphic. For example, you should have an icon graphic named `ic_launcher` sized at 96 x 96 pixels in your `res/drawable-xhdpi` folder, one named `ic_launcher` sized 72 x 72 pixels in your `res/drawable-hdpi` folder, and so on for all four icons.

If you decide to name your icon graphic differently, update your manifest. If you open it, you see in the application tag the `android:icon` attribute, which points to the appropriate image file for a particular screen density.

After you've updated the icon, launch the game and return to the app directory to see the updated icon.

Whew — now your game is finished! The preceding few chapters give you the basic functionality to make a simple, turn-based game. You can use it as a basis for more complex games of the same type, including multiplayer turn-based games. However, you may be more interested in more graphics-intensive, real-time games, such as side-scrollers or action and arcade games.

In the following chapters, I walk you through the steps to implement the popular carnival game Whack-a-Mole, which provides a strong basis for developing games of this type.

Part IV

Moving On to Your Second Game: Whack-a-Mole

The 5th Wave   By Rich Tennant

"So, what's this breakthrough in virtualization you wanted to show me?"

In this part . . .

Part IV walks you through the development of your second full game, a virtual version of the arcade action game Whack-a-Mole. You cover concepts similar to those of the first game, but use the more efficient (and more complex) `SurfaceView`. You also get a look at how to load and play sounds in your game, as well as how to save and load data. By the end of Part IV you have a second complete, playable game — and the experience of building it.

Chapter 8

Creating a Complex Title Screen

• •

In This Chapter

▶ Starting Whack-a-Mole

▶ Implementing a title screen with `SurfaceView`

▶ Adding options menus to your games

▶ Enabling and disabling sound

• •

*T*his chapter sets you on your way toward making an arcade-style game with animations and sounds: a mobile-game version of the classic carnival game Whack-a-Mole. In case you've never heard of the game or played it yourself, it typically has a play area littered with a series of holes. When the game starts, a pesky mole pops up from one or more of the holes. The player's task is to whack the mole on the head as fast as possible, using a hand or a striking object, such as a mallet. The game ends after a set time limit expires or when the player doesn't whack the moles fast enough.

In your digital version, the play screen displays a field of seven holes, with moles popping up at random locations. You start slowly and then increase the rate at which the moles appear. Figure 8-1 shows a mock-up of the play screen.

When a mole pops up from a hole, the player's score is rendered in the lower left corner; the game timer, in the lower right corner. Like Crazy Eights, this game is simple, but implementing it introduces you to some vital programming concepts. Unlike Crazy Eights, this game has animation, so it needs a more efficient drawing process. If you were to implement this game using the approach presented in the first half of this book, the game's performance would be quite choppy.

Figure 8-1:
Mock-up
of the play
screen in
Whack-a-
Mole.

You also implement important sound and menu options in this game. Between the two games, you should be able to glean enough information to jump-start your own game.

You can download sample files for this chapter at

```
www.dummies.com/go/androidgameprogramming
```

Using SurfaceView

The official Android documentation for 2-D graphics is at the Android Developers' site:

```
http://developer.android.com/guide/topics/graphics/
            2d-graphics.html
```

The "Canvas and Drawables" overview page notes that if your app or game doesn't require a high frame rate (a chess game is used as an example), the recommended practice is to extend the `View` class and call draws on the `Canvas` via the `onDraw()` method — which is exactly what you do with the Crazy Eights game. A card game isn't particularly graphics-intensive, and you don't implement animation (though you certainly could, to give it polish).

You might be perfectly content to implement your game using only `View`. If you're making a board game, card game, or even a word game, the programming approach you take to Crazy Eights in this book will probably work just fine. However, if you want to make a side-scroller (such as Super Mario Bros.) or a shoot-'em-up (like Asteroids), or even a pinball game, the standard View isn't likely to work well for you.

One common problem with using `View` in fast-paced games is that it handles user interaction in the same thread it uses for drawing graphics. Therefore, if a player touches the screen (for example, to whack a mole on the head), the interaction is handled in the same thread that's drawing. Suppose that you want to draw an *Ouch!* word balloon over the mole's head and animate him withdrawing into his hole after he gets whacked. With `View`, all that logic is queued up in the same thread. The result is either a delayed effect in the intended action or "laggy" rendering of the animation — or both. Overall, the experience is likely to be choppy and unappealing (and *not* fun).

However, the `SurfaceView` subclass of `View` handles drawing to canvas in a separate thread, so user interaction (such as touching the screen) happens in one thread and drawing happens in another. This arrangement makes the process more efficient and leads to a smoother game experience.

Using `SurfaceView` is quite a bit more complicated than `View`, but it's vital if you want to make games that provide a satisfying user experience. Don't worry: I'll walk you through it.

Before you start working with `SurfaceView`, create a new project and all its relevant infrastructure for your new game.

To create a new Android project for your Whack-a-Mole game, follow these steps:

1. **Select File⇨New⇨Android Project.**

   The New Android Project Window appears.

2. **In the Project Name field, type** WhackAMole **and then click Next.**

3. **Select Android 4.0 as the target name and then click Next.**

4. **In the Package Name field, type this line, and then click Finish:**

```
com.agpfd.whackamole
```

First, modify the manifest. For Crazy Eights, the layout is in portrait mode. In this game, however, you fix the screen in landscape mode because you'll be laying out game elements more along the horizontal axis.

Open the `AndroidManifest.xml` file in your new WhackAMole project and modify it to look like Listing 8-1.

Listing 8-1: **Manifest File for Whack-A-Mole**

```
<?xml version="1.0" encoding="utf-8"?>
<manifest xmlns:android="http://schemas.android.com/apk/
        res/android"
    package="com.agpfd.whackamole"
    android:versionCode="1"
    android:versionName="1.0" >

    <uses-sdk android:minSdkVersion="7" />

    <application
        android:icon="@drawable/ic_launcher"
        android:label="@string/app_name" >
        <activity
            android:name=".WhackAMoleActivity"
            android:screenOrientation="landscape"        →14
            android:configChanges=
                "orientation|keyboardHidden"              →15
            android:label="@string/app_name" >
            <intent-filter>
                <action android:name=
        "android.intent.action.MAIN" />
                <category android:name=
        "android.intent.category.LAUNCHER" />
            </intent-filter>
        </activity>
    </application>
</manifest>
```

Listing 8-1 controls the screen orientation:

  ✔ Line 14 specifies landscape as the screen orientation.

  ✔ Line 15 prevents the screen from reorienting when the device is rotated or the physical keyboard opens or closes.

Next, you implement `WhackAMoleView`, the primary class for handling interactions and drawing to the screen. You have to handle these tasks differently from the way they work in Crazy Eights (which has two activities, each with its own view). Here, you take an alternative approach: You have only one activity and one view, so you need a variable to keep track of them.

To create the `WhackAMoleView`, follow these steps:

1. **Right-click the package in Eclipse.**

2. **Select New⇨Class.**

3. **Enter `WhackAMoleView` as the name.**

4. **Click Finish.**

The contents of this class should match Listing 8-2. It's long, so bear with me!

Listing 8-2:   WhackAMoleView Extending SurfaceView

```
package com.agpfd.whackamole;

import android.content.Context;
import android.graphics.Bitmap;
import android.graphics.BitmapFactory;
import android.graphics.Canvas;
import android.os.Handler;
import android.os.Message;
import android.util.AttributeSet;
import android.view.MotionEvent;
import android.view.SurfaceHolder;
import android.view.SurfaceView;

public class WhackAMoleView extends SurfaceView implements
         SurfaceHolder.Callback {

    private Context myContext;                                →16
    private SurfaceHolder mySurfaceHolder;
    private Bitmap backgroundImg;
    private int screenW = 1;
    private int screenH = 1;
    private boolean running = false;
    private boolean onTitle = true;
    private WhackAMoleThread thread;

      public WhackAMoleView(Context context,                 →25
             AttributeSet attrs) {
        super(context, attrs);

        SurfaceHolder holder = getHolder();
        holder.addCallback(this);

        thread = new WhackAMoleThread(holder, context,
          new Handler() {
          @Override
```

(continued)

Listing 8-2 *(continued)*

```java
        public void handleMessage(Message m) {

        }
    });

    setFocusable(true);
}

public WhackAMoleThread getThread() {                    →40
        return thread;
}

class WhackAMoleThread extends Thread {                  →44

    public WhackAMoleThread(SurfaceHolder
        surfaceHolder, Context context,
            Handler handler) {
        mySurfaceHolder = surfaceHolder;
        myContext = context;
        backgroundImg =
            BitmapFactory.decodeResource
            (context.getResources(),R.drawable.title);
    }

    @Override
    public void run() {
        while (running) {
            Canvas c = null;
            try {
                c = mySurfaceHolder.lockCanvas(null);
                synchronized (mySurfaceHolder) {
                    draw(c);
                }
            } finally {
                if (c != null) {
                    mySurfaceHolderunlockCanvasAndPost(c);
                }
            }
        }
    }

    private void draw(Canvas canvas) {
            try {
            canvas.drawBitmap(backgroundImg, 0, 0,
                null);
            } catch (Exception e) {
            }
```

```
        }

        boolean doTouchEvent(MotionEvent event) {          →78
            synchronized (mySurfaceHolder) {
             int eventaction = event.getAction();
             int X = (int)event.getX();
             int Y = (int)event.getY();

             switch (eventaction ) {

             case MotionEvent.ACTION_DOWN:
                break;

              case MotionEvent.ACTION_MOVE:
                break;

             case MotionEvent.ACTION_UP:
                if (onTitle) {
                    backgroundImg =
                    BitmapFactory.decodeResource
                    (myContext.getResources(),
                    R.drawable.background);
                    backgroundImg =
                    Bitmap.createScaledBitmap(backgroundImg,
                    screenW, screenH, true);
                    onTitle = false;
                }
                break;
             }
          }
            return true;
        }

        public void setSurfaceSize(int width,            →104
            int height) {
            synchronized (mySurfaceHolder) {
                screenW = width;
                screenH = height;
                backgroundImg = Bitmap.createScaledBitmap(
                        backgroundImg, width, height,
                        true);
            }
        }

        public void setRunning(boolean b) {
            running = b;
        }
    }

    @Override
    public boolean onTouchEvent(MotionEvent event) {
```

(continued)

Listing 8-2 *(continued)*

```
            return thread.doTouchEvent(event);
    }

    @Override
    public void surfaceChanged(SurfaceHolder holder, int
        format, int width, int height) {
            thread.setSurfaceSize(width, height);
    }

    @Override
    public void surfaceCreated(SurfaceHolder holder) {
        thread.setRunning(true);
        if (thread.getState() == Thread.State.NEW) {
            thread.start();
        }
    }

    @Override
    public void surfaceDestroyed(SurfaceHolder holder) {
        thread.setRunning(false);
    }
}
```

Here's a brief explanation of various lines in this listing:

→**16-23** Declare all variables here. You need a local reference to the context for tasks such as loading images. You have a handle to the surface manager object, which lets you interact with important elements of the `SurfaceView`. You also have variables to hold the screen width and height, a boolean to track whether the thread that's drawing is running, a boolean to track whether you're on the title screen, and a reference to the thread that draws everything.

→**25** Your constructor gets the surface holder, assigns a callback, and creates an instance of the thread.

→**40** This method returns the thread in case you need to control it from the activity.

→**44** This line holds the main thread. In the constructor, you load the title screen image, which renders when the game starts up. The `run()` method calls `draw()`. The `draw()` method, which now draws only the background image, is surrounded by a try/catch statement, in case there are any issues creating or destroying the canvas.

→**78**   The `doTouchEvent()` method is the same as `onTouchEvent()` in Crazy Eights. Here, the only event you're handling is when the user lifts their finger from the screen (ACTION_UP). You're simply loading the game screen background, setting it as the default background, and then toggling the boolean to indicate that the player is no longer on the title screen.

→**104**   This line, which is invoked when the surface dimensions change, is initially used to get and set the width and height of the screen.

The remaining methods are used to handle changes in the state of the surface. The code may look daunting, but in the end, its effects are worth your time and trouble.

Whew! You've set up the view, which is one difficult task, and now you need to declare a layout to hold this view and implement the activity to run it.

To create the XML layout file that will hold your view, follow these steps:

1. **Right-click the `res>layout` directory in your project**

2. **Select New⇨File.**

3. **Name the file `whackamole_layout.xml`.**

4. **Click Finish.**

5. **Edit the contents of the file to match Listing 8-3.**

Listing 8-3:   Layout File for WhackAMoleView

```xml
<?xml version="1.0" encoding="utf-8"?>
<LinearLayout xmlns:android="http://schemas.android.com/
        apk/res/android"
    android:layout_width="fill_parent"
    android:layout_height="fill_parent"
    android:orientation="vertical" >

    <com.agpfd.whackamole.WhackAMoleView
        android:id="@+id/mole"
        android:layout_width="fill_parent"
        android:layout_height="fill_parent"/>

</LinearLayout>
```

This listing embeds your custom view in a `LinearLayout`. You reference this XML from your activity when you load your custom view.

Open your `WhackAMoleActivity` file and modify its contents to match Listing 8-4.

Listing 8-4: WhackAMole Activity Loading WhackAMoleView

```
package com.agpfd.whackamole;

import android.app.Activity;
import android.os.Bundle;
import android.view.Window;
import android.view.WindowManager;

public class WhackAMoleActivity extends Activity {

    private WhackAMoleView myWhackAMoleView;

    /** Called when the activity is first created. */
    @Override
    public void onCreate(Bundle savedInstanceState) {
        super.onCreate(savedInstanceState);
        requestWindowFeature(Window.FEATURE_NO_TITLE);  →16
        getWindow().setFlags
            (WindowManager.LayoutParams.FLAG_FULLSCREEN,
            WindowManager.LayoutParams.FLAG_FULLSCREEN);
        setContentView(R.layout.whackamole_layout);     →19
        myWhackAMoleView = (WhackAMoleView)
            findViewById(R.id.mole);                     →20
        myWhackAMoleView.setKeepScreenOn(true);         →21
    }
}
```

Here's a brief explanation of various lines in this listing:

→**16-17** You remove the title bar from the window to maximize screen space and make the app appear in full-screen mode.

→**19**   Set the content view to the XML layout file you just defined.

→**20**   This line gets a handle to the view defined in your XML layout file.

→**21**   You're disabling the screen time-out while the game is being played.

At this point, you're ready to run the game for the first time. It simply displays the title screen and, when you touch the screen, toggles to the empty game screen. Figure 8-2 shows the title screen in your game.

Make sure that all appropriate graphics files are in your `res>drawable` directory. Feel free to design your own graphics, or see the link in the section "Using SurfaceView," at the beginning of this chapter.

Figure 8-2:
Title screen
in Whack-a-
Mole.

If you run the game and then touch the screen, the initial game screen appears, showing only a field with seven holes, as shown in Figure 8-3.

Figure 8-3:
Empty game
screen in
Whack-a-
Mole.

You're on your way to producing a fast-paced arcade game! Because this game has sound, I show you how to add an options menu to let the user toggle the sound option.

Adding an Options Menu

You have a few choices in the design of the Options menu. You can make your own button and draw the Options button on one or more screens using the canvas.

After a player clicks the Options button, your own, custom Options menu appears. Figure 8-4 shows what it might look like.

Figure 8-4:
Mock-up of
the Options
button and
Options
menu.

The Options button is drawn in the upper left corner as a gear icon. Clicking the Options menu opens it with whatever options you want to provide. In this example, it has only a check box for toggling the sound on or off.

Another approach, if the menu shows sound as the only configurable option, is to display the speaker icon on the screen and allow the user to toggle the sound on and off without having to open a secondary menu. This concept might look like Figure 8-5.

When the sound is toggled on, the screen appears as shown earlier, in Figure 8-4. If the user clicks the speaker icon, you can then draw the same icon with a slash through it to indicate that the sound is turned off, and toggle it back on after every click.

Another approach, the preferred one in this example, is to use the default menu functionality of Android.

Figure 8-5:
Mock-up of the game screen with the Sound option visible directly onscreen.

Toggling the Sound Option

Older Android devices had a hardware Menu button that launched any menus defined by an app. Newer devices and versions of Android have generally done away with the hardware Menu button in favor of software menu buttons. You create your menu options in the WhackAMoleActivity. Open that file and add the two following variable declarations:

```
private static final int TOGGLE_SOUND = 1;
private boolean soundEnabled = true;
```

Then add the two methods shown in Listing 8-5.

Listing 8-5:   Defining an Option Menu in WhackAMoleActivity

```
public boolean onCreateOptionsMenu(Menu menu) {          →1
        MenuItem toggleSound = menu.add(0, TOGGLE_SOUND,
            0, "Toggle Sound");
        return true;
    }

public boolean onOptionsItemSelected(MenuItem item) {    →6
        switch (item.getItemId()) {
        case TOGGLE_SOUND:
                String soundEnabledText = "Sound On";      →9
```

(continued)

Listing 8-5 *(continued)*

```
                    if (soundEnabled) {
                        soundEnabled = false;
                        soundEnabledText = "Sound Off";
                    } else {
                        soundEnabled = true;
                    }
                    Toast.makeText(this, soundEnabledText,
                        Toast.LENGTH_SHORT).show();
                    break;
            }
        return false;
}
```

Here's a brief explanation of various lines in the listing:

→**2**   Override the `onCreateOptionsMenu()` method, and define a menu item for toggling the sound. To keep it simple, simply insert text in the button — later, you can add icons or other images and fully customize the menu options.

→**6**   The `onOptionsItemSelected()` method handles the selection of menu items. In this example, you have only one option, so you have only one case in your switch. If you had more options, you would add more cases.

→**9–16** When the user toggles the sound option, a toast is displayed that indicates a change; default to a string with the text `"Sound On"`. If the sound is enabled, you toggle off both the boolean and the text. Otherwise, you toggle both of them on. Then you display the toast.

You'll also need the following import statements:

```
import android.view.Menu;
import android.view.MenuItem;
import android.widget.Toast;
```

Don't do anything with the sound setting yet. When you add sounds, you'll have the infrastructure in place.

Figure 8-6 shows how the menu looks in Android 4.0.

The menu is designated by the three dots in the upper right corner (though the appearance of menus may vary depending on Android version or device). Clicking those dots makes the menu appear. In this case, a player has only one option. When the player clicks the option, a toast appears, indicating whether the sound is now on or off. Give it a try.

Figure 8-6:
The Sound
option menu
running in
Android 4.0.

Your nonfunctional game screen already appears when the title screen is clicked. Now you simply implement the logic for playing the game.

One other thing you need to do before you move on, though, is to update the launcher icons for your new game. Figure 8-7 shows the four screen density icons.

Figure 8-7:
Icons in
Whack-a-
Mole.

Here are the screen density sizes, from left to right:

- ✔ xhdpi: 96 x 96 pixels
- ✔ hdpi: 72 x 72 pixels
- ✔ mdpi: 48 x 48 pixels
- ✔ ldpi: 32 x 32 pixels

Each image needs to be in its corresponding folder in the res directory of your project. For example, the 72 x 72 icon needs to be in the res/drawable-hdpi folder. They all should have the same name, ic_launcher.png, and you should delete the default icon image used for starter Android projects. You can find the image files, along with all code referenced in this section, at the link in this chapter's introduction.

Chapter 9

Creating an Animated Play Screen

. . . .

In This Chapter

▶ Implementing simple animations

▶ Using sounds in your game

▶ Handling real-time interactivity

. . . .

*U*nderstanding how to layer images to create the visual effects you want in your game, animate elements on the screen, handle real-time inter-activity, and load and play sounds are all critical skills necessary to develop many types of games. This chapter will teach you the basic approach to all these skills and put you well on your way to developing your own game using these effects.

On to the meat of the Whack-a-Mole game!

Handling Images for the Play Screen

You actually want your players to be able to whack those onscreen moles. That's the point of the game. To do that, you need moles to pop out of holes. Figure 9-1 shows what your mole image looks like.

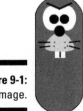

Figure 9-1:
Mole image.

Scary, isn't he? The basic approach you take is to have three layers of graphics: the background, the moles, and masks that the mole images sit behind. To make more sense of this, look at Figure 9-2.

Figure 9-2:
Play screen
with mole
and mask
for Hole
One.

I've made the mask transparent in this figure to give you an idea of how things are going to work:

1. The background image will be drawn first.

2. The moles will be drawn on top of the background images.

3. The masks will be drawn on top of the moles, obscuring them from view.

Figure 9-3 is the image you're using for the real mask, which has the same color and pattern as the grass in the background image.

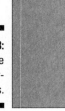

Figure 9-3:
Mask image
for obscur-
ing moles.

When you animate your moles, modifying their y-position, they're drawn on the canvas "between" the background and the mask — which makes them appear to rise up out of the holes and pop back into them.

Being a game programmer is a bit like being a stage magician. You are often creating pleasant optical illusions for your audience. You have to think about the visual effect that you want the player to experience, and then brainstorm about how you might bring that effect to life. In this case, I decided to use three layers of images to produce the desired visual effect of a mole popping out of a hole, but there's almost always many ways of accomplishing the same goal.

You've already got the background image rendered, so the next thing to draw is your moles. Because you're rescaling the background image and trying to place your masks and moles relative to the resized image, you need a number of variables to track the scaling for both resizing and placement.

In WhackAMoleView, add the following scaling variables, as well as new bitmaps for your mask and mole graphics.

```
private int backgroundOrigW;
private int backgroundOrigH;
private float scaleW;
private float scaleH;
private float drawScaleW;
private float drawScaleH;
private Bitmap mask;
private Bitmap mole;
```

You'll load your new graphics and set all your scaling variables in ACTION_UP, after the player touches the title screen for the first time.

Modify the ACTION_UP case of your doTouchEvent() method to match Listing 9-1.

Listing 9-1:   Modified ACTION_UP Loading Mole and Mask Graphics

```
case MotionEvent.ACTION_UP:
   if (onTitle) {
     backgroundImg =
          BitmapFactory.decodeResource
          (myContext.getResources(),
          R.drawable.background);
     backgroundImg =
          Bitmap.createScaledBitmap(backgroundImg,
          screenW, screenH, true);
     mask = BitmapFactory.decodeResource
          (myContext.getResources(),                    →7
```

(continued)

Listing 9-1 *(continued)*

```
                          R.drawable.mask);
        mole = BitmapFactory.decodeResource
            (myContext.getResources(), R.drawable.mole);  →9
        scaleW = (float) screenW/ (float)
            backgroundOrigW;                               →11
        scaleH = (float) screenH/ (float)
            backgroundOrigH;                               →12
        mask = Bitmap.createScaledBitmap(mask, (int)
            (mask.getWidth()*scaleW),
            (int)(mask.getHeight()*scaleH), true);         →13
        mole = Bitmap.createScaledBitmap(mole, (int)
            (mole.getWidth()*scaleW),
            (int)(mole.getHeight()*scaleH), true);
        onTitle = false;
        }
break;
```

Here is a brief explanation of what the various lines do:

→**7-10** Here you're just loading in the images for the mask and the mole.

→**11-12** These lines determine the scaling variables you'll use to resize images based on how much you scaled the background. You just divide the screen width/height of whatever device you're on by the original width/height of your background image.

→**13-16** The `createScaledBitmap()` method allows us to create new bitmaps for your mask and mole images by multiplying their original width and height by the image scaling factor.

Now that you've got the images loaded, how do you know where to draw them? Figure 9-4 shows the x and y values for the seven holes in your game background image.

But these coordinates are for your original image. You'll also need a set of scaling factors for where to draw images to the screen, based on how much you scaled the background. You also need variables for the x and y position of each of your seven moles.

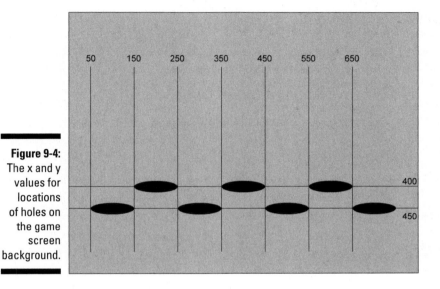

Figure 9-4:
The x and y values for locations of holes on the game screen background.

Add the following 16 variable declarations to the rest of your global variables in `WhackAMoleView`.

```
private int mole1x, mole2x, mole3x, mole4x, mole5x,
        mole6x, mole7x;
private int mole1y, mole2y, mole3y, mole4y, mole5y,
        mole6y, mole7y;
```

Now you modify the `setSurfaceSize()` method, since that's where you capture the screen width and height of the device the game is running on. Modify the `setSurfaceSize()` method of your `WhackAMoleView` to match Listing 9-2.

Listing 9-2:   Modified setSurfaceSize() Method Setting Mole Locations

```
public void setSurfaceSize(int width, int height) {
    synchronized (mySurfaceHolder) {
        screenW = width;
        screenH = height;
        backgroundImg =
            Bitmap.createScaledBitmap(backgroundImg, width,
            height, true);
        drawScaleW = (float) screenW / 800;              →7
        drawScaleH = (float) screenH / 600;
        mole1x = (int) (55*drawScaleW);                  →9
```

(continued)

Listing 9-2 *(continued)*

```
            mole2x = (int) (155*drawScaleW);
            mole3x = (int) (255*drawScaleW);
            mole4x = (int) (355*drawScaleW);
            mole5x = (int) (455*drawScaleW);
            mole6x = (int) (555*drawScaleW);
            mole7x = (int) (655*drawScaleW);
            mole1y = (int) (475*drawScaleH);
            mole2y = (int) (425*drawScaleH);
            mole3y = (int) (475*drawScaleH);
            mole4y = (int) (425*drawScaleH);
            mole5y = (int) (475*drawScaleH);
            mole6y = (int) (425*drawScaleH);
            mole7y = (int) (475*drawScaleH);
        }
    }
```

This is pretty straightforward:

→**7-8**   Setting the scaling factors for drawing images to the screen.

→ **9-22**   Setting the initial positions for each mole. They don't line up exactly with the coordinates for the holes, because you want the mole images slightly below the hole position and centered.

The values listed here, once scaled, should work fine for you.

Now you're ready to draw both your moles and your masks, as shown in Listing 9-3.

Listing 9-3:   Modified draw() Method for Drawing Moles and Masks

```
private void draw(Canvas canvas) {
    try {
        canvas.drawBitmap(backgroundImg, 0, 0, null);
        if (!onTitle) {
            canvas.drawBitmap(mole, mole1x, mole1y, null);
            canvas.drawBitmap(mole, mole2x, mole2y, null);
            canvas.drawBitmap(mole, mole3x, mole3y, null);
            canvas.drawBitmap(mole, mole4x, mole4y, null);
            canvas.drawBitmap(mole, mole5x, mole5y, null);
            canvas.drawBitmap(mole, mole6x, mole6y, null);
            canvas.drawBitmap(mole, mole7x, mole7y, null);
            canvas.drawBitmap(mask, (int) 50*drawScaleW,
                (int) 450*drawScaleH, null);
            canvas.drawBitmap(mask, (int)150*drawScaleW,
                (int) 400*drawScaleH, null);
            canvas.drawBitmap(mask, (int)250*drawScaleW,
                (int) 450*drawScaleH, null);
```

```
        canvas.drawBitmap(mask, (int)350*drawScaleW,
            (int) 400*drawScaleH, null);
        canvas.drawBitmap(mask, (int)450*drawScaleW,
            (int) 450*drawScaleH, null);
        canvas.drawBitmap(mask, (int)550*drawScaleW,
            (int) 400*drawScaleH, null);
        canvas.drawBitmap(mask, (int)650*drawScaleW,
            (int) 450*drawScaleH, null);
    }
} catch (Exception e) {
}
```

Remember that the order in which bitmaps are drawn in this method determines what will be drawn on top or bottom:

1. The background is your first layer, so it needs to be drawn first.

2. Your moles are drawn on top of the background image, using the variables you just initialized.

3. The masks are drawn last, and their coordinates are fixed, since they won't be moving.

If you run the game, as long as everything is done correctly, it won't look any different from before! But your new mole and mask images should be there.

If you want to check the proper positions of your moles, comment out the lines above that draw the masks and run the game again. You should see the moles in their proper starting positions, ready to pop up and get whacked. Just make sure you include the mask drawing lines back in before you move on.

You jump right into game play when the player touches the title screen. The next section will walk you through how to decide when and where the moles pop up, and how to make them come to life.

You can download sample files for this chapter at

```
http://www.dummies.com/go/androidgameprogramming
```

Making Simple Animations

Just as with most of your previous functionality, when you add something new, you need some new variables.

Add the following variable declarations to your `WhackAMoleView`.

```
private int activeMole = 0;
private boolean moleRising = true;
private boolean moleSinking = false;
private int moleRate = 5;
private boolean moleJustHit = false;
```

The preceding code keeps track of the movement of moles:

✔ The first variable will keep track of which mole is currently moving. You'll only have one mole moving at a time.

In an alternate version of the game, you could have multiple moles emerge from their holes at the same time, but quite a few older devices don't support *multi-touch* (the capability to capture touch inputs from more than one point on the screen), and you'd really want that capability if you were subjecting your players to multiple moles. So, for now, stick to having them deal with only one mole at a time. The `activeMole` variable tracks that.

✔ You've also got booleans indicating whether a mole is sinking or rising. You're not handling this with a single variable because sometimes you want all the moles to be neither sinking nor rising. The `moleRate` variable will handle the speed at which moles are moving. Here's where you make the game more difficult as it progresses, upping the speed of the moles after every ten successful whacks.

You'll want to experiment with the starting value of this variable:

• If it's too low, the game may seem boring at first.

• Too high, and it may get too difficult too quickly.

Play around with it and see what works for you.

✔ You're also adding the `moleJustHit` variable to track when a player successfully whacks a mole. When you get to user interactions, you'll begin to use it, but for now you'll add it in so that you have it ready to use later.

The first new method you'll add to handle the animation of the moles will be called whenever you need to pick a mole to move. You'll call it `pickActiveMole()`. Add this new method to the WhackAMoleThread in your `WhackAMoleView` and make sure it matches the contents of Listing 9-4.

Listing 9-4:   The pickActiveMole() Method

```
private void pickActiveMole() {
    activeMole = new Random().nextInt(7) + 1;
    moleRising = true;
    moleSinking = false;
}
```

When this method is called, you set the `activeMole` variable to a random integer between 1 and 7. You set moleRising to true and `moleSinking` to false. You'll update the `moleRate` variable here later when you start handling whether the user is successfully hitting or missing moles.

You'll also need the import:

```
import java.util.Random;
```

When do you want to call this new method?

- ✔ When the play screen is launched
- ✔ When a mole is successfully whacked
- ✔ When the player misses the mole and it makes it safely back to its initial position in the hole.

Let's deal with the first case, when the play screen is launched. Add a call to the `pickActiveMole()` method in the `ACTION_UP` case of `doTouch Event()`, just after the line where you toggle `onTitle` to `false` (refer to Listing 9-1 for reference).

```
onTitle = false;
pickActiveMole();
```

This gives us an active mole, but it's still not doing anything! To make those moles pop up, add a new method within the `WhackAMoleThread` in `WhackAMoleView` (just after the `setRunning()` method is fine). Call it `animateMoles()` and make the contents match Listing 9-5.

Listing 9-5:   The animateMoles() Method

```
private void animateMoles() {
if (activeMole == 1) {
    if (moleRising) {
        mole1y -= moleRate;
    } else if (moleSinking) {
        mole1y += moleRate;
    }
    if (mole1y >= (int) (475*drawScaleH) || moleJustHit) {
        mole1y = (int) (475*drawScaleH);
        pickActiveMole();
    }
    if (mole1y <= (int) (300*drawScaleH)) {
        mole1y = (int) (300*drawScaleH);
        moleRising = false;
        moleSinking = true;
    }
```

(continued)

Listing 9-5 *(continued)*

```
    }
if (activeMole == 2) {
    if (moleRising) {
        mole2y -= moleRate;
    } else if (moleSinking) {
        mole2y += moleRate;
    }
    if (mole2y >= (int) (425*drawScaleH) || moleJustHit) {
        mole2y = (int) (425*drawScaleH);
        pickActiveMole();
    }
    if (mole2y <= (int) (250*drawScaleH)) {
        mole2y = (int) (250*drawScaleH);
        moleRising = false;
        moleSinking = true;
    }
}
if (activeMole == 3) {
    if (moleRising) {
        mole3y -= moleRate;
    } else if (moleSinking) {
        mole3y += moleRate;
    }
    if (mole3y >= (int) (475*drawScaleH) || moleJustHit) {
        mole3y = (int) (475*drawScaleH);
        pickActiveMole();
    }
    if (mole3y <= (int) (300*drawScaleH)) {
        mole3y = (int) (300*drawScaleH);
        moleRising = false;
        moleSinking = true;
    }
}
if (activeMole == 4) {
    if (moleRising) {
        mole4y -= moleRate;
    } else if (moleSinking) {
        mole4y += moleRate;
    }
    if (mole4y >= (int) (425*drawScaleH) || moleJustHit) {
        mole4y = (int) (425*drawScaleH);
        pickActiveMole();
    }
    if (mole4y <= (int) (250*drawScaleH)) {
        mole4y = (int) (250*drawScaleH);
        moleRising = false;
        moleSinking = true;
    }
}
```

```
if (activeMole == 5) {
    if (moleRising) {
        mole5y -= moleRate;
    } else if (moleSinking) {
        mole5y += moleRate;
    }
    if (mole5y >= (int) (475*drawScaleH) || moleJustHit) {
        mole5y = (int) (475*drawScaleH);
        pickActiveMole();
    }
    if (mole5y <= (int) (300*drawScaleH)) {
        mole5y = (int) (300*drawScaleH);
        moleRising = false;
        moleSinking = true;
    }
}
if (activeMole == 6) {
    if (moleRising) {
        mole6y -= moleRate;
    } else if (moleSinking) {
        mole6y += moleRate;
    }
    if (mole6y >= (int) (425*drawScaleH) || moleJustHit) {
        mole6y = (int) (425*drawScaleH);
        pickActiveMole();
    }
    if (mole6y <= (int) (250*drawScaleH)) {
        mole6y = (int) (250*drawScaleH);
        moleRising = false;
        moleSinking = true;
    }
}
if (activeMole == 7) {
    if (moleRising) {
        mole7y -= moleRate;
    } else if (moleSinking) {
        mole7y += moleRate;
    }
    if (mole7y >= (int) (475*drawScaleH) || moleJustHit) {
        mole7y = (int) (475*drawScaleH);
        pickActiveMole();
    }
    if (mole7y <= (int) (300*drawScaleH)) {
        mole7y = (int) (300*drawScaleH);
        moleRising = false;
        moleSinking = true;
    }
}
}
```

This method is long, but it's got a lot of repetition, so it's not that difficult to follow. You've got a conditional for each active mole ID, and they're all doing the same thing:

1. If a mole is moving, it will either be rising (moving up) or sinking (moving down). You'll use two variables to track those states:

    - If `moleRising` is `true`, you decrement the y-position of that particular mole, which makes it move toward the top of the screen. Remember that y=0 is at the top of the screen.

    - If `moleSinking` is `true`, you increment the y-position of the mole, pushing it toward the bottom of the screen.

2. You check to see if the mole has either been hit or returned to its original y-position.

    In either of those cases you call `pickActiveMole()`.

3. The final conditional is to check if the mole has reached its highest position on the screen (that is, it has fully popped out of its hole).

    If so, you toggle the `moleRising` and `moleSinking` variables so that the mole will move toward the bottom of the screen.

You should be able to run the game now and see the moles popping up and returning to their holes, one at a time. Again, play with the mole rate to see what you think is a good starting speed. Next you specify how the game responds when the player touches the screen on a mole out of its hole.

Handling User Interaction

To handle when the player whacks a mole, you need to detect when their finger touches the screen in the region where an active mole is out of its hole. You also want a snazzy graphic to display to give the feeling of whacking a mole some real punch, something like Figure 9-5.

You also want a nice sound for the whack to give that satisfying feedback of hitting a mole on the head, but that's a topic for the next section.

Figure 9-5:
Image to
display
when the
user whacks
a mole.

For now, you need to load a new bitmap, and you also need a few more variables for detecting an active whack, as well as tracking how many moles the player has hit or missed. Add the following variable declarations to WhackAMoleView.

```
private Bitmap whack;
private boolean whacking = false;
private int molesWhacked = 0;
private int molesMissed = 0;
```

You'll load the whack image when the player transitions to the play screen after touching the title screen. Modify your ACTION_UP case of doTouch-Event() again so that it matches Listing 9-6.

Listing 9-6:   The animateMoles() Method

```
case MotionEvent.ACTION_UP:
    if (onTitle) {
        backgroundImg = BitmapFactory.decodeResource
            (myContext.getResources(),
            R.drawable.background);
        backgroundImg =
            Bitmap.createScaledBitmap(backgroundImg,
            screenW, screenH, true);
        mask = BitmapFactory.decodeResource
            (myContext.getResources(), R.drawable.mask);
        mole =
            BitmapFactory.decodeResource
            (myContext.getResources(), R.drawable.mole);
        whack = BitmapFactory.decodeResource
            (myContext.getResources(), R.drawable.whack);
        scaleW = (float) screenW/ (float) backgroundOrigW;
        scaleH = (float) screenH/ (float) backgroundOrigH;
        mask = Bitmap.createScaledBitmap(mask,
            (int)(mask.getWidth()*scaleW),
            (int)(mask.getHeight()*scaleH), true);
        mole = Bitmap.createScaledBitmap(mole,
            (int)(mole.getWidth()*scaleW),
            (int)(mole.getHeight()*scaleH), true);
        whack = Bitmap.createScaledBitmap(whack,
            (int)(whack.getWidth()*scaleW),
            (int)(whack.getHeight()*scaleH), true);
        onTitle = false;
        pickActiveMole();
    }
    whacking = false;
    break;
```

All the lines do here is load the `whack` bitmap and set the whacking variable to `false`. You do this because you only want the graphic to display when the player has a fingertip down on the screen. Whenever the finger lifts, you want the game to stop displaying the graphic.

Now you need the logic for detecting whether the player's finger is touching the region where an active mole is present. For that, you need two global variables to track where the user touched the screen. Add the following two variables to your `WhackAMoleView`.

```
private int fingerX, fingerY;
```

Add a new method called `detectMoleContact()` (just after `pickActive Mole()` is fine). Make sure the contents match Listing 9-7.

Listing 9-7:   The detectMoleContact() Method

```
private boolean detectMoleContact() {
    boolean contact = false;
    if (activeMole == 1 &&
            fingerX >= mole1x &&
            fingerX < mole1x+(int)(88*drawScaleW) &&
            fingerY > mole1y &&
            fingerY < (int) 450*drawScaleH) {
        contact = true;
        moleJustHit = true;
    }
    if (activeMole == 2 &&
            fingerX >= mole2x &&
            fingerX < mole2x+(int)(88*drawScaleW) &&
            fingerY > mole2y &&
            fingerY < (int) 400*drawScaleH) {
        contact = true;
        moleJustHit = true;
    }
    if (activeMole == 3 &&
            fingerX >= mole3x &&
            fingerX < mole3x+(int)(88*drawScaleW) &&
            fingerY > mole3y &&
            fingerY < (int) 450*drawScaleH) {
        contact = true;
        moleJustHit = true;
    }
    if (activeMole == 4 &&
            fingerX >= mole4x &&
            fingerX < mole4x+(int)(88*drawScaleW) &&
            fingerY > mole4y &&
            fingerY < (int) 400*drawScaleH) {
```

```
            contact = true;
            moleJustHit = true;
        }
        if (activeMole == 5 &&
                fingerX >= mole5x &&
                fingerX < mole5x+(int)(88*drawScaleW) &&
                fingerY > mole5y &&
                fingerY < (int) 450*drawScaleH) {
            contact = true;
            moleJustHit = true;
        }
        if (activeMole == 6 &&
                fingerX >= mole6x &&
                fingerX < mole6x+(int)(88*drawScaleW) &&
                fingerY > mole6y &&
                fingerY < (int) 400*drawScaleH) {
            contact = true;
            moleJustHit = true;
        }
        if (activeMole == 7 &&
                fingerX >= mole7x &&
                fingerX < mole7x+(int)(88*drawScaleW) &&
                fingerY > mole7y &&
                fingerY < (int) 450*drawScaleH) {
            contact = true;
            moleJustHit = true;
        }
        return contact;
}
```

This method returns a boolean indicating whether contact was found:

1. For each active mole ID, you check to see whether the coordinates of the finger position are both

    - Between the mole's x-position and its width

    - Between its current y-position and the bottom lip of its hole

2. If those conditions are met, you set contact and moleJustHit to true.

    Remember that the moleJustHit variable is used in your animate Moles() method to pick a new mole if one has just been whacked.

You call your new animateMoles() method from the run() method of your thread, so that it updates every time the canvas is redrawn. Modify the run() method to match Listing 9-8.

Listing 9-8:   Modified run() Method

```
@Override
public void run() {
    while (running) {
        Canvas c = null;
        try {
            c = mySurfaceHolder.lockCanvas(null);
            synchronized (mySurfaceHolder) {
                animateMoles();
                draw(c);
            }
        } finally {
            if (c != null) {
                mySurfaceHolder.unlockCanvasAndPost(c);
            }
        }
    }
}
```

Detection needs to take place when the player touches the screen, so you need to modify the ACTION_DOWN case of doTouchEvent(). Modify the case to match Listing 9-9.

Listing 9-9:   Modified ACTION_DOWN Case

```
case MotionEvent.ACTION_DOWN:
    fingerX = X;
    fingerY = Y;
    if (!onTitle && detectMoleContact()) {
        whacking = true;
        molesWhacked++;
    }
    break;
```

Here you capture the x and y positions of the finger. Then, if you are not on the title screen and your detectMoleContact() method returns true, you set whacking to true and increment the number of moles whacked.

You want to draw the whack image while whacking is true, so add the following few lines to your draw() method. Make sure they're last, because you want this graphic always drawn on top of everything else:

```
if (whacking) {
    canvas.drawBitmap(whack, fingerX -
    (whack.getWidth()/2),
    fingerY -(whack.getHeight()/2), null);
}
```

By drawing the graphic shifted half the width from the finger position's x and half the height from the finger position's y, you center it directly under the finger, giving the illusion of an explosion splaying out from underneath the player's finger. Give it a try!

The last thing to do before working with sounds is to display the number of whacks and misses. The game isn't tracking misses yet, so add that functionality to your `pickActiveMole()` method, as seen in Listing 9-10.

Listing 9-10: Modified pickActiveMole() Method

```
private void pickActiveMole() {
    if (!moleJustHit && activeMole > 0) {
        molesMissed++;
    }
    activeMole = new Random().nextInt(7) + 1;
    moleRising = true;
    moleSinking = false;
    moleJustHit = false;
    moleRate = 5 + (int)(molesWhacked/10);
}
```

You added a few lines at the beginning of this method to increment the `molesMissed` variable if you're picking a new mole and one wasn't just hit and an active mole has been selected.

Notice that I also added a line at the end to adjust the rate at which the moles move. Basically this logic increments the speed the moles move by 1 pixel for every 10 moles whacked. Again, depending on how quickly you want the difficulty of the game to ramp up, you can adjust this rate to whatever you think is the most fun.

Now that you're tracking the number of whacked and missed moles, draw that information to the screen. Remember that to draw text to the canvas you need a `Paint` object. Let's draw the text in black, so add the following variable declaration to your `WhackAMoleView`.

```
private Paint blackPaint;
```

Then instantiate it and initialize its parameters by added the following lines at the end of the `setSurfaceSize()` method.

```
blackPaint = new Paint();
blackPaint.setAntiAlias(true);
blackPaint.setColor(Color.BLACK);
blackPaint.setStyle(Paint.Style.STROKE);
blackPaint.setTextAlign(Paint.Align.LEFT);
blackPaint.setTextSize(drawScaleW*30);
```

You'll need the following imports as well:

```
import android.graphics.Paint;
import android.graphics.Color;
```

You're initializing your Paint parameters here so that you can get the scaling factor to adjust the text size when it's drawn to the screen. To draw the text, modify your draw() method to include the following two lines before the ones that draw the mole and mask images.

```
canvas.drawText("Whacked: " + Integer.toString(molesWhacked),
        10, blackPaint.getTextSize()+10, blackPaint);

canvas.drawText("Missed: " + Integer.toString(molesMissed),
        screenW-(int)(200*drawScaleW),
        blackPaint.getTextSize()+10, blackPaint);
```

These two lines draw the Whacked and Missed mole counts at the top of the screen. Now that you've got all the major game elements drawn, animated, and working the way you want, you'll add a couple of sounds to enhance the play experience before finishing up the game.

Loading and Playing Sounds

For sound resources, you have a number of options. You can purchase pre-made sound effects, hire a contractor to make them specifically for your game, or make your own. Obviously the last option is the cheapest, but it can also be fun.

For your first few games, I'd advise against spending a ton on art and music resources, and while making your own can seem less professional, it's certainly a safer investment.

The freeware audio editing program Audacity (audacity.sourceforge.net) is a great resource for producing and editing your own sound effects. I used them to generate the two effects you're using in your game. You've got one for a successful whack event and one for a miss.

Android supports a wide range of audio formats but you're using the Ogg Vorbis (.ogg) format. It has excellent compression quality and tends to have fewer technical issues in Android in my experience. For a comprehensive list, see

```
http://developer.android.com/guide/appendix/media-
            formats.html
```

Sound resources reside in the res/raw directory of your project. If this directory doesn't exist, create it:

1. **Right-click the res directory.**
2. **Select New⇨Folder**
3. **Name the new folder raw.**

You can either download the resources for the game via the link provided at the beginning of this chapter, or produce your own. Either way, you need to have two sound files named miss.ogg and whack.ogg in your res/raw directory before you begin modifying the code for sound effects.

There's an arcane art to making your own sound effects. I kept it pretty simple:

✔ The whack noise was made simply by snapping a piece of paper in front of a microphone (I held both ends of the paper, moved them together, then quickly snapped the sheet flat).

✔ The miss noise is simply a high-pitched "hee-hee" sound produced by voice.

Feel free to purchase or produce your own if you don't like mine.

You use the SoundPool object in Android to load and play your sounds, so you need to declare more variables at the beginning of your WhackAMoleView.

```
private static SoundPool sounds;
private static int whackSound;
private static int missSound;
public boolean soundOn = true;
```

You'll also need the import statement:

```
import android.media.SoundPool;
```

You'll instantiate the `SoundPool` and load your sounds from file in the `WhackAMoleThread` constructor. The final version of your `WhackAMoleThread` constructor should match Listing 9-11.

Listing 9-11: WhackAMoleThread Constructor Loading Sounds

```
public WhackAMoleThread(SurfaceHolder surfaceHolder,
        Context context, Handler handler) {
    mySurfaceHolder = surfaceHolder;
    myContext = context;
    backgroundImg = BitmapFactory.decodeResource
            (context.getResources(), R.drawable.title);
    backgroundOrigW = backgroundImg.getWidth();
    backgroundOrigH = backgroundImg.getHeight();
    sounds = new SoundPool(5,
            AudioManager.STREAM_MUSIC, 0);            →9
    whackSound = sounds.load(myContext, R.raw.whack, 1); →10
    missSound = sounds.load(myContext, R.raw.miss, 1);  →11
}
```

The SoundPool is instantiated on Line 9, and your two sound effects are loading into the pool via Lines 10 and 11. You want to play the whack sound whenever the player successfully touches a region with an active mole, the same place in the code where you draw the whack graphic, and that's in your `ACTION_DOWN` case of `doTouchEvent()`.

The final version of your `ACTION_DOWN` case should match Listing 9-12.

Listing 9-12: Playing the Whack Sound Effect

```
case MotionEvent.ACTION_DOWN:
    fingerX = X;
    fingerY = Y;
    if (!onTitle && detectMoleContact()) {
        whacking = true;
        if (soundOn) {
            AudioManager audioManager = (AudioManager)
                    myContext.getSystemService
                    (Context.AUDIO_SERVICE);
            float volume = (float)
                    audioManager.getStreamVolume
                    (AudioManager.STREAM_MUSIC);
            sounds.play(whackSound, volume, volume, 1, 0,
                    1);
        }
        molesWhacked++;
    }
    break;
```

You create an instance of `AudioManager` to get the volume for the music stream. There are volume levels for other streams, such as the device's ring tone, but you've set up your `SoundPool` to use the same stream as the one for music, which is the recommended practice for sound effects in games. You get the volume for that stream, then use it to play the sound.

The other sound effect should be played when the player misses a mole and it reaches the bottom of its hole. You can play the sound in your `pickActiveMole()` method, the same place you check that a mole made it to its minimum height. Modify your `pickActiveMole()` method to match Listing 9-13.

Listing 9-13: Playing the Miss Sound Effect

```
private void pickActiveMole() {
    if (!moleJustHit && activeMole > 0) {
        if (soundOn) {
        AudioManager audioManager = (AudioManager)
            myContext.getSystemService
            (Context.AUDIO_SERVICE);
            float volume = (float)
audioManager.getStreamVolume(AudioManager.STREAM_MUSIC);
        sounds.play(missSound, volume, volume, 1, 0, 1);
        }
        molesMissed++;
    }
    activeMole = new Random().nextInt(7) + 1;
    moleRising = true;
    moleSinking = false;
    moleJustHit = false;
    moleRate = 5 + (int)(molesWhacked/10);
}
```

You insert the same logic as you did for playing the whack sound, in the same location where you're incrementing the `molesMissed` variable. These additions result in the sound effects playing when you want them to, but there are a couple more things you need to do with regard to sounds.

The first is to enable your game to control the correct volume stream using the device hardware buttons. If you load up the game on a device, you'll probably notice that if you press the up or down hardware buttons that control volume, by default they adjust the ring volume and not the volume of the sound in your game. To remedy this, you need to tell your game to adjust the music stream volume with the hardware buttons. This is done with a single line of code in the `WhackAMoleActivity`. Modify the `onCreate()` method of `WhackAMoleActivity` to match Listing 9-14.

Listing 9-14:   Controlling Volume

```
@Override
public void onCreate(Bundle savedInstanceState) {
    super.onCreate(savedInstanceState);
    requestWindowFeature(Window.FEATURE_NO_TITLE);
    getWindow().setFlags
            (WindowManager.LayoutParams.FLAG_FULLSCREEN,
            WindowManager.LayoutParams.FLAG_FULLSCREEN);
    setContentView(R.layout.whackamole_layout);
    myWhackAMoleView = (WhackAMoleView)
            findViewById(R.id.mole);
    myWhackAMoleView.setKeepScreenOn(true);
    setVolumeControlStream(AudioManager.STREAM_MUSIC);
}
```

That last line of code sets the volume control for the hardware buttons to the music stream while your game is running. The last thing you need to handle with regard to sound is enabling and disabling it via your menu option. Modify the onOptionsItemSelected() method in WhackAMoleActivity to match Listing 9-15.

Listing 9-15:   Enabling and Disabling Sound

```
public boolean onOptionsItemSelected(MenuItem item) {
    switch (item.getItemId()) {
    case TOGGLE_SOUND:
        String soundEnabledText = "Sound On";
        if (soundEnabled) {
            soundEnabled = false;
            myWhackAMoleView.soundOn = false;            →7
            soundEnabledText = "Sound Off";
        } else {
            soundEnabled = true;
            myWhackAMoleView.soundOn = true;             →11
        }
        Toast.makeText(this, soundEnabledText,
                Toast.LENGTH_SHORT).show();
        break;
    }
    return false;
}
```

All you did was add Lines 7 and 11 to toggle the sound setting in your WhackAMoleView when the user changes the setting in the options menu.

Try it out and see how you like the sounds. Make sure you test toggling the sound from the options menu.

A quick word about music

You won't be adding music to this particular game (at least not in this example), but if you decide to go this route, you'll want to use MediaPlayer for your music files.

SoundPool is more appropriate for sound effects, but is not effective for long music files or those that need to loop for many iterations.

For reference on how to use MediaPlayer, see

```
http://developer.android.com/
    reference/android/media/
    MediaPlayer.html
```

Handling End of Game

The last thing you need to do to make the game playable is to handle the end of game state. Let's do that when the player misses their fifth mole.

Instead of using the pre-built dialog boxes as in Crazy Eights, here you draw your own custom dialog box onscreen when the game ends, and prompt the player to start a new one. Figure 9-6 shows what your custom dialog box will look like.

Figure 9-6: Custom Game Over dialog box.

You need a boolean variable to track when the end-game state is reached and a bitmap for your dialog box, so add the following declarations to your variables in `WhackAMoleView`.

```
private boolean gameOver = false;
private Bitmap gameOverDialog;
```

You'll detect the game over condition in the pickActiveMole() method, where you increment the number of missed moles. Modify your pick ActiveMole() method to match Listing 9-16.

Listing 9-16: Detecting the End of a Game

```
private void pickActiveMole() {
    if (!moleJustHit && activeMole > 0) {
        if (soundOn) {
            AudioManager audioManager = (AudioManager)
                myContext.getSystemService
                (Context. AUDIO_SERVICE);
            float volume = (float)
            audioManager.getStreamVolume
            (AudioManager.STREAM_MUSIC);
            sounds.play(missSound, volume, volume,
            1, 0, 1);
        }
        molesMissed++;
        if (molesMissed >= 5) {                          →11
            gameOver = true;
        }
    }
    activeMole = new Random().nextInt(7) + 1;
    moleRising = true;
    moleSinking = false;
    moleJustHit = false;
    moleRate = 5 + (int)(molesWhacked/10);
}
```

You added the check starting at Line 11 to see if the number of missed moles is equal to or greater than 5. If so, you toggle your gameOver variable. You only want to be updating the game state and animating moles if the game is still going, so let's modify the run() method of your thread to only animate the moles if gameOver is true.

Modify the run() method in WhackAMoleThread to match Listing 9-17.

Listing 9-17: Modified run() Method

```
@Override
public void run() {
    while (running) {
        Canvas c = null;
        try {
            c = mySurfaceHolder.lockCanvas(null);
            synchronized (mySurfaceHolder) {
                if (!gameOver) {                          →8
```

```
                    animateMoles();
                }
                draw(c);
            }
        } finally {
            if (c != null) {
                mySurfaceHolder.unlockCanvasAndPost(c);
            }
        }
    }
}
```

You just added a conditional on Line 8 to call `animateMoles()` only when `gameOver` is not `true`. Next you'll only check for mole whacks if `gameOver` is `false` when the user touches the screen.

Modify the `ACTION_DOWN` case of `doTouchEvent()` to match Listing 9-18.

Listing 9-18: Modified ACTION_DOWN for End of Game

```
case MotionEvent.ACTION_DOWN:
    if (!gameOver) {
        fingerX = X;
        fingerY = Y;
        if (!onTitle && detectMoleContact()) {
            whacking = true;
            if (soundOn) {
            AudioManager audioManager = (AudioManager)
                myContext.getSystemService
                (Context.AUDIO_SERVICE);
                float volume = (float)
                audioManager.getStreamVolume
                (AudioManager.STREAM_MUSIC);
                sounds.play(whackSound, volume, volume,
                1, 0, 1);
            }
            molesWhacked++;
        }
    }
    break;
```

Here you just wrapped all the logic in `ACTION_DOWN` in a conditional so that it only works if `gameOver` is `false`. You'll load your dialog-box graphic along with your other play screen graphics in `ACTION_UP`. You also add a check to see whether the game has ended. If it has, you reset all the relevant variables and set `gameOver` to `false` so the user can play another round.

Listing 9-19: Modified ACTION_UP for End of Game

```
case MotionEvent.ACTION_UP:
    if (onTitle) {
        backgroundImg = BitmapFactory.decodeResource
            (myContext.getResources(),
            R.drawable.background);
        backgroundImg = Bitmap.createScaledBitmap
            (backgroundImg, screenW, screenH, true);
        mask = BitmapFactory.decodeResource
            (myContext.getResources(), R.drawable.mask);
        mole = BitmapFactory.decodeResource
            (myContext.getResources(), R.drawable.mole);
        whack = BitmapFactory.decodeResource
            (myContext.getResources(), R.drawable.whack);
        gameOverDialog = BitmapFactory.decodeResource
            (myContext.getResources(),
            R.drawable.gameover);
        scaleW = (float) screenW/ (float) backgroundOrigW;
        scaleH = (float) screenH/ (float) backgroundOrigH;
        mask = Bitmap.createScaledBitmap(mask, (int)
            (mask.getWidth()*scaleW),
            (int)(mask.getHeight()*scaleH), true);
        mole = Bitmap.createScaledBitmap(mole, (int)
            (mole.getWidth()*scaleW),
            (int)(mole.getHeight()*scaleH), true);
        whack = Bitmap.createScaledBitmap(whack, (int)
            (whack.getWidth()*scaleW), (int)
            (whack.getHeight()*scaleH), true);
        gameOverDialog = Bitmap.createScaledBitmap
            (gameOverDialog,
            (int)(gameOverDialog.getWidth()*scaleW),
            (int)(gameOverDialog.getHeight()*scaleH),
            true);
        onTitle = false;
        pickActiveMole();
    }
    whacking = false;
    if (gameOver) {
        molesWhacked = 0;
        molesMissed = 0;
        activeMole = 0;
        pickActiveMole();
        gameOver = false;
    }
    break;
```

As with your other images, you load the dialog box when the play screen is viewed for the first time, and you resize it based on your scaling factor.

The last few lines you added reset `molesWhacked`, `molesMissed`, and `activeMole`, then call `pickActiveMole()` and reset `gameOver` to `false`.

Next you want to draw the dialog box if `gameOver` is `true`. Add the following lines to your `draw()` method (make sure you add them at the end, so that the game draws the dialog box on top of everything else).

```
if (gameOver) {
    canvas.drawBitmap(gameOverDialog, (screenW/2) -
        (gameOverDialog.getWidth()/2), (screenH/2) -
        (gameOverDialog.getHeight()/2), null);
}
```

That should be it! When the player misses the fifth mole, the screen should look like Figure 9-7.

Figure 9-7:
Play screen
when the
game is
over.

When the player touches the screen, a new game should start, with all the variables reset to zero. You've got another playable game now, although there are still lots of improvements that could be made to make the game more enjoyable and user-friendly. For example, the game starts immediately when you transition from either the title screen or the Game Over dialog box. Typically for arcade games (especially fast-paced ones) there will be a

"Ready!" message on the screen with a brief pause, a countdown, or both. This gives the player a chance to get ready for the oncoming wave.

As an exercise, I'd encourage you to implement such a pre-game pause in Whack-a-Mole, using what you've learned so far, and pay attention to how it affects the flow of the game after it's implemented. Tiny improvements add up. There's often an impulse to immediately upload your game when it's in a playable state, but you really should give it to friends and family to test, while paying attention to how they interact with the game. The smoother and more playable your game is, the more fun it will be, and the more people will want to play it.

As the game stands, it's pretty one-note. Most players, including kids, would get bored fairly quickly. Think of ways you might add variety and complexity to the game. You could add birds flying by in the sky for the player to whack as well, or super-moles that take two whacks to tackle. You could also divide the game into stages, resetting the speed to a lower rate with the next stage. I'm sure you can think up more variations that would carry your simple base game to another level.

But you're not quite done with Whack-a-Mole yet. Another important thing you'll probably want to be doing in your games is persisting data. That's what Chapter 10 is all about.

Chapter 10

Storing and Retrieving Game Information

In This Chapter

▶ Using Android's `SharedPreferences` file

▶ Reading and writing XML

▶ Creating SQLite databases

*P*laying games on a mobile device comes with the inherent issue that the device is often used for other things — like phone calls — which means your game is more likely to be interrupted at some point than it would be on devices like PCs or consoles. Even when the game itself is not disrupted, there's usually information that you would like to *persist* (store between sessions), even if the gaming sessions are bite-size.

Common examples of data you'd want to persist include

✔ Options (such as sound/music settings)

✔ High scores

✔ The *state* of an individual game (where game elements were located; what the score was, and so on)

When it comes to storing and retrieving data, you have several options:

✔ `SharedPreferences` (key-value pairs for primitive data types)

✔ Write to file (either on internal or external storage)

✔ Database (the default supported database type for Android is SQLite)

✔ The cloud (you can use the network to store the data remotely)

For practicality's sake, this chapter deals only with the first three options. Networked games include a lot of popular types of games on mobile platforms, but they're beyond the scope of this book. However, I do show you how to persist the sound option across user sessions, using the first three data-storage mechanisms. You can choose which one is right for the type of information you choose to store.

You can download sample files for this chapter at `http://www.dummies.com/go/androidgameprogramming`

Using Shared Preferences for Data Storage

The `SharedPreferences` framework in Android allows you to store primitive data types such as `int`, `float`, and `boolean`, as key-value pairs. The storage is *sandboxed* (isolated) relative to your app and isn't visible to other applications (including those that access your storage).

This arrangement makes `SharedPreferences` ideal for storing a handful of user settings. Information stored in `SharedPreferences` persists between sessions, so users don't have to keep changing settings every time they open the app. This approach will work great for your game's sound option.

The first item to specify is a `String` value for the name of your `SharedPreferences` file. Add the following variable declaration to your `WhackAMoleActivity`.

```
public static final String PREFERENCES_NAME =
        "MyPreferences";
```

Here's where you store the setting for sound whenever the player selects the option to toggle the sound from the Options menu: You add a few lines to the `TOGGLE_SOUND` case of your `onOptionsItemSelected()` method. Make sure your modified method matches Listing 10-1.

Listing 10-1: Storing the Sound Setting When Changed

```
public boolean onOptionsItemSelected(MenuItem item) {
    switch (item.getItemId()) {
    case TOGGLE_SOUND:
        String soundEnabledText = "Sound On";
        if (soundEnabled) {
```

```
              soundEnabled = false;
              myWhackAMoleView.soundOn = false;
              soundEnabledText = "Sound Off";
          } else {
              soundEnabled = true;
              myWhackAMoleView.soundOn = true;
          }
          SharedPreferences settings =
              getSharedPreferences(PREFERENCES_NAME, 0);    →13
          SharedPreferences.Editor editor =
              settings.edit();                              →15
          editor.putBoolean("soundSetting",
              soundEnabled);                                →16
          editor.commit();                                  →17
          Toast.makeText(this, soundEnabledText,
              Toast.LENGTH_SHORT).show();
          break;


      }
      return false;
}
```

Here is a brief explanation of what the various lines do:

→13   Creates a reference to your `SharedPreferences` file.

→15   Calls `edit()` on the settings instance to get an editor, which you need to make changes.

→16   Puts your key-value pair in the settings file. You updated the setting earlier in this case and changed the value in your `WhackAMoleView`.

→17   Here the `commit()` method must be called on the editor to finalize the changes in the file.

You'll also need the following import:

```
import android.content.SharedPreferences;
```

That's how you save the settings with `SharedPreferences`.

How do you retrieve the information? You want to load the settings values when the application is launched, so you modify your `onCreate()` method in `WhackAMoleActivity` to match Listing 10-2.

Listing 10-2: **Retrieving the Sound Setting When the Game is Launched**

```
@Override
public void onCreate(Bundle savedInstanceState) {
    super.onCreate(savedInstanceState);
    requestWindowFeature(Window.FEATURE_NO_TITLE);
    getWindow().setFlags
            (WindowManager.LayoutParams.FLAG_FULLSCREEN,
            WindowManager.LayoutParams.FLAG_FULLSCREEN);
    setContentView(R.layout.whackamole_layout);
    myWhackAMoleView = (WhackAMoleView)
            findViewById(R.id.mole);
    myWhackAMoleView.setKeepScreenOn(true);
    setVolumeControlStream(AudioManager.STREAM_MUSIC);
    SharedPreferences settings =
            getSharedPreferences(PREFERENCES_NAME, 0);      →11
    soundEnabled =
            settings.getBoolean("soundSetting", true);
    myWhackAMoleView.soundOn = soundEnabled;
}
```

Here's the process in Listing 10-2:

1. Starting with Line 11, you get an instance of your `SharedPreferences` file to work with.

2. You retrieve the sound setting from the file using your key and set your local variable to the retrieved value.

   The `true` in the `getBoolean()` method is the default setting for the value.

3. In the last line, you set the value of `soundOn` in your view to the retrieved value.

The first time the game is run, if the preferences file does not exist, the default value for sound is used. In this case the default is on. After you've made these changes, fire up the game and try toggling the sound settings. Now, if you toggle the sound off, and then completely kill the game by backing out with the Back button, the sound setting should be saved when you re-launch the game.

You can use `SharedPreferences` for many kinds of information, including most of the common usages for games discussed at the beginning of this chapter. But storing a list of high scores or even more complex information will probably get tedious. Read on for an efficient approach to storing and retrieving the information from a file, using a common data structure known as XML.

Using XML for Data Storage

The second method this chapter covers for reading and writing data is using XML.

If you want to see how this method works, comment out the code just added (using `SharedPreferences`) in Listing 10-2.

XML stands for eXtensible Markup Language. It's basically a generalized markup language (like HTML) that allows you to make up your own custom tags. One nice advantage of XML documents is that they are both human- and machine-readable (provided the designer named the tags sensibly!).

The data can be organized hierarchically (grouped with parent and child nodes), but to keep things simple, here you only tell your code to read and write in a single piece of data — the sound setting.

For more complex examples, visit www.w3schools.com/xml.

Again, all your changes will be in the `WhackAMoleActivity`. You start by adding a `writeXML()` method with the contents shown in Listing 10-3.

Listing 10-3:   Storing Data with writeXML() Method

```
public void writeXML() {
    try {                                              →2
        String profileFileName = "settings";           →3
        FileOutputStream fOut =
            openFileOutput(profileFileName + ".xml",
                MODE_WORLD_WRITEABLE);
        StringBuffer profileXML = new StringBuffer();   →5
        profileXML.append("<sound_setting>" +
            soundEnabled + "</sound_setting>\n");       →6
        OutputStreamWriter osw = new
            OutputStreamWriter(fOut);                   →8
        osw.write(profileXML.toString());               →9
        osw.flush();
        osw.close();
    } catch (IOException ioe) {
        ioe.printStackTrace();
    }
}
```

Here is a brief explanation of what the various lines do:

→**2**   The logic is surrounded by an I/O `try`/`catch`.

→**3**   Here you create a name for your output file, and then create an output stream.

→**5**   Here you create a `StringBuffer` which allows us to produce a variable-length string.

→**6**   Next you append your actual sound setting, wrapped in XML tags you have called `"sound_setting"`. For each piece of data, you need a separate `append` statement such as this.

→**8**   The `OutputStreamWriter` allows you to write out the file. You create an instance here, passing in your `FileOutputStream`.

→**9-11** These three lines actually write out your file; then they flush and close the stream.

You'll also need the following imports:

```
import java.io.FileOutputStream;
import java.io.OutputStreamWriter;
```

At this point, you call your new method when the user toggles the sound option from the menu, just as you did with `SharedPreferences`. Modify your `onOptionsItemSelected()` method to match Listing 10-4

Listing 10-4:   Modified onOptionsItemSelected() Method

```
public boolean onOptionsItemSelected(MenuItem item) {
    switch (item.getItemId()) {
    case TOGGLE_SOUND:
        String soundEnabledText = "Sound On";
        if (soundEnabled) {
            soundEnabled = false;
            myWhackAMoleView.soundOn = false;
            soundEnabledText = "Sound Off";
        } else {
            soundEnabled = true;
            myWhackAMoleView.soundOn = true;
        }
        writeXML();                                          →13
        Toast.makeText(this, soundEnabledText,
            Toast.LENGTH_SHORT).show();
        break;

    }
    return false;
}
```

All the code in Listing 10-4 does is add Line 13 to call your `writeXML()` method.

Next you need a method for reading the XML data from file and updating your sound setting. Add the `readXML()` method to your `WhackAMoleActivity` with the contents matching Listing 10-5.

Listing 10-5:   The readXML() Method

```
private void readXML() throws XmlPullParserException,
        IOException {
    String tagName = "";                                           →2
    XmlPullParserFactory factory =
            XmlPullParserFactory.newInstance();                    →3
    factory.setNamespaceAware(true);
    XmlPullParser xpp = factory.newPullParser();
    try {
        InputStream in =
            openFileInput("settings.xml");                         →7
        InputStreamReader isr = new
          InputStreamReader(in);
        BufferedReader reader = new BufferedReader(isr);
        String str;
        StringBuffer buf = new StringBuffer();
        while ((str = reader.readLine()) != null) {
            buf.append(str);
        }
        in.close();
        xpp.setInput(new StringReader(buf.toString()));
        int eventType = xpp.getEventType();
        while (eventType != XmlPullParser.END_DOCUMENT) {
          if(eventType == XmlPullParser.START_DOCUMENT) {
          } else if(eventType ==
          XmlPullParser.END_DOCUMENT) {
          } else if(eventType == XmlPullParser.START_TAG)
          {
              tagName = xpp.getName();
          } else if(eventType == XmlPullParser.END_TAG) {
          } else if(eventType == XmlPullParser.TEXT) {

              if (tagName.contains("sound_setting")) {
                  soundEnabled =
                      Boolean.parseBoolean
                      (xpp.getText().toString());
              }
          }
          eventType = xpp.next();
        }
```

(continued)

Listing 10-5 *(continued)*

```
        } catch (Exception FileNotFoundException){
            System.out.println("File Not Found");
        }
}
```

Here is a brief explanation of what the various lines do:

→**2**   You need a String to hold the current tag being read.

→**3-5**   This line creates a factory for generating a pull parser, which is an interface for parsing an XML document. The next couple of lines create the parser with the correct parameters.

→**7**   Starting here, you create the necessary components to read in the document as a stream and parse it one line at a time. The conditionals look at what part of the document you're parsing, and detect whether you come across a tag that contains "sound_setting". If the tag is found, the parser reads the contents of that tag, parses it as a boolean data type, and sets your current sound setting to the value of the boolean.

You'll also need the following imports:

```
import org.xmlpull.v1.XmlPullParser;
import org.xmlpull.v1.XmlPullParserException;
import org.xmlpull.v1.XmlPullParserFactory;
import java.io.IOException;
import java.io.InputStream;
import java.io.InputStreamReader;
import.java.io.BufferedReader;
import java.io.StringReader;
```

You can obviously structure your XML documents much more elaborately to store complex game states and use this basic example as a starting point for parsing them.

The last piece is to call your readXML() method, and you want to do that right when the game is launched. Modify your onCreate() method to match Listing 10-6.

Listing 10-6:   Modified onCreate() Calling readXML()

```
@Override
public void onCreate(Bundle savedInstanceState) {
    super.onCreate(savedInstanceState);
    requestWindowFeature(Window.FEATURE_NO_TITLE);
```

```
getWindow().setFlags
    (WindowManager.LayoutParams.FLAG_FULLSCREEN,
    WindowManager.LayoutParams.FLAG_FULLSCREEN);
setContentView(R.layout.whackamole_layout);
myWhackAMoleView = (WhackAMoleView) findViewById
    (R.id.mole);
myWhackAMoleView.setKeepScreenOn(true);
setVolumeControlStream(AudioManager.STREAM_MUSIC);
try {
    readXML();
} catch (XmlPullParserException e) {
    e.printStackTrace();
} catch (IOException e) {
    e.printStackTrace();
}
myWhackAMoleView.soundOn = soundEnabled;
}
```

The readXML() method throws two types of exceptions, so you need to sur-round your call with a try and two catches, one for each exception type. After calling readXML(), your local soundEnabled variable will have the stored value, so you can then just set the variable in your view and everything should work fine.

Using this method of storing and retrieving data is overkill for something simple like a sound setting, but it makes more sense for things like high scores or complex game states, much like the next method this chapter goes over: databases.

Using a SQLite Database for Data Storage

The officially supported database for Android is SQLite, which means that functionality for creating and manipulating SQLite databases is built into Android.

SQLite is a smaller version of full-blown SQL databases, but they should have all the functionality you really need. The information in SQLite databases created from a particular application are *sandboxed*, which means the data is only available to that application, and not outside the application.

To create and interact with a SQLite database, you need to create a new class that handles typical database operations. It's going to extend the SQLiteOpenHelper class that's part of the Android SDK.

I include some methods that you won't be using right away, but which come in handy if you find your code has to do a lot more heavy lifting with databases.

To create the new class, right-click the package icon in Eclipse and select New➪Class. Name the class DatabaseAdapter, and then modify the contents to match Listing 10-7.

Listing 10-7: DatabaseAdapter Class

```java
package com.agpfd.whackamole;

import android.content.ContentValues;
import android.content.Context;
import android.database.Cursor;
import android.database.SQLException;
import android.database.sqlite.SQLiteDatabase;
import android.database.sqlite.SQLiteOpenHelper;
import android.util.Log;

public class DatabaseAdapter
{
    public static final String KEY_ROWID = "_id";
    public static final String KEY_SOUND_SETTING =
        "sound_setting";
    private static final String TAG = "DBAdapter";
    private static final String DATABASE_NAME =
        "settingsdata";
    private static final String SETTINGS_TABLE =
        "settings";
    private final Context context;

    private DatabaseHelper DatabaseHelper;
    private SQLiteDatabase db;

    public DatabaseAdapter(Context context) {
        this.context = context;
        DatabaseHelper = new DatabaseHelper(context);
    }

    private static class DatabaseHelper extends
            SQLiteOpenHelper {                                    →27

        private static final int DATABASE_VERSION = 1;
```

```
        private static final String
            CREATE_SETTINGS_TABLE =                    →31
            " create table " + SETTINGS_TABLE +
            " (_id integer primary key
             autoincrement," +
            " sound_setting text not null);";

        public DatabaseHelper(Context context) {
            super(context, DATABASE_NAME, null,
            DATABASE_VERSION);
        }

        @Override
        public void onCreate(SQLiteDatabase database) {
            database.execSQL(CREATE_SETTINGS_TABLE);
        }

        @Override
        public void onUpgrade(SQLiteDatabase database,
            int oldVersion, int newVersion) {
            Log.w(TAG, "Upgrading database from
            version" + oldVersion + " to "+
            newVersion + ", which will destroy all
            old data");
            database.execSQL("DROP TABLE IF EXISTS
            todo");onCreate(database);
        }
    }

public DatabaseAdapter open() throws
        SQLException {                                 →53
        db = DatabaseHelper.getWritableDatabase();
        return this;
    }

    public void close() {
        DatabaseHelper.close();
    }

    public long insertRecord
    (String newSoundSetting) {                         →60
    ContentValues initialValues = new
            ContentValues();
    initialValues.put(KEY_SOUND_SETTING,
            newSoundSetting);
    return db.insert(SETTINGS_TABLE, null,
            initialValues);
```

(continued)

Listing 10-7 *(continued)*

```
    }

    public boolean updateRecord(long rowId, String
        newSoundSetting) {
        ContentValues args = new ContentValues();
        args.put(KEY_SOUND_SETTING, newSoundSetting);
        return db.update(SETTINGS_TABLE, args,
            KEY_ROWID + "=" + rowId, null) > 0;
    }

    public void insertOrUpdateRecord(String
        newSoundSetting) {                               →73
        String INSERT_OR_UPDATE_RECORD =
          "INSERT OR REPLACE INTO " + SETTINGS_TABLE + "
            (" + KEY_ROWID + "," + KEY_SOUND_SETTING + ")
            " +
            "VALUES (1," + "'" + newSoundSetting + "');";
        db.execSQL(INSERT_OR_UPDATE_RECORD);
    }

    public boolean deleteRecord(long rowId) {
        return db.delete(SETTINGS_TABLE, KEY_ROWID +
          "=" + rowId, null) > 0;
    }

    public Cursor getAllRecords() {
        return db.query(SETTINGS_TABLE, new String[] {
                    KEY_ROWID,
                    KEY_SOUND_SETTING
                    },
            null,
            null,
            null,
            null,
            null);
    }

    public Cursor getRecord(long rowId) throws
        SQLException {
        Cursor mCursor =
            db.query(true, SETTINGS_TABLE, new String[] {
            KEY_ROWID,
            KEY_SOUND_SETTING
```

```
        },
                KEY_ROWID + "=" + rowId,
                null,
                null,
                null,
                null,
                null);
        if (mCursor != null) {
            mCursor.moveToFirst();
        }
        return mCursor;
    }
}
```

The Android documentation recommends this approach for using SQLite. You create this separate class to assist with database operations. Although you won't be using all the methods in this class, here's a brief overview of what's in this class:

→27   After specifying your imports and global variable declarations, you define a DatabaseHelper class.

→31   This variable holds a string that defines the raw SQL command for creating the only table your database will have, the settings table. For reference on SQLite syntax and queries, visit http://www.sqlite.org/.

→53   This is a method for opening the database, which is necessary for reading and writing from it. The following method is for closing the database, which should be done only when your code is finished interacting with the database.

→60   The next two methods, insertRecord() and updateRecord() do what they say. You want to insert a record if you already know that one doesn't exist, and update a record if you already know that one exists. But what do you do if you don't know whether the record exists? That's why you have the next method.

→73   This method executes a raw SQL command on the database, passing in your sound setting as text and setting the value of the first row in the database to the value of the sound setting. If the record exists, it's updated; if not, it's created. This is the method you use when your game has to access the database.

The rest of the methods are fairly straightforward. I include them for your convenience if your game has to handle more extensive interaction with a database and needs them. For the moment, you need use only one more of them, the `getRecord()` method.

Here's a closer look at how your code interacts with the database from `WhackAMoleActivity`. First you want to update or insert a new record into the database when the user changes the sound setting. Modify your `onOptionsItemSelected()` method in `WhackAMoleActivity` to match Listing 10-8.

Listing 10-8: Modified onOptionsItemSelected() Using the Database

```
public boolean onOptionsItemSelected(MenuItem item) {
    switch (item.getItemId()) {
    case TOGGLE_SOUND:
        String soundEnabledText = "Sound On";
        if (soundEnabled) {
            soundEnabled = false;
            myWhackAMoleView.soundOn = false;
            soundEnabledText = "Sound Off";
        } else {
            soundEnabled = true;
            myWhackAMoleView.soundOn = true;
        }
        DatabaseAdapter db = new DatabaseAdapter(this);   →13
        try {
            db.open();
        }catch(SQLException sqle){
            throw sqle;
        }
        db.insertOrUpdateRecord(Boolean.
            toString(soundEnabled));                       →19
        db.close();
        Toast.makeText(this, soundEnabledText,
            Toast.LENGTH_SHORT).show();
        break;

    }
    return false;
}
```

Here's what happens with Listing 10-8:

1. The game starts its interaction with the database when Line 13 creates an instance of your `DatabaseAdapter` class.

2. The code opens the database before calling the insertOrUpdateR-ecord() method on Line 19.

3. The code closes the database and shows the Toast, just as it does with your other data-storage methods.

You need to retrieve the information stored in the database when the game launches, so the next order of business is to modify your onCreate() method in WhackAMoleActivity to fetch the sound setting. Modify your onCreate() method to match Listing 10-9.

Listing 10-9:   Retrieving Data From the Database

```
@Override
public void onCreate(Bundle savedInstanceState) {
    super.onCreate(savedInstanceState);
    requestWindowFeature(Window.FEATURE_NO_TITLE);
    getWindow().setFlags
            (WindowManager.LayoutParams.FLAG_FULLSCREEN,
            WindowManager.LayoutParams.FLAG_FULLSCREEN);
    setContentView(R.layout.whackamole_layout);
    myWhackAMoleView = (WhackAMoleView)
            findViewById(R.id.mole);
    myWhackAMoleView.setKeepScreenOn(true);
    setVolumeControlStream(AudioManager.STREAM_MUSIC);
    DatabaseAdapter db = new DatabaseAdapter(this);      →11
    try {
        db.open();                                       →13
    }catch(SQLException sqle){
        throw sqle;
    }
    Cursor c = db.getRecord(1);                          →17
    startManagingCursor(c);
    if (c.moveToFirst())
    {
        do {
            soundEnabled =
                    Boolean.parseBoolean((c.getString(1))
        } while (c.moveToNext());
    }
    db.close();
    myWhackAMoleView.soundOn = soundEnabled;
}
```

Here's what happens in Listing 10-9:

1. Line 11 creates an instance of your `DatabaseAdapter`.

2. Line 13 opens the database.

3. Line 17 calls `getRecord()` from your `DatabaseAdapter`, passing in a row number of 1.

   You only have one row, so you can use this as the default.

4. The method returns a `Cursor`, a standard data structure for traversing records in a database.

   The `startManagingCursor()` method enables the current activity to handle the lifecycle of the cursor; `moveToFirst()` moves to the first record.

5. The code stores the string in your single row and parses it as a `boolean` data type, setting your `soundEnabled` variable to the value of the string.

   If the game were fetching more information from the database, this logic would loop through as many records as needed.

6. The code closes the database.

If you've worked through the last six chapters, you've got two playable games under your belt after some hands-on experience with

✔ Implementing games with simple interactions with a touchscreen interface

✔ Implementing more complex real-time games with `SurfaceView`

✔ Handling images and sounds

✔ Storing and retrieving data in your game

At this point, if you've done all that wrestling, you've got the chops to dive into developing your own game. Chapter 11 discusses strategies and tools for trying to make money with your game; then I show you how to package, publish, and update your game.

If you don't plan on monetizing your game, you might just want to skip ahead to Chapter 12.

Part V
Managing Your Game in the Market

The 5th Wave   By Rich Tennant

"So, tell me about this new refinement to your attack mode."

In this part . . .

Part V covers issues related to your game after it's finished and ready for upload. If you want to try to make money from your game, here's where you scrutinize the different monetization models, how they work, and their various pros and cons. I walk you through the process of setting up a developer account on Google Play, readying your game for upload, and adding all the resources necessary for your market listing.

Chapter 11

Making Money with Your Game

In This Chapter

▶ Checking out your competitors

▶ Understanding different monetization methods

▶ Choosing the monetization method that's best for your game

*Y*ou've got a great game design, the tools to implement it, and it's nearly ready for publication. If you took the long view before you started designing, you thought about whether you wanted to try to make money from your game, or even start a fledgling business. Maybe you just want to make games for fun and share them with the world for free. But if you do want to try to monetize your game, the first thing to do is to know the market — especially your direct competition. Then you can decide the best way to monetize your specific game and implement a plan to do so. In some cases, this means using a third-party SDK to serve ads in your game. In others it means using the Android SDK, though some methods don't require any additional code at all.

But first things first. How (or even if) you decide to monetize may come down to an assessment of what else is already in the marketplace, so that's where we'll start.

Knowing Your Competition

The very first thing to do is to fire up Google Play (`play.google.com`) in your favorite web browser. Figure 11-1 shows a snapshot of Google Play as of this writing.

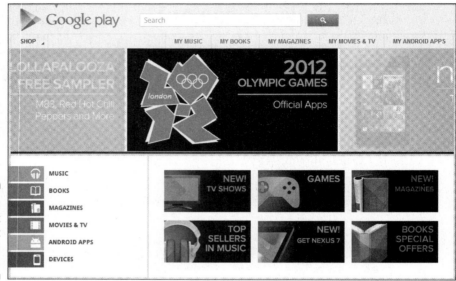

Figure 11-1:
Current
snapshot
of Google
Play.

Google Play used to be called the Android Market, but recently Google rebranded the market and consolidated it into a one-stop shop for many other types of digital media, including books, music, movies, and television shows.

In general, this move is good for the typical Android developer, because it means there are other draws that bring customers to the marketplace. Users may visit Google Play looking for a new song, and in doing so may come across an interesting-looking app to try out (yours!). Android apps have their own subsection of Google Play; click Android Apps to browse the various game categories.

Viewing the top-ranked games in a given category (such as Brain & Puzzle) will give you an idea of what's popular in that category. You can go one of two ways with this information:

 ✔ Adopt a strategy of jumping on the bandwagon.
 ✔ Take the road less traveled and make a game that is less likely to compete directly with popular existing games.

If you have a very specific game in mind, such as a variant of a popular game, use Google Play's search functionality to see if one or more versions already exist. For example, a current search of "crazy eights" returns at least half a dozen versions of the game (including a Christmas-themed one!). You may decide that if the market is already too crowded with versions of the game you want to implement, you should try something else.

If you do want to go head-to-head with existing games, be aware that they've already got a huge head start on you. They may already have built up a significant and loyal user base. You'll want to look closely at the listing of each competitor's game in Google Play. Figure 11-2 shows the current listing of my game Golf Solitaire Free.

Figure 11-2: Google Play listing of my game Golf Solitaire Free.

When looking at your potential competitor's listings, pay particular attention to the following points:

✔ The rating for the app.

This app has an average rating of 4.3 stars, which is very strong.

✔ Number of ratings and installs.

Very few people take the time to rate and/or comment on an app, so the number of ratings is always a small fraction of the overall number of people playing the game. A large number of ratings means the game is popular. With 1,862 ratings and between 100,000 and 500,000 installs, this is an indication that the game is solidly popular. Not one of the elite 1 percent, but very solid.

✔ Date of most recent comments and/or updates.

✔ The graph indicating how the game is *trending* (that is, are the downloads recently increasing or decreasing).

Unfortunately for me, Golf Solitaire Free is trending downward most recently, but such an indicator can be good for you if your competitor's game is waning; it might show you an opening.

Besides looking at the individual listings for your competitor's game, you have one more obvious and necessary task: downloading and playing their games! You might find some competing games so professional and polished that you decide (as an individual or small team developer) that you might not be able to make a competitive product. More often than not, though, you'll find many games with bugs or deficiencies, and you might decide you can make a better game. Read through the user comments to get an idea of specific complaints or feature requests. If you can give people what they want, you might just win them away from the competition.

I'll end this section with a case study: my multiplayer crossword game WordWise. Figure 11-3 shows screenshots of the title and play screens for the game.

Figure 11-3:
Screenshots of my crossword puzzle game WordWise.

In early 2010, I realized that there was no multiplayer crossword game of this kind for Android. Words With Friends was incredibly popular on the iPhone, and its fans were constantly asking if and when a port to Android was coming. I thought that if I moved to fill the void quickly, I could build up a loyal user base and scoop competitors entering the Android market late with a game of this style. I developed the front end while a friend and fellow developer implemented the server.

A brief word about intellectual property

I'm not a lawyer, and most likely, neither are you. Tread carefully if you decide to make a version of a previously existing game.

✔ If the game is old and in the public domain — chess or checkers come to mind — you're fine making your own version.

✔ Avoid using the same look and feel as an existing game — and implementing even a similar look and feel may get your game pulled from the market, or you may find yourself the recipient of a cease-and-desist letter.

So-called "clones" (similar implementations of popular games) are often a divisive subject among game developers. Some argue there's nothing wrong with building upon what already exists and improving it. Others spurn making any game that is clearly similar to an existing game.

Obviously, similarity is a matter of degree; some clones are more blatantly similar than others. If you do decide to make a game that's very much like another, you'll want to research the legal implications, and you may want to go so far as to consult legal counsel.

We released the Android version in May 2010 and the iPhone version later that year. We were indeed the first on Android with this style of game, and the first cross-platform version as well. Revenue was strong for about six months. We encountered competition from a rival app called WordFeud, but we had built up a loyal user base that liked some features of our app better. We had focused less on the social aspect of the game and built it for slightly more serious players. Most games of this type allow endless attempts at making correct words. We gave the players two chances at making a legal play. Failing to make a legal play in two attempts resulted in a forfeited turn.

Everything went reasonably well until Words With Friends was finally ported to Android in early 2011. Our revenue flatlined overnight. As independent developers, we were not able to compete directly with a product that had worldwide name recognition, a built-in audience of millions on the iPhone platform, and a huge marketing budget.

However, WordWise wasn't a waste of time or effort. By identifying a gap in the market, we were able to do reasonably well for about a nine-month period. We knew all along that there was a danger that a much larger competitor would land in the market and blow us out, but that was a risk we decided to take. WordWise is still on the market, though it no longer makes any significant revenue. We leave the server up for existing players, but don't actively update the product since it is no longer profitable.

If I had it to do all over again, I would have stressed the social aspect of the game more aggressively, implementing sharing and chat features from the first implementation. If you end up working on multiplayer games, don't underestimate the power of social interactions in spreading the popularity of your game and making it a more cohesive player experience.

The really important thing to note about this example is that we were aware of *the absence of a particular type of game in the market and an existing demand.* We exploited that knowledge to develop a game that performed well for a decent stretch of time, making it worth our while to implement it. Now that Android is a much more popular platform than it was in 2010, finding gaps is more difficult. Android has also drawn the attention of major game-industry heavyweights. So competition is much fiercer than it once was. That doesn't mean you still can't make a hit game, just that it's more difficult than it was just a couple of years ago.

As of this writing, Google's management of the market has also made it more difficult for smaller developers to get seen. New and updated apps used to show up in a Just In category, but because of abuse (some developers were publishing meaningless updates just to get an app bumped to the head of the queue), Google eliminated the category. For now, the market favors popular ports of existing games from other platforms, or games published by companies with multi-million dollar marketing budgets.

Your best bet is to search for existing games of the kind that you like to play:

- ✔ If either you can't find a game exactly like what you want, or the current crop just isn't very good, that situation might signal an exploitable spot in the market.

- ✔ Instead of competing with the game-industry giants, you can also look for regional or specialty games that might have been overlooked.

  For example, I live in Louisiana, and there's a popular card game specific to this area called Boo-Ray (*bourré,* in French). As of this writing, I can't find a Boo-Ray app on Google Play. The audience would be small, but it would likely also be enthusiastic.

- ✔ Just come up with a game concept so original and thrilling that it blows everyone away and becomes the next big hit.

No matter what your strategy, if you're going for the big time, you have to decide how you're going to make money from your game — and you have lots of options.

Monetization Models

Finding the right monetization strategy for your game may be more of an art than a science:

- ✔ In some cases, a particular model stands out as a perfect fit for a particular type of game. For instance, in-app purchases are particularly well suited to games with lots of items and upgrades, such as farm simulators or role-playing games.

- ✔ Most of the time, the best way to make money from your game may not be glaringly obvious.

Nothing says these models are mutually exclusive. I've done reasonably well with a mixed model — releasing free, ad-based versions of most of my games along with a paid, ad-free version. Throughout the discussion of the various models, if you have a particular game in mind that you want to develop, think about which model(s) would be the best fit.

Approach monetization from the perspective of the player. Would you click an ad if it was related to something you were interested in? Or would ads simply annoy you? What would get you to spend money on a game, or within a game? What method is the best fit for your game?

Free

The first option is to give your game away for free.

Wait . . . what?

How do you make money from something that you're giving away? Stay tuned: The next few sections talk about "free" games that aren't really free because they can

- ✔ Try directly (within the game itself) to upsell the user to a paid version.

- ✔ Serve ads that attempt to generate revenue.

- ✔ Sell virtual goods that cost real money. This is known as the "freemium" model.

Keep in mind that a game doesn't have to directly solicit money from the player in order to generate revenue.

The first game you make, unless it's the most mind-bendingly awesome game in the world, you should release for free. Why?

✔ If you're new to game programming, it's unlikely that you're going to hit a home run the first time you step into the batter's box. More than likely your game will be a bit rough around the edges, though hopefully it's still very good. When you release a game for free, with no strings attached, it's going to get a lot more downloads and see a lot more play. That in turn will give you a lot more feedback on what you can improve.

✔ It's going to build up a user base, hopefully one that will seek our future games that they will be willing to fork out money for.

If you think you've got a hit on your hands, by all means monetize your first game right out of the chute. But if you're new to the whole game, releasing that first game for free, without a monetization method but to gain experience, just might be the best plan.

Paid

The most obvious way to try to make money from something is to sell it! In Chapter 12, when I talk about publishing through Google Play, you get a look at how to set the price of an app upon publication. Google automatically handles conversion into foreign currencies for countries where your game will be available for sale.

If you're going to sell games, you need to be aware of sales tax issues. Sales tax law for Internet sales and digital goods is still a pretty murky subject, so if you're in doubt at all, consult your local government authority, legal counsel, and/or a CPA. Google Checkout treats *you* as the vendor, not Google, so for sales in the US, they aren't collecting sales tax. You may need to collect and remit sales tax to your state or municipality.

The two main questions you need to figure out are (a) whether you should offer a paid version of your game, and (b) if so, how much will you charge? Paid apps and games are going to have a much smaller audience. People will be much more willing to download something without the expense or hassle of paying for it. So the number of people playing your game will be smaller than it would have been if you'd released the game for free.

When people do pay for something, their expectations are higher. It's a general phenomenon that paid versions of apps and games have higher average ratings than their free counterparts. This seems a little strange at first glance, but it seems that people tend to perceive something as having higher quality if it was more difficult to obtain. This attitude also means that your users may demand personalized customer support, and they may request additional features or changes to the game.

Okay, you should try to develop good standing with your user base when you can. You may get unreasonable demands, even some harsh criticism, but try to use that feedback to make your current and future games better. Overall you'd be surprised how worked up some people can get over something they paid less than a dollar for, but it certainly happens!

Speaking of which, what are you going to charge for your game? Big-budget console games go for up to sixty dollars these days. People are certainly willing to spend a significant amount of money on entertainment and gaming. But something of a double standard is at work when it comes to mobile apps. Many developers, particularly for the iPhone market, have complained of a "race to the bottom": In a bid to be competitive and undercut others on the market, many games (even very high-quality ones) have priced themselves down to the minimum, 99 cents. This has almost led to the perception that one US dollar is right around the standard expected price for a paid game.

✓ The minimum price for an app on Google Play is $0.99 USD

✓ The maximum price is $200 USD.

You may not want to go quite as high as the max, but you may not want to simply default to the minimum. If you do, you may be undercutting yourself.

With my first few games, I experimented with price points ranging from $0.99 to $2.99. I typically ended up settling on $1.99:

✓ I tended to get more sales when the price was lower, but not enough to make up for the price cut. Remember, you have to sell twice as many games at $0.99 as you do at $1.99 for that price point to make sense. That wasn't the case for me, so I stuck with the slightly higher price point.

✓ Of course, $2.99 seemed to be more than most people were willing to pay, and my sales dropped dangerously low. Don't be afraid to experiment a little.

You can't toggle between an app being paid and free in Google Play:

✓ If at any time you designate your app as free in the market, you cannot then make it a paid app.

✓ You can change a paid app to free, but once it's free, it will always be free (unless you rename the package and completely republish it).

Free-to-Paid

A very popular model for monetizing games is to release a free version of the game with the intent of selling a paid version of the game. Many of the earliest games for personal computers used a *shareware* model, with copies of the software distributed for free, usually with a pitch for the user to buy a full licensed version.

However, within this model, there are several possible options for monetization, including:

✔ The free version links to the paid version in the marketplace.

✔ The free version allows conversion from within the game (via an in-app purchase) to unlock itself into the full version.

✔ The game is actually the full version, but users may be prompted to send the developer money via a *donate* feature.

I've never heard of this method being used successfully, though that doesn't mean it hasn't been. I'm just including it here for completeness.

Keep in mind that these techniques are not mutually exclusive. Figure 11-4 shows the title screen of my free version of Golf Solitaire.

Figure 11-4:
Title screen
for Golf
Solitaire
Free.

This version monetizes three ways:

✔ Ads

✔ Upselling to the paid version

✔ Promoting other games

In Figure 11-4, the "Play 18 Holes" button is grayed out. The full version of the game includes all 18 holes. By teasing the user with this functionality, the phantom button provides an incentive for the user to buy the full version.

This is a somewhat controversial design. For example, when we tried to publish this version in the iTunes marketplace, the app was rejected, because Apple does not allow non-functional UI elements.

This title screen also includes a button that links to the full, ad-free version of the game in Google Play. The following code snippet shows how to link to another app in Google Play.

```
Intent intent = new Intent(Intent.ACTION_VIEW,
Uri.parse("market://search?q=pname:com.golfsolitaire
        polyclef"));
try {
    myContext.startActivity(intent);
} catch (Exception e) {
}
```

The preceding code snippet explains how an active link to Google Play is made:

✔ First you need to create an intent of the type ACTION_VIEW.

✔ The second parameter is a link to parse, in this case a market query with the package name com.golfsolitaire and the publisher polyclef. We then call startActivity() from the current context, passing in the new intent.

This code will launch Google Play with the search parameters we specified, displaying the full version of the game. You'll want to include similar code attached to a button's click functionality or your screen's onTouch() method.

Deciding what functionality to include?

✔ Typically you want to give the player enough of a taste to decide whether they like the game enough to buy the full version. This normally means the first few levels or rounds of a typical game.

✔ Another option, which I've never personally used, is time-based (that is, letting the player play the game for a fixed amount of time).

I'd recommend free-to-paid as a strategy. A free version of a game will see many more downloads than a purely paid one, so you'll get a lot more exposure. And hopefully a good amount of that exposure will lead to conversions to the paid version of your game.

Ad-based

Using ads to monetize your game is another popular strategy. There are several appealing reasons to use ads:

- As mentioned earlier, free games get a lot more downloads, and thus more exposure and play.

- Software piracy is a problem; just how big a problem is controversial, and you can find arguments on all sides. But ads neatly sidestep the issue of piracy. In fact, you may even want to upload your game to a torrent site if it's got ads in it!

- Several mobile market research studies have indicated that Android users are less likely to pay for apps than their counterparts on other platforms. This is probably in large part due to the wide penetration of Android across all demographics. In any case, people do like free content, and an ad-based solution might fit the bill.

Ads don't come without risks, though:

- Just as with ad blockers for the web, users may find a way to keep your ads from displaying, though you'll find most won't care to go to that trouble.

- Another potential problem just has to do with how much money you can expect to make. Just as in the early days of Internet advertising, the first couple of years of mobile advertising saw a big influx of advertisers, and thus revenue.

  Unlike the situation on the web, however, ad providers haven't done nearly as good a job at targeting ads to users of games, so (at least in my experience) the returns are not nearly what they once were. That doesn't mean you can't still make money from an ad-based game, but you're probably going to need the game to have hundreds of thousands or millions of downloads if you want to make a full-time go at mobile game development.

Ads in mobile apps and games make money the same way that web-based ads do

- Per impression (when an ad is simply viewed)
- Per click (when the user actually clicks on an ad)

  By far more money is made per click.

Be careful about how and where you place ads, or you'll end up hurting yourself and the mobile-ad business as well:

✔ You don't want to place ads near UI elements so that the ads may be accidentally clicked. These "spurious" clicks may earn you a little more money in the near term, but since they are accidental, they don't help the businesses that placed them. And worse, you may draw lower user ratings from players, or even get the attention of Google.

✔ Violating the market's policies can get you a warning or even have your app pulled or your account suspended. Even though Google is less restrictive than most other mobile markets, they still have content guidelines you need to adhere to:

```
play.google.com/about/developer-content-policy.html
```

The technical aspects of integrating ads into your games are usually pretty easy and straightforward. Each ad provider will supply you with a downloadable SDK with instructions about how to integrate its service into your game.

If you want to use more than one ad provider, I'd suggest AdWhirl, which is known as an *ad mediator*, a service that lets you use multiple ad providers in a single app and control the ratio of ads served by each provider. You can also serve up *house ads*, banner ads that promote your own games. You can either

✔ Promote other games that you have on the market

✔ Contact fellow developers to promote each other's games.

In-app Purchases

When a user makes a financial transaction within your app or game, this is known as an in-app purchase.

The two main uses of in-app purchases with regard to games are to

✔ Upgrade from a free version to a paid version within the same app.

✔ Purchase additional levels.

✔ Purchase virtual goods.

Different markets or services may have different policies regarding how in-app purchases are used, so be sure you read the guidelines!

Some games are going to be natural fits for in-app purchases, such as RPGs (which have lots of in-game items like weapons or armor that could easily be offered for potential purchase). Sometimes you want to be creative when it comes to monetization, but you also don't want to just jump on the bandwagon because other game companies have had success with a given method, especially if it doesn't really fit into how your game plays. Don't shoehorn in-app purchases into your game to an irritating extent (for example,

I don't recommend making people pay extra for a queen in chess!), but you may want to integrate in-app purchases into your design if it comes naturally.

Alternatives to Google Play

Google Play isn't the only way to distribute Android games, though it is the most popular. The reason is that when people get an Android device and go looking for content, they are usually going to take the path of least resistance — and that means using the market that's preinstalled on their device. In most cases, that's Google Play, but third-party markets exist as well.

As of this writing, the second largest market for developers is Amazon's App Store. They've successfully entered the tablet market, which enables them to sell lots of devices with their own app store preinstalled.

Uploading and maintaining your games on multiple markets can be a pain, especially if those markets have different requirements for promotional resources like icons, banners, and descriptions. But you just might find that it's worth your while if you put in the effort. Chapter 12 walks you through creating a developer account on Google Play, as well as uploading and updating your app there. But don't forget that you have options.

Chapter 12

Publishing and Updating Your Game

In This Chapter

▶ Exporting a signed application

▶ Setting up your Google Play developer account

▶ Supporting your game after it's published

Your game won't be seen by anyone until you upload it to a market. I'll show you how to get your game into Google Play. If you're like me, you don't work for a multimillion-dollar game company with a massive marketing budget. If that's the case, then your market listing is the most valuable marketing tool you have. The first thing people will see is the name and icon for your game, but if they visit the market listing, that's where you need to get them interested enough to download your game.

So first things first — namely, the nuts and bolts of the upload process, and then a look at all the different options you have for your listing.

Creating a developer account for Google Play

You need a regular Google Account in order to register for a Google publisher account. Odds are you already have a Google Account, but if you don't, you can create one during the registration process for a developer account.

To start the developer registration process, go to

```
https://play.google.com/apps/publish
```

Follow these steps:

1. **Enter basic contact information about yourself and your company (if you're associated with one).**

2. **Read and agree to the Developer Distribution Agreement.**

3. **Pay a $25 fee.**

   This requires a Google Checkout account; if you don't have one, you can set one up during the process.

When your account has been processed and you've been notified via e-mail, return to `https://play.google.com/apps/publish`, which takes you to your Android Developer Console.

From there, you can do lots of useful things:

✔ Upload new apps and updates

✔ View usage statistics and feedback

✔ Track sales

If you want to sell your games, the first thing to do after your developer account is approved is to create a Google Checkout Merchant account. Google Play uses Google Checkout for all financial transactions.

To set up a Google Checkout Merchant account

1. **Access the developer console.**

2. **Click the Edit Profile link at the top**

3. **Select Setup a Merchant Account at Google Checkout.**

   You're walked through the steps for setting up a merchant account;

When that's done, you can use the developer console to

✔ List games for sale

✔ View sales reports

Generating a Key with Keytool

Google Play requires that each application you upload into their market be digitally signed with a certificate associated with a private key.

The tools required to generate the key are provided in the Java Development Kit (JDK) installed in Chapter 3.

To make sure that you have the proper Keytool installed and working, you can type the following from the command line:

```
$ keytool -help
```

If the Keytool is working, you'll see a list of possible commands. If not, you'll need to troubleshoot your JDK installation.

The first thing to do is generate a private key to be stored somewhere on your local development machine; you use it each time you sign a game for release. An example of the command for generating a private key with Keytool is the following:

```
$ keytool -genkey -v -keystore my-release-key.keystore
          -alias alias_name -keyalg RSA -keysize 2048
          -validity 10000
```

For reference about what each of these options and parameters do, see

```
http://docs.oracle.com/javase/6/docs/technotes/tools/
          windows/keytool.html.
```

When you run this command, you're prompted to enter a password that's at least six characters long, followed by a number of questions about you and your organization.

By default, the key should be generated in the same directory where the Keytool is located, though you may specify the target directory as an input parameter. You may want to move the newly-generated key to another location (such as a password-protected directory).

Exporting a Signed Application

When you have a valid key, you can use it to sign your application at the same time you compile it into an .apk (Android Application Package) file, which is the standard file format for Android.

You could export an unsigned .apk file and sign it manually (this is what I used to do in the early days). But these days you can sign the application the same time you compile it with Eclipse.

Let's say you want to sign and export your Whack-a-Mole game. Follow these steps:

1. **Right-click the project in the Package Explorer and select Android Tools⊏Export Signed Application Package...**

   You should see the wizard for exporting a signed application, which should look something like Figure 12-1.

Figure 12-1:
The Export
Android
Application
wizard in
Eclipse.

2. **Click Next.**

   You're prompted to enter the location of the key you just created, along with its password (Figure 12-2).

3. **Enter the location of the key and its password, then click Next.**

   You're prompted to select the alias and enter the password (Figure 12-3).

4. **Select the alias and enter the password, then click Next.**

   The final screen in the wizard prompts you for the location for the exported file.

5. **Enter or browse to the location where you want to store the exported game.**

   You're notified on this screen that the certificate will expire in 24 years, which should be plenty of time. If you've already exported the file before, you'll get a warning that you're about to overwrite the existing version.

6. **Click Finish.**

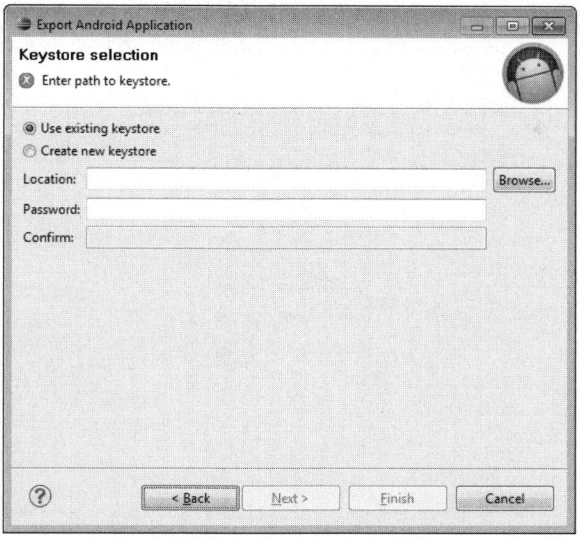

Figure 12-2:
Entering the
key location
and pass-
word.

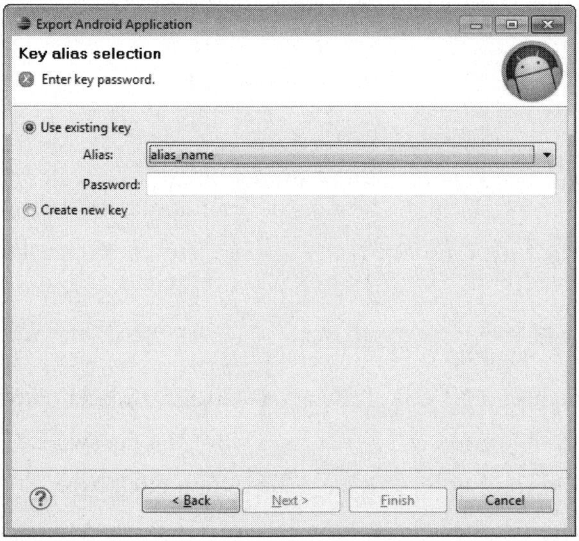

Figure 12-3:
Selecting
the alias
and pass-
word.

That's it! You now have a signed `.apk` file ready for upload into Google Play.
Combine it with a developer account and you're set.

Uploading Your Game to Google Play

When your developer account is set up, you can upload your first game.

The following files and information are required:

- ✔ The `.apk` file for the game.
- ✔ At least two screenshots of your game.

  Screenshots must be one of these sizes:
  - 320x480
  - 480x800
  - 480x854
  - 1280x720
  - 1280x800

  Your screenshots can be either portrait (tall) or landscape (wide), even though they won't appear in landscape orientation in the developer console.

  Include at least one screenshot of actual game play, so prospective players can get an idea of what playing the game looks like before they download.

- ✔ A high-resolution (512x512) application icon. This is the icon used by Google Play and should be the same as your application icon.
- ✔ An app title and description. The title can be up to 30 characters long, while the description can be up to 4,000 characters.

I recommend adding these optional items:

- ✔ A promotional graphic (180x120), kind of like a small banner for your game.
- ✔ A feature graphic (1240x500). This is the large graphic seen on your game's listing in Google Play when viewing in a browser.

  A slick, appealing high-resolution graphic on your market listing is the first thing users will see, so you want to make a good impression.
- ✔ A promotional video. You can produce a video and upload it to YouTube, then submit the link associated with your game in the developer console. The video will be available to users in Google Play so that they can view it before deciding whether or not to download your game.

A video can serve two main purposes:

- Showing off your game. Try not to show video clips of confusing levels or lots of things going on to the point where you can't see what's happening. An opening level is usually good. Try to avoid cut-scenes or cinematics if you have them. People usually want to see how the game will play. If the video is too different from the game experience, players might not be happy with you.

- Presenting a sort of tutorial. Especially if your game is novel, players may need a gentle introduction into how it works. If the game is especially difficult to understand, you'll want in-game tips, hints, and tutorials, but the listing video is also a good place to explain the basics of the game.

Keep your video short:

- A minute or less for just a game play intro.

- Three minutes or less for a more in-depth, tutorial-like video.

Actually capturing video from a device can be difficult:

- ✔ You can use an emulator and video screen capture software on your development machine. Emulator performance is often very choppy, so the quality of your video might suffer.

- ✔ You can try to capture the video from a hardware device, but taking video of electronic devices is also difficult, usually resulting in poorly-lighted, grainy video.

- ✔ If you have access to studio-quality production of demo videos, go for it!

A bad video may be worse than no video at all, so try to determine if you can actually produce something that's going to showcase your game, rather than make it look shoddy.

A privacy policy can indicate how you will use any personal information that may be gathered by your game. This usually isn't an issue unless your game is multiplayer and has a login system with usernames and passwords, or is location-based and somehow uses the player's location or other information in game play. If you are gathering any information you will want to link to a privacy policy, as well as detailing the policy within the app itself.

Uploading the APK

Your APK should be signed and stored in a handy location when you begin the upload procedures. Follow these steps:

1. **From the main page in the developer console, click the Upload Application button.**

   The first thing you will be prompted to do is upload your `.apk` file, as in Figure 12-4.

Figure 12-4:
The Upload
new APK
dialog in the
Google Play
developer
console.

Upload new APK

Required: Select your application's APK

Choose File No file chosen   Upload

Optional: Add an expansion file
If your app exceeds the 50MB APK limit, you can add expansion files. Learn more

Add file

Close

You don't actually have to upload your .apk at this time. You can close the dialog and fill out the rest of the information and settings about your game, and upload the .apk later.

2. **To upload your** `.apk` **file now, click Choose File, browse to the location where you stored the .apk, then once it's chosen click Upload.**

As the dialog states, if your `.apk` file exceeds Google Play's limit of 50MB, you can upload expansion files. For a small game, it's unlikely that you'll exceed 50MB, which can actually encompass an awful lot of images, sound, and music. If you do have more resources than that, you'll want to click Learn more to determine how to use additional files not integrated into your `.apk`.

Adding product details

When the `.apk` is uploaded, you'll need to add other resources and details to your game's listing. Some of these will display in the Google Play listing that users will see, and others will be used by Google.

Creating and uploading screenshots

The Android tools for Eclipse make it easy to take quality screenshots. You should see a button in the upper-right corner of your Eclipse window that opens the DDMS (Dalvik Debug Monitor Service) perspective. The DDMS actually includes a suite of tools that allows you to monitor the performance of your game as well as spoofing certain features available on hardware devices. Those uses are too big a topic to cover here, but another handy feature of the DDMS is screen capture. Follow these steps:

1. **Click the DDMS button in Eclipse.**

   The perspective should show

   - A window named Devices

   - Tabs in the main window that display other information about the current device.

   All devices you have attached to your development machine or emulators you have running will display here.

2. **Select the device you want to capture a screen shot from by clicking the device icon and serial number in the Devices window.**

   When a device is selected, the screen capture icon, which looks like a camera, should be active (Figure 12-5).

3. **To take a screenshot, click the screen capture icon.**

   Whatever is currently displaying on your device will be captured and displayed in a new window (Figure 12-6).

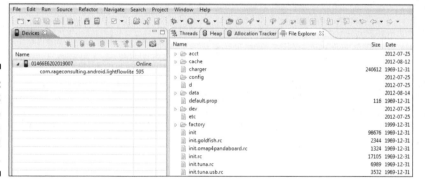

Figure 12-5:
DDMS
perspective
showing a
selected
device.

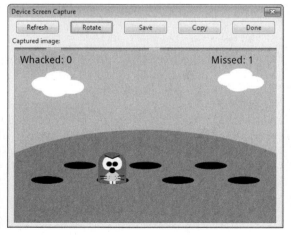

Figure 12-6:
The Device
Screen
Capture
window.

To rotate the image into landscape, click Rotate. The screen capture may produce artifacts, especially if your animation is fast and the emulator is running slowly, so you may need to try a number of times before getting a shot you like. When you click Refresh, the screen capture updates with whatever is currently on the screen. I find it useful to start a game and click the Refresh button until I find a shot I like.

4. **When you have a shot you like, click Save and browse to the location where you would like to save the shot and click the Save button in the dialog.**

   Again, you need a minimum of two screenshots. I usually like to include three to five, but you'll likely want at least one of your play screen out of your two shots.

Uploading icons and other graphics

Figure 12-7 shows the Upload assets section of the developer console when uploading an `.apk` file.

Figure 12-7:
The Upload assets section of the Google Play developer console.

> ▶ **Google play** | ANDROID DEVELOPER CONSOLE
>
> **Edit Application**
>
> [Publish] [Save]
>
> | Product details | APK files |
>
> **Upload assets**
>
> | Screenshots at least 2 | Add a screenshot: [Choose File] No file chosen | [Upload] | **Screenshots:** 320 x 480, 480 x 800, 480 x 854, 1280 x 720, 1280 x 800 24 bit PNG or JPEG (no alpha) Full bleed, no border in art You may upload screenshots in landscape orientation. The thumbnails will appear to be rotated, but the actual images and their orientations will be preserved. |
>
> | High Resolution Application Icon [Learn More] | Add a hi-res application icon: [Choose File] No file chosen | [Upload] | **High Resolution Application Icon:** 512 x 512 32 bit PNG or JPEG Maximum: 1024 KB |
>
> | Promotional Graphic optional | Add a promotional graphic: [Choose File] No file chosen | [Upload] | **Promo Graphic:** 180w x 120h 24 bit PNG or JPEG (no alpha) No border in art |
>
> | Feature Graphic optional [Learn More] | Add a feature graphic: [Choose File] No file chosen | [Upload] | **Feature Graphic:** 1024 x 500 24 bit PNG or JPEG (no alpha) Will be downsized to mini or micro |
>
> | Promotional Video optional | Add a promotional video link: [http://] | | **Promotional Video:** Enter YouTube URL. |
>
> | Privacy Policy [Learn more] | Add a privacy policy link: [http://] ☑ Not submitting a privacy policy URL at this time | | |
>
> | Marketing Opt-Out | ☑ Do not promote my application except in Google Play and in any Google-owned online or mobile properties. I understand that any changes to this preference may take sixty days to take effect. | | |

There are buttons for each set of assets that allow you to browse your local machine to where you stored them, select them, then upload them. For the hi-res icon (512x512) it's a good idea to design your icon first using this size, then scale it down to as low as 32x32 to make sure it still looks good.

Browse around both the web and device versions of Google Play to look at other games' promotional graphics, to see what works and what doesn't. Try to look at a wide variety of listings to give yourself ideas about what you think does and doesn't work.

Writing your game's description

The graphics in a listing are the first things that will catch someone's eye, but the description is another crucial aspect to marketing your game. You want to get people interested in downloading and trying your game out. As long as the game is fun, the hardest part is often getting them to click that Install button.

Follow these guidelines for writing a great, alluring description for your game:

✔ Sound enthusiastic, but not too cheesy. Watch those exclamation points!

✔ Keep it succinct. In the early days of the market, the description length was appallingly small. These days, 4,000 characters are quite a lot, but that doesn't mean you have to use it all. In fact, a lot of potential down-loaders might be turned off by a wall of text. You want to hook them, not give them eyestrain.

✔ Be descriptive. Don't think you're going to get people to download your app by being vague and mysterious.

Let's try to write some hypothetical descriptions for Whack-a-Mole and see what might or might not work:

✔ *This is an awesome game that people of all ages will want to play! Do you like fun!?! This addictive game will keep you or your kids entertained for hours on end. Go ahead and download it now...you won't be disappointed!*

You shouldn't have too many problems figuring out what's wrong with a description like this. About the only thing going for it is its brevity. The description sounds like a carnival barker, but its biggest sin is that it doesn't tell you anything substantive about the game itself, or what it's like to play.

✔ *Moles have invaded your back yard! Whack them on the head to knock them back underground. Whack-a-Mole updates the classic carnival game with a fully touch-screen interface that looks and plays great on any Android device. The more moles you whack, the faster they come. Fast-paced fun for players of all ages!*

This is pretty good, though admittedly not perfect. You are doing some things right here, though: introducing the theme of the game, describing the actual game play, and describing the interface and compatibility across a wide range of devices. The description gives a good sense of what playing the game is like, and does so in a brief, solid paragraph.

If you just don't feel comfortable with words, or you're distributing the app in a market in which you don't speak the native language, get some help. Just as with other resources, you can hire someone, or find a friend or family member who can help you out. If you butcher the description, it's going to result in fewer downloads, so take the time to do it right.

Don't clog descriptions with release notes, bug fix comments, or replies to your users. Google Play now allows dedicated places for each of these. When you do post version changes or bug fixes, be succinct and descriptive. Users don't care about the technical details, only that you fixed the bug that wouldn't let them save their high scores. Use your game description space for its intended use: describing and getting people interested in downloading your game.

In the same section where you enter the game description and recent changes text, there is a space for promo text, limited to 80 characters. This is typically used when a game happens to be featured as a top app in a given category. Hopefully that will happen for you, since it's a great form of exposure. Just to be prepared for such an eventuality, you should also have content for the promo text. Eighty characters isn't much, so this is almost like the tag line for a movie, a briefer version of your game description. For Whack-a-Mole you might try something like this:

Whack the moles! Try this fast-paced carnival action game for Android.

This is 70 characters. As you can see, there's not much room, but you'll want enough to describe the game very briefly and make someone click the link to the market listing.

Setting other market listing options

When you've entered the text for the descriptions, you'll need to select the application type and category. The app type you select should be Game. The Game application type has these subcategories. You'll want to choose the subcategory that best fits your game:

✔ Arcade & Action

✔ Brain & Puzzle

✔ Cards & Casino

✔ Casual

✔ Live Wallpaper

✔ Racing

✔ Sports Games

✔ Widgets

The market doesn't currently support multiple categories, so even if your game overlaps categories, you can choose only one. You might want to choose the category with less competition, and thus more visibility. And you are able to change this setting at any time, so you can experiment a little.

Next you'll need to set the Copy Protection, Content Rating, and Pricing. Figure 12-8 shows these publishing options in the developer console.

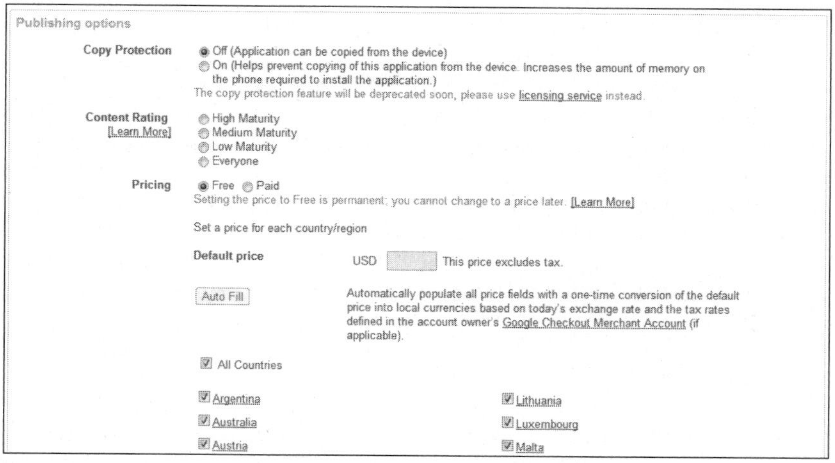

Figure 12-8:
Publishing
options for
your game.

Copy Protection

Copy Protection was Google's first pass at keeping apps from being pirated. It increases the size of your uploaded app and doesn't actually provide very much in the way of protection. Besides, as the console notes, it's being done away with. Google currently recommends that you use their licensing service (see http://developer.android.com/guide/google/play/licensing/index. html). Remember, these options are for paid apps. While the licensing option might provide marginally more protection than the previous incarnation, the bottom line is that if people want to pirate your game, they will. You have to ask yourself whether any kind of copy protection or *DRM* (digital rights management) is worth the time and effort required to implement it. I'd argue that for your first game, or even first few games, the answer is no.

You're probably just not going to get enough exposure, and when you're just starting out (realistically speaking), it's unlikely that your first game will be enough of a hit to make piracy a real issue. If you're really worried about it, go ahead and implement licensing or your own anti-piracy measures. Just remember that the time you invest could be spent polishing or marketing your game.

Content Rating

Content Rating deals with the age-level appropriateness of the content in your game.

Be careful here. If your game is rated too broadly and users complain to Google, that might be an issue for you.

The main areas of concern for a game (just as for movies and other media) are the usual suspects:

- ✔ **Violence.** Per Google's guidelines, if your game contains cartoon or fantasy violence (such as whacking a mole on the head), the maturity level should at least be set to Low Maturity. Of course, if you've got zombies eating brains and entrails, or other gratuitous depictions, you likely need to go up to High Maturity. Get feedback from beta testers across a wide range of demographics. In other words, try to get your mom to play it and see what she says. Moms' reactions are a good baseline for determining what the baseline maturity level should be.

- ✔ **Profanity or crude humor.** If your game requires shooting boogers from a giant nose to kill enemies, or contains any words that are considered taboo or possibly offensive, rate it at least Medium Maturity.

- ✔ **Sexual content.** It will usually be obvious if your game has a sexual theme (which I would generally advise against overdoing). But if the elves in your RPG have substantial cleavage or the dialog in your game is a little suggestive, you might not offend most folks. Default on the side of safety and rate your app for more mature audiences if there's any kind of question.

Of course, these areas are all subjective, which is why it's important to get a lot of input from other people.

Steer clear of more mature themes for your first couple of games. You'll avoid any potential controversy, but the big upside is that your available audience will be much larger.

Another aspect of maturity levels to note is location. If you happen to be developing a location-based game (such as a scavenger hunt that uses the GPS), the game cannot be rated Everyone. It must be rated at least Low Maturity. This is presumably because of issues related to tracking the location of minors.

Pricing

The Pricing section is your option to set the price.

If the game is free, it must always be free.

If you are selling the game, follow these steps: enter a default price in US dollars in the price field. Below that is a list of other countries where you can make the game available for sale. By default, all locations are checked. After entering a price in US dollars, you can click the Auto Fill button to convert the price into values for local currencies in other locations.

As of this writing, the Auto Fill feature didn't quite work right for 99 cents, rounding certain currencies down below the minimum price so that you had to edit them manually.

The price excludes tax. You can set up automatic tax allocation through Google Checkout. Just be sure you consult your accountant or attorney about collecting taxes in your state or region. Google's not going to do it for you.

Contact information

When you've set these options, you'll need to enter contact information for you or your company, for support purposes. You don't need to enter a telephone number unless you want to provide telephone support. There are the standard acknowledgements that the game meets the proper content guidelines at the very bottom of the page. When you check those, return to the top of the page and click Publish.

Congratulations! Your app will be live on Google Play almost immediately. However, if there are any issues with your submission, the console will indicate them with warnings to fix them. Otherwise your game is out there for the whole Android ecosystem to download and play.

When you publish and the listing is visible, you'll want to check it via both the web and device versions of Google Play to see how it looks. You'll also want to test downloading your game to see what the process is like from a user's perspective.

When you've published a game, it will stay in your developer console forever. You can't delete listings. You can unpublish games (by clicking the Unpublish button for a listing), but the actual listing will always stay in Google's system for reference and support.

Supporting and Updating Your Game After Publication

If your game gets any significant amount of downloads, you'll get e-mails. Some will be praising you and your game and thanking you for making it. These will be in the minority, probably about 5 percent. The rest will either be criticism of varying levels of specificity and helpfulness, or requests for help. You should try to respond to every e-mail you get, and unless you're getting millions of downloads, this should be very doable. You represent your game and to a lesser extent the Android platform, so when you reply to your users in a professional manner, it reflects well on everyone and can help boost your reputation and sometimes your game's user rating.

Some users might be rude. Resist the urge to be rude back. The more professional you act, the more professional you'll be, and you don't want comments on your app that say you insulted someone (even if that someone might have deserved it).

If there's a feature request or someone suggests a change to the UI or other functionality, make sure to listen. They probably care enough about the game to want to see it better, and if they took the time to write you then their suggestion warrants some consideration. You can't please everyone, but if the suggestion is sound and doable, you probably want to spend the time making the change. If it's a bug, you definitely want to spend the time hunting down the problem and making the change.

I've seen a fair amount of discussion among mobile game developers regarding whether it's worth the effort to update your game on a regular basis, or concentrate on that next game you're working on. A number of developers have data to indicate that updates don't affect the bottom line all that much, in terms of retaining old customers and gaining new ones. It's certainly a tradeoff. In general I'd advise that you update significant bugs and functionality that won't take that long to implement, but I wouldn't prioritize updating an old game at the expense of working on a new one.

When you do have a new version, you'll need to increment both the version code and version name in the manifest file of your project. For example, if your previous version code was 1, you should increment it to 2. If your version name was 1.0, you should update to 1.1, and so on. Follow these steps:

1. **You'll need to export your signed application each time you have a new updated .apk.**

2. **When you visit the application listing for your app in the developer console, click the APK files tab.**

   Figure 12-9 shows this view for my game Golf Solitaire.

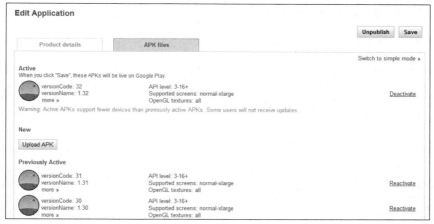

Figure 12-9:
The APK
files tab
in the
Google Play
developer
console.

   You'll see the current active version along with all previously active versions.

3. **Click the Upload APK button to browse to the location where your new .apk file is stored to upload it.**

   When uploaded, you can set the new version to the active version, deactivating the old one.

4. **Click Save when you're done.**

   The new version will become active almost immediately.

If you need to revert to a previous version, just use the same interface to deactivate the new version and activate an old one.

Part VI
The Part of Tens

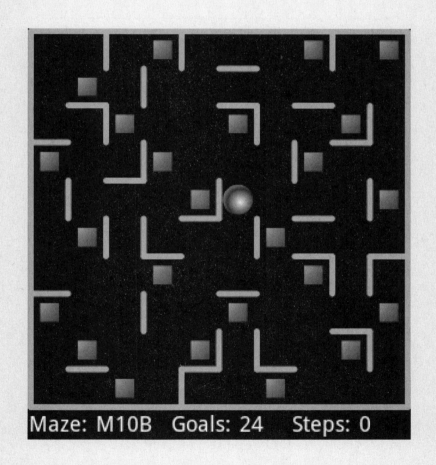

Maze: M10B   Goals: 24   Steps: 0

In this part . . .

Part VI provides you with a wealth of resources to help you on your path to creating awesome Android games. I introduce you to a bunch of open-source games that other developers have been kind enough to share, spanning virtually every game genre you can imagine. I also brief you about game engines and other tools that help streamline the process of creating games. By the time you've explored this book, dug through the sample code of these projects, and leveraged some of the tools discussed, you'll be well equipped to build great games yourself.

Chapter 13

Ten Open-Source Game Projects

*O*ften the best way to get where you're going, especially when developing games, is to build on what others have done already. Even if you do start completely from scratch, looking at how someone else already accomplished something similar can speed up your development time or give you new ideas and insights.

The following ten Android game projects are all open-source. That means the source code and all resources for the game are made freely available. Be sure to *check the license for each*, though. Just because they're free of charge doesn't mean that you can simply copy and paste their code over into your game.

I've included a good cross-section of genres and approaches, so if the two games built in this book weren't the kinds of games you necessarily want to build, chances are that at least one of these free projects fills that bill.

Lunar Lander

The Android SDK comes bundled with example projects that exemplify best practices with regard to developing certain types of apps. One of the earliest examples of this is the Lunar Lander game, shown in Figure 13-1. The project is organized very similarly to our Whack-a-Mole game and uses SurfaceView. If you're interested in building a 2D simulation game with real-time controls, you should definitely check this example out.

Figure 13-1:
Lunar
Lander.

Like other game samples in the SDK, this game tends to use keyboard input. If your test device is touchscreen-only, you'll need to run the sample game in an emulator.

To load an existing sample from the Android SDK, follow these steps:

1. **In Eclipse, right-click the project explorer and select Import.**
2. **Select Existing Android Code Into Workspace and then click Next.**
3. **Browse to the directory in which you installed the Android SDK.**

   Samples are located in `/samples/<android-sdk-version>`. You probably want to use samples from the latest version.
4. **Click Finish.**

If your project includes errors at this point, make sure your build target is the same as the SDK version the sample is from:

1. **Right-click the imported project and select Properties.**
2. **Select Android from the left menu.**
3. **Check the box associated with the build version that matches the sample directory of the project.**

Replica Island

We didn't cover how to implement a side-scrolling platformer. If you're interested in implementing this type of game, you'll definitely want to check out Replica Island, shown in Figure 13-2. The game stars the Android robot himself, navigating maze-like environments filled with obstacles and items to gather. The game was developed by Chris Pruett when he worked for Google, and became a popular free game in the market.

Figure 13-2: Replica Island.

The source and all related project files are here:

http://code.google.com/p/replicaisland.

Alien Blood Bath

This game isn't nearly as cute and family-friendly as Replica Island, although it follows in the same side-scrolling platformer genre. Alien Blood Bath (shown in Figure 13-3) is a rewrite of the Windows game of the same name.

Figure 13-3:
Alien Blood
Bath.

Probably not hard to figure out what the theme and the game play are like on this one!

The project files are available here:

```
http://code.google.com/p/alienbloodbath
```

OpenSudoku

If bathing in the blood of aliens isn't your thing — but brain-bending puzzles are — then check out OpenSudoku, an open-source version of the popular grid-and-numbers game. (See Figure 13-4.) It features 90 puzzles with three difficulty levels.

Google Play has lots of existing Sudoku games, but working through this code and implementing your own puzzles and variations will definitely be useful if you want to build games in this genre.

The project files are available here:

```
http://code.google.com/p/opensudoku-android
```

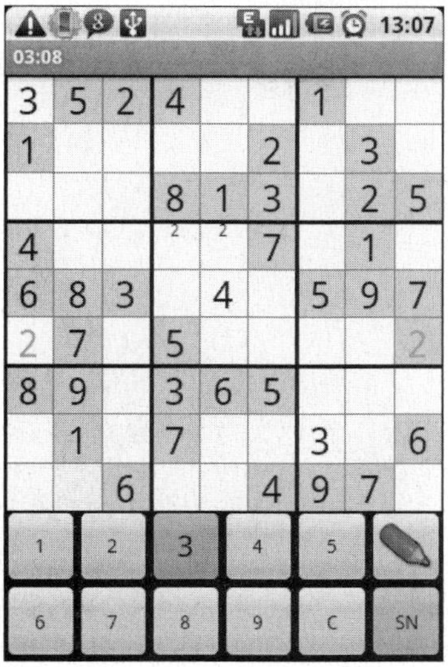

Figure 13-4:
Open-
Sudoku.

Lexic

Lexic (see Figure 13-5) is a word game in which the player is given three minutes to find as many words as possible on a grid of randomized letters (another popular subgenre of word games).

Figure 13-5:
Lexic.

The code isn't very well commented, but it's still a useful starting place if you want to build a word game.

The source code is here:

```
http://code.google.com/p/lexic
```

Newton's Cradle

Newton's Cradle is the popular desk toy — metal balls suspended from strings knocking into one another — brought to life on Android. (See Figure 13-6.) This is a great (and simple) place to start looking into the workings of a simple physics-based game.

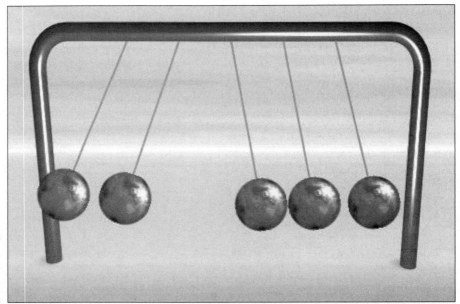

Figure 13-6: Newton's Cradle.

The source is here:

```
http://code.google.com/p/newtonscradle
```

Vector Pinball

With purposefully simple graphics, Vector Pinball gives you an efficient primer on how to translate arcade classics into cool mobile games. (See Figure 13-7.) Vector Pinball actually uses a wrapper around the Box2D physics engine, so it's a reliable resource for building games with physics.

The source is here:

```
https://github.com/dozingcat/Vector-Pinball
```

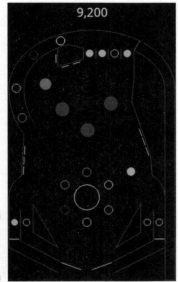

Figure 13-7:
Vector
Pinball.

asqare

Match-3 games make up an incredibly popular genre of casual games: The player moves simple elements in a grid until three or more of the same kind are in a row. I have a couple of games that fall into this class or are mashups of other games that use this concept. Some of the most popular casual games of all time are match-3. Asqare (don't know where they got that spelling) does a great job of showing how to implement this type of game, with simply-colored sprites. (See Figure 13-8.) Use it as a basis for inspiration for your own themed match-3 game, and you just might have a hit on your hands!

The source is here: `http://code.google.com/p/asqare/`.

Figure 13-8:
asqare.

tiltmazes

Almost everyone has a wooden labyrinth game sitting around in the attic or the garage: The player uses knobs to tilt the game surface, trying to navigate a metal ball through the maze. (See Figure 13-9.) This open-source version uses the accelerometer to allow the player to tilt the device to roll the virtual ball around to collect tokens.

Figure 13-9:
tiltmazes.

If you want to incorporate alternate input sensors such as the accelerometer into your game, this game is a good reference point.

The source code is here:

```
http://code.google.com/p/tiltmazes
```

GL ES Quake

We didn't cover 3D game development in this book, but if you're feeling adventurous, this version of the popular id Software game Quake, ported to the Android platform, might be the place to look. (See Figure 13-10.)

OpenGL ES (for Embedded Systems) is a scaled-down version of the OpenGL 3D graphics API and is the supported standard for Android. It's a big leap from 2D to 3D, and the complexity and demands of the hardware increase quite a bit. But mobile devices do keep getting more and more powerful, so if this is the direction you want to go, dive right in.

The source code is here:

```
http://code.google.com/p/glesquake
```

Figure 13-10:
Quake.

Chapter 14

Ten Game Engines and Tools

In This Chapter

▶ Finding good game engines

▶ Getting software for creating your own image and sound resources

▶ Investigating tools for promoting and monetizing your games

A *game engine* is a pre-built set of tools to help you build a game without having to reimplement tasks that are common to almost every game. A lot of good game engines are available for Android; I've listed a good sampling here, though it's certainly not exhaustive.

You also might want to take advantage of some freely available SDKs that can improve non-game aspects of your game product — such as marketing and analytics. I've included some tools here that can help you promote your game to other users and gather information on when and how your game is being played.

Also, if you want to make your own image and sound resources, you'll need tools that are up to the task. If you already own great image-editing software and know how to use it, that's great. But if not, and you're on a budget, I point you toward some formidable free resources that can help you do the needed world-building.

libgdx

This game engine allows cross-platform game development for both Android and desktop games. Just a few lines of code allow you to run your game on your desktop machine, which makes prototyping and testing much easier. libgdx has Box2D support for physics, and TMX tilemap support, which allows for easy, rapid development of games that use tiles, such as RPGs.

Some very popular games on Google Play were developed using libgdx, and I have used it for my physics-based game Save the Egg. It will definitely save you a lot of time and effort in the making of a professional game, and it is pretty well documented with a large community of developers. It's an easy download (see Figure 14-1.) See

```
http://code.google.com/p/libgdx
```

Figure 14-1:
libgdx
website.

AndEngine

This is another great free game engine for Android, developed by Nicolas Gramlich (see Figure 14-2). It includes many of the features you want in a game engine and has an active development community at www.andengine.org/forums. See

    https://github.com/nicolasgramlich/AndEngine

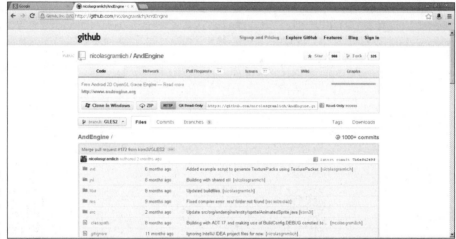

Figure 14-2:
AndEngine
website.

Unity

Besides the free engines, powerful proprietary game engines exist for use with Android. Unity, for example, has been around for a long time and has extended its game engine for use with Android. The baseline version is free to use; upgrades to the Pro version are available, as is support for many more optimizations and higher-level features. See

    http://unity3d.com/unity/publishing/android

OpenFeint

Often you'll want to include features that allow players to recommend the game to one another and compare their performance via shared leaderboards (ranked listings of scores from other players). OpenFeint is a free SDK that supports friend recommendations, leaderboards, and achievements.

Social features can often take your game to the next level of popularity (and profitability!), so using these freely available tools and help files just might be a very good idea (see Figure 14-3). See

```
http://support.openfeint.com/dev/welcome
```

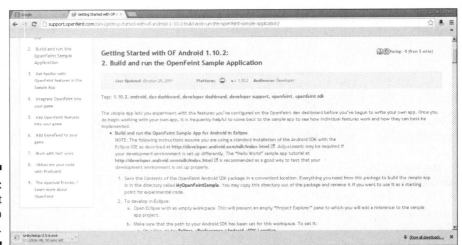

Figure 14-3: OpenFeint setup instructions.

Flurry

As feature-rich as the Google Play developer console is, it's been slow to offer native support for a lot of usage statistics and bug reports. Even now, the console could use some help in that department; there's still a lot of value in including analytics in your game to help improve (and possibly monetize) it. Flurry offers a painless way to build in analytics.

With just a couple of lines of code, Flurry provides a treasure trove of default user data — for openers, number of sessions per day per user and length of sessions. And if that's not enough information for you, Flurry allows you to capture information about custom events — say, how many attempts it takes users on average to defeat a particular level or enemy, or how often they use a particular set of controls. Information is power, and gathering detailed analytics may help you improve your game immensely (see Figure 14-4). Flurry now also provides an ad network and other monetization tools, so that's something else you might want to look into. See

```
http://www.flurry.com
```

Figure 14-4: Flurry.

Audacity

Elsewhere in the book, I mention the options of either purchasing sound effects and music or producing your own. You really should try making your own sound effects, and read up on the history of sound effects in movies like *Star Wars*. You'd be surprised at how some of them are made!

In any case, if you do go the roll-your-own route, Audacity is a great free tool for editing audio. (See Figure 14-5.) It's been around a long time and has a very avid user base. See

```
http://audacity.sourceforge.net
```

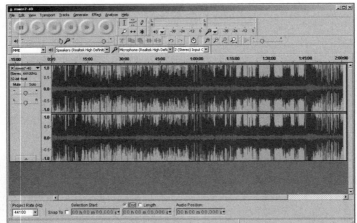

Figure 14-5:
Audacity
interface.

sfxr

This is a cool little tool that I came across a while back. (See Figure 14-6.) You can use it to create common sound effects from old-school-style video games, like coin-ups, laser blasts, and jumping sounds. If you're working on retro games, this is a must. Even if you're not, you may find a place for the kinds of effects generated by sfxr in your game. See

```
http://code.google.com/p/sfxr
```

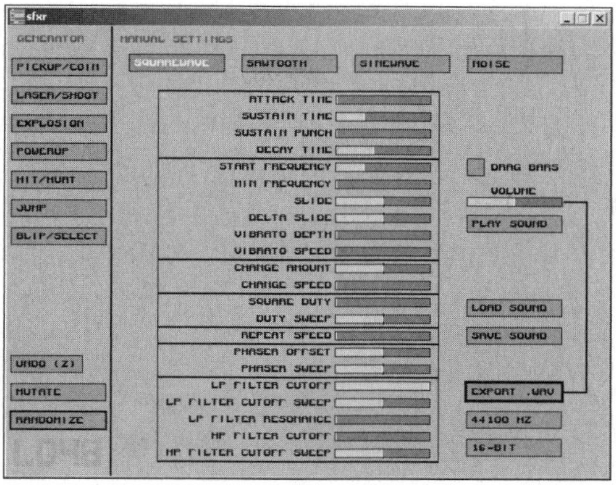

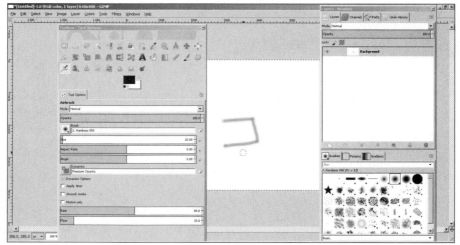

Figure 14-6:
sfxr
interface.

GIMP

GIMP is short for GNU Image Manipulation Program. It's a powerful, free image editor on par with many proprietary programs (see Figure 14-7). The last time I used it, the learning curve was a bit steep. If you're working with fairly complex images and effects, you'll want to invest the time in learning GIMP. Otherwise you might want to use a simpler, friendlier tool for your image needs. See

```
www.gimp.org
```

Figure 14-7:
GIMP
workspace.

Inkscape

If you're comfortable working with vector graphics, Inkscape is a great little tool for image creation and editing. It's pretty user-friendly and has a lot of features. (See Figure 14-8.) You can export your creations to .PNG format for use in your Android games. Work through some of the tutorials and you'll find that you can create some pretty nice images even if you're not a professional artist. See

```
inkscape.org
```

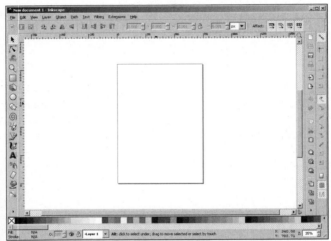

Figure 14-8:
Inkscape
workspace.

AdWhirl

In Chapter 11, I mention *ad mediation* — the process of using multiple ad networks in a single app, controlling the ratios to maximize your profit from ads. At any given time, some networks may be generating more revenue than others, so it may make sense to monitor and adjust which ad provider's ads are being served up by your app. (See Figure 14-9.) This may sound confusing, but it's really not — especially not when you have a good tool to help you handle it.

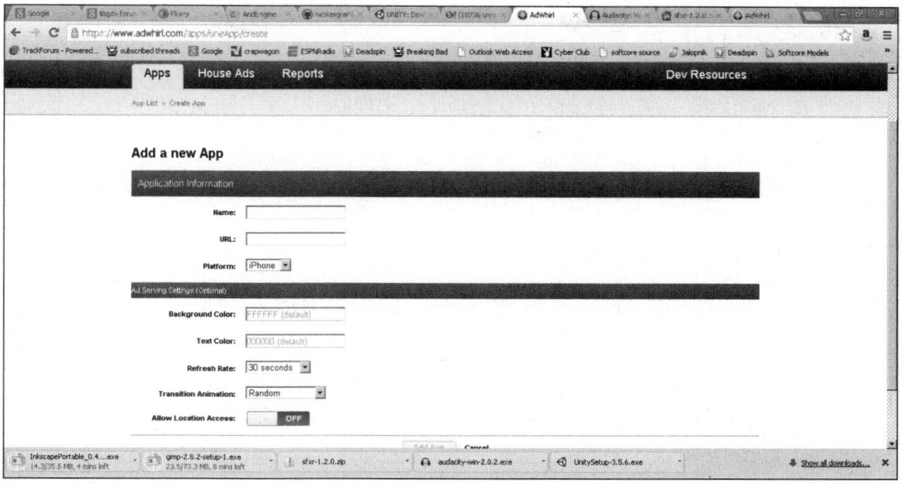

Figure 14-9:
Add an
AdWhirl
app.

AdWhirl is a free tool that allows you to use a wide cross-section of ad networks in your game, as well as house ads promoting your other apps. If you're thinking at all about monetizing your game via ads, you'll want to look into AdWhirl. See

```
adwhirl.com
```

Chapter 15

Ten More Places to Distribute Your Game

In This Chapter

▶ Discovering other app markets

▶ Distributing your game yourself through your website

▶ Getting creative with alternative distribution methods

The most common and popular way of getting your game seen and downloaded is through Google Play, the official Android market administrated by Google. But it's definitely not the only place to distribute your game. Because of Android's relatively open nature, many third-party app stores have popped up, eager to give Google competition in the app market business.

People will tend to default to whatever comes pre-installed on their devices, so app markets that are bundled with the device have an enormous advantage over others that need to be installed. That doesn't mean they're not viable alternatives to be explored.

This chapter takes a look at some of these third-party app markets, as well as a couple of other distribution channels that you may not have considered. Remember that each market may have its own unique resource requirements (for example, some markets may require five screen shots of your game, while some may require none). There is some overhead in maintaining your game in multiple markets, but if you have the time and energy, it may be worth it.

Amazon

The Amazon market for Android apps (Figure 15-1) is probably the most viable secondary market for Android apps and games right now. The reason is that Amazon has its own line of Android devices and preinstalls their own market on these devices. They've also done a great job promoting early exclusives for popular games to drum up interest. Right now some of my games sell more copies on the Amazon market than Google Play! Amazon also features a Free App of the Day promotion which encourages daily visits, and if you're lucky, your game might be featured. Typically you won't see direct sales the day of the promotion, but the increased exposure should boost your long-term sales. You'll find the Amazon market at:

```
www.amazon.com/appstore
```

Figure 15-1:
Amazon.com.

Handango

Handango's been in the mobile app market for a long time, before the smartphone revolution. (See Figure 15-2). They've adapted pretty well to the explosion in the mobile app and game market, and you should find them fairly reputable and reliable. You'll find their market here:

www.handango.com

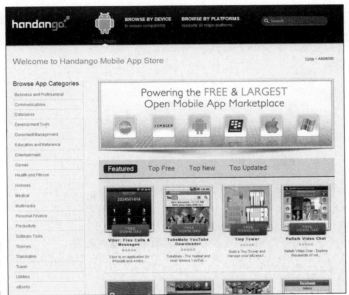

Figure 15-2: Handango.

Opera Mobile App Store

Opera is a software company based in Norway that's best known for their browser. However, they've also gotten in on the mobile app market and have a very nice site (see Figure 15-3).

Figure 15-3:
Opera.

Opera Mobile App Store is here:

```
http://apps.opera.com/en_us
```

GetJar

Like other mobile app markets, GetJar lets you browse by compatibility with your device (see Figure 15-4). Installing the market client is easy, making the process of installing apps from GetJar relatively painless.

Figure 15-4:
GetJar.

The GetJar market is here:

```
www.getjar.com
```

SlideME

SlideME is the first market in the list that's dedicated solely to Android apps and games (Amazon's app store is dedicated to Android as well, but they obviously sell other stuff online). As such, users looking for your Android game may have an easier time navigating a dedicated market. (See Figure 15-5.)

Figure 15-5:
SlideME.

The SlideME market is here:

```
www.slideme.org
```

Appoke

Appoke bills itself as a "social app store" for Android devices. That means users rely on their social network to find out what apps and games their friends and family have installed and how those apps and games are rated. (See Figure 15-6.) Neat!

Figure 15-6:
Appoke.

Find the Appoke market at:

www.appoke.com

AppBrain

AppBrain is yet another app market devoted solely to Android. The market links to feeds with "Hot Apps", "Latest Apps", and "Latest Reviews", as well as the usual categories like Arcade & Action games and Communication. (See Figure 15-7.) Find the AppBrain market at:

```
www.appbrain.com
```

Figure 15-1:
AppBrain.

AndroLib

AndroLib is not so much an alternative market as a browser for Google Play. This was more relevant in the days before the Google Play web site came along, but you still may prefer it as an interface into Google Play, especially if you're frustrated with poor search results in Google Play. (See Figure 15-8.)

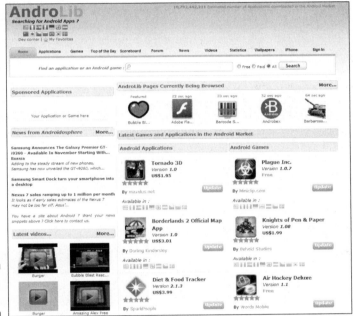

Figure 15-1:
AndroLib.

The AndroLib market browser is here:

www.androlib.com

Your Website

If you have a website for your game business (and I highly recommend that you get one if you don't), consider distributing your game there. Ecommerce solutions exist for selling your app via your website, which can be a little clunky. However, if your game is free, there's really no reason not to offer it freely on your website. It's just another download point for users to get your game.

BitTorrent Sites

BitTorrent is one of the most popular internet protocols for file sharing, which is most often used for sharing pirated materials. But you may be able to leverage file sharing to work in your favor. Especially in the case when your game is free (and possibly ad-supported), you really don't care how it's distributed.

Get together with other developers and bundle several games together. Bundled games are generally more popular than single games on such sites.

Chapter 16

Ten Websites for Android Game Developers

In This Chapter

▶ Finding web resources for Android development

▶ Discovering websites that talk about and review Android games

▶ Keeping up-to-date on the latest Android news and community feedback

I've tried to give you foundations for creating your own great games for the Android mobile platform, but what if you have more questions? In this chapter, I'll point you to some great resources for connecting with other Android developers who may have already solved whatever issue you're having, or who can help you troubleshoot. There are thousands of Android developers out there at various levels of experience; many of them will be willing to help you out. Don't overlook this amazing resource! When I first started, many of these sites were invaluable in helping me learn the basics, then later to troubleshoot some of the thorniest problems I encountered.

This section will also point you to websites devoted specifically to reviewing Android apps and games.

 Consider approaching some of these sites once your game is completed and published. A nice review on an established site can go a long way in garnering downloads.

This section also includes sites for Android news and community forums. to help you keep up-to-date on the latest in the Android world. In some forums, it may be appropriate to mention or promote your game. That's another good source of exposure.

Stack Overflow

This is an excellent collaborative question and answer site for programming.
A couple of years ago, Google announced that it would be an official support
environment for Android.

Most problems you'll encounter will probably have an answer somewhere in
the Stack Overflow forums (see Figure 16-1). But if not, post yours and someone will probably come along and help. I've used this resource extensively
and it has been invaluable. They also have a cool achievements/incentives
design to let you know who the most trusted commenters are. Check it out at

```
www.stackoverflow.com
```

Figure 16-1:
Stack
Overflow
forums.

Android Developer

This is the official developer website for Android. The site is where you'll download the Android SDK, which I mentioned very early on in this book. But this site has extensive resources on design principles regarding Android apps, along with tons of helpful videos and downloads, plus the latest news (see Figure 16-2). Don't just visit to grab the SDK. Spend some time looking through the other offerings at

`www.developer.android.com`

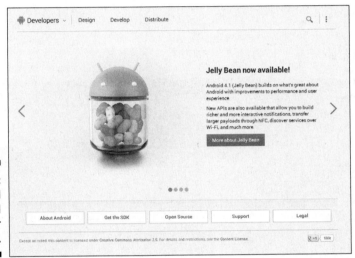

Figure 16-2: The official Android developer website.

anddev.org

When I first got started in Android development, this was the first site I found. It was (and still is) an awesome resource. There are forums dedicated to asking and answering specific problems related to Android programming (see Figure 16-3), as well as very helpful tutorials covering a wide range of topics.

Because the website is associated with the 2D game engine AndEngine, you can also find lots of resources devoted to that tool, if you are interested in using it.

The site is at

```
www.anddev.org
```

Figure 16-3:
anddev.org
community
forums.

Android Developers Blog

Part of being a good game developer is keeping up-to-date on the latest news and information regarding the platforms you work on. The Android Developer's Blog is straight from the horse's mouth (see Figure 16-4), with members of the Android development team at Google posting the latest news regarding the platform.

You'll probably want to put this in your feed. Find it at

`www.android-developers.blogspot.com`

Figure 16-4:
Messages from the Android development team.

Appolicious

This is a Yahoo-sponsored app recommendation and review site with a social bent (see Figure 16-5). The site is yet another way to

✔ See what apps are trending.

✔ Assess your competition

✔ Get your own game reviewed.

Find it at

www.androidapps.com

Figure 16-5:
Appolicious
advice,
backed by
Yahoo.

Android Tapp

Android Tapp is a site devoted to reviews for Android apps (see Figure 16-6). Once your game is completed or near completion, you want to consider submitting the .apk to review sites to stir up initial interest.

The early days after release are the most important.

Android Tapp is one of the more established review sites, so check it out at

www.androidtapp.com

Figure 16-6: Reviews and news from Android Tapp.

Phandroid

This website is a great place to find the latest news on Android (see Figure 16-7). In addition, their forums are very active and are a great place to talk about Android games and gaming and possibly promote your newest creation. Check it out at

```
www.phandroid.com
```

Figure 16-7:
Fan fun and
facts at
Phandroid.

xda developers

This website is a great resource for developers and users of custom ROMs and non-factory modifications of the Android OS. Even if you're not interested in custom ROMs, you should visit the site (see Figure 16-8). They have discussions broken down by device, which is a great resource if you're having particular issues testing your game on a specific piece of hardware. If you can't find an answer to a particularly difficult technical issue, look or post here:

`www.xda-developers.com`

Figure 16-8: Check xdadevelopers for device-specific help.

Droid Gamers

Andrew Huff runs this great website devoted to all things related to Android and gaming (see Figure 16-9). You'll find news, reviews, interviews, and more, specifically for games on Android.

You should definitely visit and bookmark this one. Drop Andrew an e-mail if you've got a new release coming out or some other Android game-related news!

Visit them at

www.droidgamers.com

Figure 16-9:
Droid
Gamers
covers
gaming from
virtual start
to virtual
finish.

Android and Me

This is another great resource for keeping up with the latest in the Android world. The site is very slick and well-designed, and up-to-date with the latest in the Android world (see Figure 16-10). Check out the site at

www.androidandme.com

Figure 16-10:
Android and Me delivers the latest news.

Glossary

Active installs

The number of devices that currently have your app or game installed. *Total* installs (installations of the program) includes active installs plus the number of devices that installed, and then uninstalled, your app or game.

Analytics

Program(s) for gathering information about usage patterns of your app or game (such as what demographics of users are playing your game, for how long, where, and when). Google provides some analytics in the developer console, but you can also use third-party packages such as Flurry (`flurry.com`) or write your own.

Asynchronous games

Games played off-line in which one player may take a turn, notify the other player, and wait for the other player to make a move in response.

Build

A given version of an app or game that has been compiled into an executable file.

Carrier

A telecommunications company that provides telephone and Internet services to mobile devices.

Emulator

Software that simulates the function of another piece of hardware or software. An Android emulator, used for testing apps, simulates an Android device in your desktop environment.

Fault tolerance

One measure of a system's robustness — specifically, how well the system continues to function under a wide range of circumstances, including damage or partial loss of functionality.

Firmware

Software stored in read-only memory (ROM) and designed not to be routinely modified.

Health bar

Visual indicator of a character's life total in a video game.

Integrated Development Environment (IDE)

A software tool for developing software. Usually includes a source code editor, debugging tools, profiling tools, and other features to increase the speed and ease of software development.

Iterating

Repeated process of revising and testing to develop an app or game.

Long-tail distribution

A set of things in which there are a large number of a few types, a moderate number of types with medium frequency, and a "long tail" of many types with only a few in number. Digital markets allow for long tails to be more profitable than traditional markets because inventory space is cheaper and search is easier. App stores almost universally have a long-tail distribution.

Mobile ecosystem

The current state of the mobile marketplace and user base, including hardware, software, infrastructure, distributers, and users.

Non-market app

An app or game that is distributed and installed from somewhere other than an app store, such as from a development environment.

Porting a game

The process of converting a game that runs on one platform (such as PC) to run on another (such as Android).

Retention rate

Analytic figure that represents the percentage of users who download a game and continue to keep it installed, rather than uninstalling it.

Rooting

Configuring a hardware device to gain administrator access, allowing the user greater control over the software that is installed, including the operating system.

Source code

Instructions in a human-readable computer language that are compiled into a machine-readable format.

Synchronous games

Games played in real time, in which all players must be playing the game at the same time.

Virtual controls

Input methods that simulate physical hardware. For example, your game may have a virtual joystick or buttons that are manipulated via a touchscreen interface.

Index

• X •

Apple & Mac

iPad 2 For Dummies,
3rd Edition
978-1-118-17679-5

iPhone 4S For Dummies,
4th Edition
978-1-118-03671-6

iPod touch For Dummies,
3rd Edition
978-1-118-12960-9

Mac OS X Lion
For Dummies
978-1-118-02205-4

Blogging & Social Media

CityVille For Dummies
978-1-118-08337-6

Facebook For Dummies,
4th Edition
978-1-118-09562-1

Mom Blogging
For Dummies
978-1-118-03843-7

Twitter For Dummies,
2nd Edition
978-0-470-76879-2

WordPress For Dummies,
4th Edition
978-1-118-07342-1

Business

Cash Flow For Dummies
978-1-118-01850-7

Investing For Dummies,
6th Edition
978-0-470-90545-6

Job Searching with Social
Media For Dummies
978-0-470-93072-4

QuickBooks 2012
For Dummies
978-1-118-09120-3

Resumes For Dummies,
6th Edition
978-0-470-87361-8

Starting an Etsy Business
For Dummies
978-0-470-93067-0

Cooking & Entertaining

Cooking Basics
For Dummies, 4th Edition
978-0-470-91388-8

Wine For Dummies,
4th Edition
978-0-470-04579-4

Diet & Nutrition

Kettlebells For Dummies
978-0-470-59929-7

Nutrition For Dummies,
5th Edition
978-0-470-93231-5

Restaurant Calorie Counter
For Dummies,
2nd Edition
978-0-470-64405-8

Digital Photography

Digital SLR Cameras &
Photography For Dummies,
4th Edition
978-1-118-14489-3

Digital SLR Settings
& Shortcuts
For Dummies
978-0-470-91763-3

Photoshop Elements 10
For Dummies
978-1-118-10742-3

Gardening

Gardening Basics
For Dummies
978-0-470-03749-2

Vegetable Gardening
For Dummies,
2nd Edition
978-0-470-49870-5

Green/Sustainable

Raising Chickens
For Dummies
978-0-470-46544-8

Green Cleaning
For Dummies
978-0-470-39106-8

Health

Diabetes For Dummies,
3rd Edition
978-0-470-27086-8

Food Allergies
For Dummies
978-0-470-09584-3

Living Gluten-Free
For Dummies,
2nd Edition
978-0-470-58589-4

Hobbies

Beekeeping
For Dummies,
2nd Edition
978-0-470-43065-1

Chess For Dummies,
3rd Edition
978-1-118-01695-4

Drawing For Dummies,
2nd Edition
978-0-470-61842-4

eBay For Dummies,
7th Edition
978-1-118-09806-6

Knitting For Dummies,
2nd Edition
978-0-470-28747-7

Language & Foreign Language

English Grammar
For Dummies,
2nd Edition
978-0-470-54664-2

French For Dummies,
2nd Edition
978-1-118-00464-7

German For Dummies,
2nd Edition
978-0-470-90101-4

Spanish Essentials
For Dummies
978-0-470-63751-7

Spanish For Dummies,
2nd Edition
978-0-470-87855-2

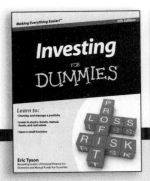

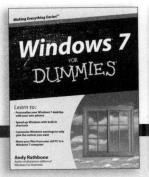

Math & Science

Algebra I For Dummies,
2nd Edition
978-0-470-55964-2

Biology For Dummies,
2nd Edition
978-0-470-59875-7

Chemistry For Dummies,
2nd Edition
978-1-1180-0730-3

Geometry For Dummies,
2nd Edition
978-0-470-08946-0

Pre-Algebra Essentials
For Dummies
978-0-470-61838-7

Microsoft Office

Excel 2010 For Dummies
978-0-470-48953-6

Office 2010 All-in-One
For Dummies
978-0-470-49748-7

Office 2011 for Mac
For Dummies
978-0-470-87869-9

Word 2010
For Dummies
978-0-470-48772-3

Music

Guitar For Dummies,
2nd Edition
978-0-7645-9904-0

Clarinet For Dummies
978-0-470-58477-4

iPod & iTunes
For Dummies,
9th Edition
978-1-118-13060-5

Pets

Cats For Dummies,
2nd Edition
978-0-7645-5275-5

Dogs All-in One
For Dummies
978-0470-52978-2

Saltwater Aquariums
For Dummies
978-0-470-06805-2

Religion & Inspiration

The Bible For Dummies
978-0-7645-5296-0

Catholicism For Dummies,
2nd Edition
978-1-118-07778-8

Spirituality For Dummies,
2nd Edition
978-0-470-19142-2

Self-Help & Relationships

Happiness For Dummies
978-0-470-28171-0

Overcoming Anxiety
For Dummies,
2nd Edition
978-0-470-57441-6

Seniors

Crosswords For Seniors
For Dummies
978-0-470-49157-7

iPad 2 For Seniors
For Dummies, 3rd Edition
978-1-118-17678-8

Laptops & Tablets
For Seniors For Dummies,
2nd Edition
978-1-118-09596-6

Smartphones & Tablets

BlackBerry For Dummies,
5th Edition
978-1-118-10035-6

Droid X2 For Dummies
978-1-118-14864-8

HTC ThunderBolt
For Dummies
978-1-118-07601-9

MOTOROLA XOOM
For Dummies
978-1-118-08835-7

Sports

Basketball For Dummies,
3rd Edition
978-1-118-07374-2

Football For Dummies,
2nd Edition
978-1-118-01261-1

Golf For Dummies,
4th Edition
978-0-470-88279-5

Test Prep

ACT For Dummies,
5th Edition
978-1-118-01259-8

ASVAB For Dummies,
3rd Edition
978-0-470-63760-9

The GRE Test For
Dummies, 7th Edition
978-0-470-00919-2

Police Officer Exam
For Dummies
978-0-470-88724-0

Series 7 Exam
For Dummies
978-0-470-09932-2

Web Development

HTML, CSS, & XHTML
For Dummies, 7th Edition
978-0-470-91659-9

Drupal For Dummies,
2nd Edition
978-1-118-08348-2

Windows 7

Windows 7
For Dummies
978-0-470-49743-2

Windows 7
For Dummies,
Book + DVD Bundle
978-0-470-52398-8

Windows 7 All-in-One
For Dummies
978-0-470-48763-1

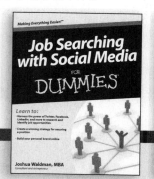

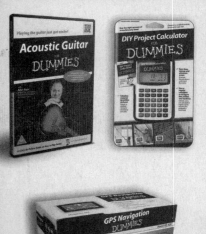